D1557928

The Suspicion of Virtue

The Suspicion of Virtue

Women Philosophers in Neoclassical France

JOHN J. CONLEY, S.J.

Cornell University Press

ITHACA AND LONDON

First published 2002 by Cornell University Press

Printed in the United States of America

Library of Congress Cataloging-in-Publication Data
Conley, John J.
    The suspicion of virtue : women philosophers in neoclassical France /
John J. Conley.
        p.   cm.
Includes bibliographical references (p.   ) and index.
    ISBN 0-8014-4020-3 (cloth)
    1. Women philosophers—France—Biography.   I. Title.
    B1815 .C66 2002
    194'.082—dc21   2002005556

Cornell University Press strives to use environmentally responsible suppliers and materials to the fullest extent possible in the publishing of its books. Such materials include vegetable-based, low-VOC inks and acid-free papers that are recycled, totally chlorine-free, or partly composed of nonwood fibers.

Cloth printing   10 9 8 7 6 5 4 3 2 1

Dedicated with gratitude
to my grandmother,
Mrs. Helen E. Broderick
("Nana")

Contents

Preface

This book began by accident.

In 1991 I presented a paper on the aesthetics of Madame de Staël to the Society for the Study of Women Philosophers. A member of the audience asked if I had ever studied any of the salon women earlier in the seventeenth century. My curiosity piqued, I began to haunt the old Lennox collection at the New York Public Library.

When I discovered Madame de Sablé, I thought that I had found an anomaly: a *salonnière* who deconstructed virtue. Then I stumbled on Madame Deshoulières, a materialist who claimed that virtue was only instinct. Soon appeared the Augustinians, Madame de la Sablière and Mademoiselle de la Vallière, with the triumph of theological over natural virtues. Then I unearthed Madame de Maintenon, with dialogue after dialogue sketching the anatomy of politeness.

Toward the end of the journey, so many unexpected women philosophers had emerged that this book could only focus on one social group: the aristocratic laity of Paris. The nuns of Port-Royal, the court of Mademoiselle de Montpensier, and the bourgeois associates of Mademoiselle de Scudéry await another book.

This journey of discovery was not a solitary one. I would like to thank the Folger Institute for a seminar grant in 1998, Fordham University for a sabbatical in 1999–2000, and St. Joseph's University for a position as visiting professor in 2000–2001. I thank the staffs of the various libraries where I conducted my research: Fordham University Library, the New York Public Library, Bibliothèque Nationale de France, Bibliothèque Mazarine, and Bibliothèque de la Société des Amis de Port-Royal. I thank colleagues who had the kindness to read earlier drafts of the work: Christopher Cullen, S.J.; Daniel Fincke; Joseph Koterski, S.J.; Catharine Randall; and Alison Weber. I thank my editor at Cornell University Press, Catherine Rice, who guided this book through publication. I warmly thank the members of the

Society for the Study of Women Philosophers, who have encouraged my research over the years.

An earlier version of Chapter 2 appeared in "Madame de Sablé's Moral Philosophy: A Jansenist Salon," by John J. Conley, which appears in *Presenting Women Philosophers* by Cecile T. Tougas and Sara Ebenreck. Reprinted by permission of Temple University Press. Copyright 2000 by Temple University. All rights reserved.

I stand on the work of many contemporary scholars who have retrieved the writing of early modern women philosophers. The research of Eileen O'Neill and Mary Ellen Waithe has been especially influential. I also stand on the work of pioneering nineteenth-century French editors, especially Victor Cousin, who meticulously collected, saved, and published the works of so many *salonnières* from this period.

The aristocratic society represented by these philosophers has long since vanished. We no longer plot the downfall of the king between Alexandrine couplets. Versailles now charges admission. But we still struggle to be just, temperate, and courageous. And the moralists of the salon still question our very quest for virtue.

JOHN CONLEY

New York

Note on Translation

I have translated the French texts into contemporary English throughout. When relevant, I have provided key French terms to clarify the original vocabulary and concept of the philosopher. In my translation I have attempted to provide as clear and as accurate a representation of the author's thought as is possible. At times this emphasis on accuracy has sacrificed certain of the authors' literary conventions. There is no effort, for example, to reproduce the complex rhyme scheme of Deshoulières in the translation of her poetry. I have used inclusive language for the translation of anthropological terms (such as *l'homme*), but out of respect for the integrity and the theology of the texts, I have maintained the gendered references to God and other religious entities.

In order to facilitate access to these rare texts in the original, I have provided four appendices to the book. The appendices present the integral French original of key works in moral theory by four women studied in the book: Madame de Sablé, Madame Deshoulières, Madame de la Sablière, and Madame de Maintenon. The Internet *Gallica* project of the Bibliothèque Nationale de France currently provides free Internet access to the works of Mesdames de Sablé and Deshoulières. The ARTFL project of the University of Chicago currently provides subscription Internet access to many other philosophical works by French women in the early modern period.

The Suspicion of Virtue

CHAPTER I

Introduction: Salon Philosophy

Once there were homes where it was permitted to speak and to think. The Muses kept company with the Graces. We went there to take lessons in politeness. We left them as if we had just left Plato's banquet.

— MADAME DE LAMBERT (1724)

In the Parisian church of Saint Etienne-du-Mont, a wooden pulpit dominates the nave. Built by Germain Pillon in 1651, the pulpit was decorated by the sculptor Lestocart. The interior panels depict the evangelists, Saint Augustine, and scenes from the life of the church's patron, Saint Stephen. On the pulpit exterior a group of statues personifies the virtues as women. Prudence holds open her book. Justice bears a sword. Temperance pours wine out of her jug. Dressed as an Amazon, Fortitude wields a club. Faith holds high a cross. Hope clings to an anchor. Charity consoles her children, nursing one infant and hugging the other.

Gendered, the pulpit sums up the ambition of the Catholic Reform: that the preaching of the gospel, as interpreted by Church tradition and as manifest in the lives of the saints, might strengthen the assembly in moral and theological virtue.

The sculpted ensemble of the Virtues represents more than the goals of Counter-Reformation preaching. It indicates the primacy of virtue in the moral philosophy of the period. Neo-scholastic authors routinely argued how the theological virtues, infused by the Holy Spirit, perfected the moral virtues pursued by Christian and pagan alike. In the psyche as in the cosmos, grace built on nature. Drawing on Stoic and Epicurean sources, humanist authors celebrated the need to cultivate moral habits, praising fortitude or temperance respectively as the key virtue.

The serene edifice of the virtues did not pass uncontested. A series of

1

neoclassical philosophers challenged the claims of moral virtues and of virtue theorists. From materialist or Augustinian perspectives, they unmasked the virtues as outcroppings of the vice of pride or, at least, they radically altered the standard hierarchy of the virtues in the religious and philosophical theory of the period.

This book focuses on the critique of virtue developed by five women philosophers of the neoclassical period: Madame de Sablé, Madame Deshoulières, Madame de la Sablière, Madame de Maintenon, and Mademoiselle de la Vallière.

Besides gender, the choice of this particular group of authors followed several other criteria. Chronologically, all these authors composed their works in the heyday of French neoclassicism, specifically during the reign of Louis XIV (1643–1715). Stylistically, they all wrote nonfiction works that offered a sustained argument about the nature of virtues and related themes in moral philosophy. Intellectually, they demonstrated a knowledge of philosophical texts and of the philosophical disputes of the period. To various degrees they participated in the Augustinian revival within French Catholicism.[1] Socially, they represent a homogeneous milieu: the aristocratic laywomen who dominated the Parisian salons of the seventeenth century.

Despite the diverse genres of their writings, they shared a similar perspective on disputed questions in moral psychology. They attacked the standard portrait of virtue in neoclassical France and proposed an alternative account of the moral dispositions falsely praised as virtuous by Christian humanism.

While the women philosophers studied in this book follow the texts and arguments of the leading male philosophers of the period, they are not mere commentators of Descartes or other canonical male authors. They employ a number of non-treatise genres to explore philosophical issues: the portrait, the maxim, the dialogue, the ode. They concentrate on certain branches of philosophy (ethics, theology) and pay little attention to others (logic, epistemology). Compared with their male counterparts, they disproportionately emphasize certain topics in their moral analysis. Politeness and friendship are typical. Many defend the need to reform education for women so that women may have greater access to the arts and the sciences. The distinctive voice developed by this circle of women authors reflects the gendered philosophical culture of the neoclassical period and the institutional pivot of that culture: the salon.

PHILOSOPHICAL FORMATION AND GENDER

The development of a philosophical culture by women in neoclassical France faced serious obstacles.[2] Women found themselves excluded from three key institutions that fostered philosophical literacy. The university categorically barred women from enrollment or even from auditing lectures. The seminary, an educational innovation of the Council of Trent, was reserved to male candidates for ordination. The scientific academy, a new venue for more informal philosophical exchange, usually banned women from membership. The Académie française, centerpiece of the French network of academies, imposed a complete ban.

The exclusion of women from these three vectors of neoclassical philosophy left its imprint on the philosophical works written by them during this period. Few women wrote in the form of the treatise, the favored literary genre for the university and the seminary. Few acquired the competence in science academy members displayed in their philosophical debates. Only the rare woman learned Latin, the *lingua franca* of the philosophical and theological establishment. Few developed a thorough knowledge of the "Aristotelianism" that formed the working creed of the university. The tendency of women philosophers to write in brief genres, to prefer a literary over a scientific mode of argument, and to stress ancient (Plato, Augustine) and modern (Descartes) sources over medieval scholastic ones reflects women's limited access to the philosophical venues of the period.

THEOLOGICAL CULTURE

Several institutions contributed to the development of the philosophical culture of women. One of the most influential was the convent school.[3] New religious orders, especially the Ursulines and the Visitandines, established a network of schools for aristocratic and bourgeois girls, one that complemented the older Benedictine convent schools. The new orders established a more extensive curriculum. Emphasis on literary composition broadened the earlier focus on penmanship and basic literacy. Courses in history and mathematics complemented the established concern for the domestic arts and the fine arts. The crystalline literary style of La Vallière and Maintenon reflects their early education by Ursuline nuns imbued with the canons of neoclassicism.

The convent school did not provide formal instruction in philosophy. However, the centerpiece of its curriculum, catechetical instruction, initiated students into a set of philosophical terms and concerns. In religion class, the student learned the standard neoscholastic philosophy of the Church. She studied the metaphysical distinction between substance and accident in order to understand the doctrine of Transubstantiation. She learned the difference between form and matter to grasp the theory of the sacraments. She studied the basic principles of natural law, the virtues, and the gifts of the Holy Spirit. An elaborate casuistry explained the application of the Decalogue to her everyday moral dilemmas. Additional course work in etiquette and in morals strengthened the moral component of the curriculum. The pronounced predilection among women philosophers of the period for moral and theological issues reflects the prominence of ethical instruction in convent education.

Allied to religious instruction was the practice of spiritual reading. St. François de Sales's *Introduction to the Devout Life* (1601)[4] became a staple in the library of every cultivated Catholic woman. Not only did the treatise introduce women to methods of meditation; it provided a detailed deontology for the laywoman, according to her state in life. Many schools mandated the reading of spiritual works with an unusual philosophical pedigree. Students at Maintenon's Saint-Cyr were required to read Augustine's *Soliloquies*.[5] Pupils under Jacqueline Pascal at Port-Royal used John of Climacus's *Ladder of Spiritual Ascent* for moral instruction.[6] The elaborate discussions of virtues and vices presented by many of these ascetical works shaped the moral philosophy later defended by the alumnae of the convent schools.

Several religious movements provided women with a certain philosophical and theological culture outside the classroom. Three movements in particular attracted aristocratic women of the period: Jansenism, Quietism, and libertinism. Each movement expressed a distinctive scale of virtues and vices in its model of the moral life. Each also defended a particular position on the most controverted metaphysical issue of the era: the relationship between necessity, divine or material, and human freedom.

Centered on the works of Cornelius Jansenius (1585–1638), a Louvain theologian and the Bishop of Ypres, the Jansenist movement promoted a rigorist version of Augustinian theology. Led in France by Abbé Saint-Cyran (1581–1643), the Jansenists insisted on humanity's complete dependence for salvation on God's sovereign gift of grace. Riddled by concupiscence, fallen human nature could only exercise its freedom to choose evil. The salvation of a small elect was due to God's inscrutable choice, not to any claims of human merit. In the moral domain the Jansenists insisted that the saved must pursue a life strictly based on God's law and firmly opposed to the world, especially to the typical vices of the court. In politics they insisted on the subordination of the civil to the religious. In foreign affairs they felt France should lead a coalition of Catholic princes against the Protestant, Orthodox, and Islamic powers; in domestic policy they emphasized moral reformation, starting with the court and the episcopate.

From the time of Richelieu, court officials detected a current of political subversion in the Jansenist movement. The emphasis on the role of the laity and the stubborn refusal to accept the papacy's successive condemnations of Jansenius seemed to promote a democratization of the Church. The palpable attraction of the movement for members of the Fronde, the aristocratic coalition opposed to royal absolutism, appeared to confirm that the egalitarian ecclesiology of the Jansenists covertly fostered a republican model of government.

From the movement's inception, women played a central role in the diffusion of Jansenist theories and practices. Headed by the reforming abbess Mère Angélique (1591–1661), the convent of Port-Royal emerged as the center of the Jansenist movement. Port-Royal's spacious Parisian church attracted a large aristocratic public to its services, sermons, and retreats. Its convent school, renowned for its pedagogical innovations and its moral rigor, enrolled numerous daughters of the aristocracy and the bourgeoisie. Four of its nuns achieved literary renown through the circulation of their theological writings in manuscript and printed form: Mère Angélique, Mère Agnès (1593–1671), Mère Angélique de Saint-Jean (1624–1684), and Soeur Jacqueline de Sainte-Euphémie (Jacqueline Pascal, 1625–1661). Madame de Sablé was only one of a phalanx of aristocratic women who wrote works inspired by the Jansenist critique of virtue and conducted salon debates on the dilemma of free will, apparently minimized or denied by Jansenist theology.

More a devotional than a doctrinal movement, Quietism affected the piety of aristocratic circles in the later decades of the seventeenth century. Led in France by Madame Guyon (1647–1717), a charismatic lecturer and prolific author, Quietism argued that the best prayer for a Christian was purely passive: a simple abandonment to God's will in quiet attentiveness. The use of imagination or discursive reasoning in prayer, common in the period's methods of meditation, was condemned as a block to effective union with God. Anthropologically, Quietism discounted the value of the human faculties, especially the intellect and the imagination. The will was to annihilate itself in the mystery of God. Morally, Quietism criticized attempts to acquire virtue by ascetical effort or by periodic resolutions of the will. The supreme Quietist virtue was humility, construed as total abandonment to God's providence.

Guyon attracted a wide aristocratic following for her methods, especially in the devout circles at court. Until she turned against Quietism in the 1690s, Madame de Maintenon defended Guyon and proudly carried Guyon's pamphlet *A Short Method of Prayer* on her person. Critics of Jansenism, especially the Jesuits, argued that this ideal of spiritual passivity radically undercut the moral life by dismissing the need to acquire the moral virtues. They also contended that this emphasis on the propriety of mystical prayer for all Christians fostered spiritual illusion and undermined the mediating role of authority and sacrament in the spiritual life.

Numerous women moralists of the period, such as Madame de la Sablière, bear clear traces of Quietist spirituality in their critiques of the ascetical quest to cultivate the natural virtues, in their negative evaluations of the faculties of imagination and reason, and in their emphasis on contemplative union with God as the proper goal of all Christians, not only of a cloistered elite.

More a set of attitudes than a doctrinal movement, libertinism was the face of religious skepticism in court and salon society. The "libertines" engaged in amorous intrigue, but their justification of sexual license rested on a distinctive metaphysical and religious outlook. They disdained basic theological tenets of Christianity, especially those that made claims of the miraculous. They rejected the Christian moral code as an irrational restraint on the personal pursuit of pleasure. Their denial of, or at least skepticism regarding, personal immortality constituted their most radical philosophical tenet. Many libertines, such as Madame Deshoulières, were Epicureans, declared partisans of Lucretius and Gassendi. They argued that material causation explains all states and actions, even the most apparently spiritual. In such a materialist perspective, the goal of the moral life is the rational pursuit of pleasure, the theological virtues are illusory, and the natural virtues are only manifestations of animal instinct. Other libertines, following Montaigne, remained determined skeptics on metaphysical and religious issues, declaring all such questions unresolvable.

Libertinism proved especially attractive to aristocratic women because it could only thrive in one of the social arenas open to them (indeed, dominated by them): the salon. Because of its moral and religious subversion, libertinism could not operate openly in the Church or in the ecclesiastically controlled university. Private and privileged (by dint of its aristocratic protectors), the salon provided an ideal site for the open exchange of skeptical theories. Deshoulières's salon was only one of several where libertines discussed favorite texts and critiqued the official religious and moral orthodoxy of the period. These salons also debated the apparent contradiction between the libertines' moral defense of personal freedom and their determinist account of human action.

BOOK AND ACADEMY

The philosophical culture of women did not depend solely on the indirectly philosophical influences of religious and literary education. A variety of avenues permitted aristocratic women of the period direct access to philosophical texts and issues.

The wide diffusion of books in French, especially Parisian, society permitted an increasingly literate public to read the works of ancient and modern philosophers. Inexpensive translations of Greek and Latin classics became an ornament of even the most modest salons and manor houses. Even as an impoverished adolescent in the provinces, Maintenon not only read, but memorized, Plutarch in translation.[7] An elite of women scholars (Mme Dacier;[8] Mlle de Rochechouart, Abbess of Fontevrault;[9] Mme Deshoulières[10]) impressed French academic circles with their translations from Latin and, more rarely, Greek texts. Successive waves of salon enthusiasm for Stoic and Epicurean philosophies arose largely from the reading of and commentary on translations of classical philosophical works.

More important was the decisive shift of philosophical writing from Latin into the French vernacular in the middle of the seventeenth century. Descartes's *Discours de la méthode* (1637) and Pascal's *Provinciales* (1656) were the most influential in a flood of French works published in philosophy and theology. Decried as dangerous vulgarizations of debates better left to the Latinophone clergy and professorate, the works immediately attracted a sizeable female readership, many of whom became ardent champions of Cartesian metaphysics and Jansenist theology. In his feminist tract *L'égalité des deux sexes* (1673),[11] Poullain de la Barre lists the most popular philosophical works read by contemporary women. The majority are written by Descartes: *Le discours de la méthode, Les méditations, Le traité de l'homme, Le traité des passions, Lettres à la reine de Suède et à la princesse de Bohème.* One is by a disciple of Descartes: Louis de la Forge's *Le traité de l'esprit de l'homme.* The last has a Jansenist provenance: Arnauld and Nicole's *La logique de Port-Royal.*

The enthusiastic response of women readers to vernacular philosophical works was not accidental. Numerous male philosophers deliberately wrote in French in part to attract the interest of women. In a letter to Père Vatier, Descartes defended the simplicity of the *Discours*'s philosophical arguments by appealing to the book's targeted female audience:

> It's not possible to make clear with certitude the arguments that prove God's existence according to my method, without clearly stating those arguments that show the incertitude in all of our knowledge of material things. It didn't seem right to me to put all these thoughts into a book that I wanted even women to understand.[12]

Pascal also indicated the importance of women readers in his polemic against moral laxism.[13]

Malebranche even argued that some physiological quirk in women explained their superiority in judging moral and aesthetic disputes:

> This delicacy of fibers in the brain is obviously present in women. This gives them their great intelligence for anything striking the senses. It's up to women to determine fashion, to judge language, to decide on good manners. They

have more knowledge, more cleverness, and more delicacy about these matters than men do.[14]

According to such arguments, women may not be superior to men as writers or philosophers, but they are in aesthetic judgment. The growing role of women as critics and editors of the works of prominent male authors seemed to confirm this preeminence in the area of taste. The dedication of numerous philosophical works to a *salonnière* like Sablé proclaimed the new status of aristocratic women as umpires in intellectual disputes.

With the rise of a vernacular canon, extensive philosophical culture was no longer confined to a handful of nuns and noblewomen versed in Latin. The emergence of French-language intellectual journals like the *Journal des Savants* (founded in 1665) also permitted women to engage more easily in philosophical discussions.

An informal Parisian network of tutors and courses provided women with an alternative philosophical education that bypassed the university and the official academies. These unofficial courses usually involved a charismatic lecturer who offered a series of philosophical and scientific conferences for an audience composed of both women and men. The courses often attempted to vulgarize the history of philosophy or contemporary philosophical controversies so that a genteel, but not especially cultivated, public could grasp the nature of the discipline.

The passionate interest of salon women in "Cartesianism" reflects the influence of these informal lycea. In his Parisian residence Jacques Rouhault[15] offered an annual cycle of lectures that defended Cartesian metaphysics and physics. An accomplished pedagogue, Rouhault sweetened the austerity of the subject matter by entertaining experiments with test-tubes and quicksilver. The yearly "Magnet Night" always swelled the already large audience of both sexes for his courses. His companion Cartesian treatise, *Traité de physique*,[16] sold briskly with his students. His disciple Clerselier[17] performed a similar service in disseminating Cartesianism through popular lectures and brochures.

The most astonishing of these informal academies was that conducted by Louis de Lesclache[18] for more than thirty years (1635–1669). From the opening of his lecture cycle on moral philosophy, Lesclache attracted a large female audience. One of his celebrated pupils, Bernarde Giraud, offered her own lectures under Lesclache's aegis and ultimately married him. He taught primarily the history of philosophy, attempting to reduce each school to a series of distinctive theses. Although fair to each philosophical system, he clearly sympathized with Aristotelianism as the most plausible of the schools. An astute popularizer, he published a companion volume, *Abrégé de la philosophie en tables,*[19] which contrasted the philosophical systems in a series of synoptic tables. The book sold thousands of copies and earned Lesclache a fortune.

When women authors of the period declared their allegiance to Cartesianism, the term could refer to the texts and theories of Descartes himself. But it often referred to the theories of his popularizing disciples or to a cluster of ideas categorized as "Cartesian" by a synthesizer like Lesclache.

Complementing the philosophical formation offered in the entrepreneurial academies, a network of scientific institutions offered lectures and experiments open to a public of both sexes.[20] Du Verney gave courses on anatomy at the Jardin du Roi. Lémery offered conferences on chemistry. At the royal observatory, Cassini invited a lay public to evenings of telescope observation followed by question-and-answer sessions on astronomy. In *Éloge des savants*,[21] Fontenelle noted the large number of women, typified by Mme de la Sablière, attending these scientific conferences and laboratory sessions. The scientific instruction often touched explicitly on philosophical issues. Lémery, for example, used his lectures on chemistry to criticize the dualism of Descartes and to defend the atomism of Gassendi.

The rise of a new class of erudite women rekindled the long-simmering *querelle des femmes*. Misogynists like Grenaille[22] battled egalitarians like Poullain de la Barre[23] over the old question of the equality or disparity of the sexes. Using the Renaissance convention of appeals to a wide range of authorities, parties to the dispute tried to determine God's position in the *querelle:* "Genesis clearly shows that God created Eve after Adam. Therefore, woman is inferior to man." "Ah, but Genesis clearly states that God created Eve at the apex of the seven days of creation. Thus, woman is superior to man." "Didn't Saint Paul say that wives should obey their husbands?" "But didn't Saint Paul also say that in Christ there is neither male nor female?" "The twelve male apostles." "The seven female virtues." "The powers of Saint Peter." "The prerogatives of the Blessed Virgin Mary." "God the Father." "But doesn't God have a Mother?"

If the rusty rhetoric of the *querelle* had scarcely changed in a century, the disputants were no longer evenly matched. The very existence of a group of educated French women competent in literature and philosophy constituted prima facie evidence on behalf of the egalitarians. In *La morale du sage*,[24] Marie-Éléonore de Rohan, Abbess of Malnoue, argued that the current generation of woman poets and scholars had destroyed the centuries-old myths concerning woman's alleged intellectual incapacity. Empirical evidence had overwhelmed prejudicial theory. She claimed that the current gap between men's and women's scientific achievements could be explained solely by the inadequacy of women's scientific education. Like other feminist authors of the period, Rohan concluded that the triumphant entry of women into the world of *belles lettres* proved that gender inequality was a product of nurture rather than nature.

SALON AS PHILOSOPHICAL SITE

At the center of the philosophical culture of French neoclassical women stood one dominant institution: the salon.[25]

Usually conducted by an aristocratic woman in her Parisian *hôtel*, the salon brought together men and women, clergy and laity, for intellectual debate and artistic performance, as well as for amorous adventure and parlor games. Although the salon had roots in the learned "courts" of Marguerite de Valois[26] and other Renaissance royalty, it developed its distinctive profile in seventeenth-century Paris.

The salon reflected the rise of a specific social class: the French aristocracy who migrated from the provinces to Paris in the seventeenth century. The exodus from the provincial manor house to several select Parisian neighborhoods (the Marais, l'Île de la Cité, Faubourg Saint-Jacques, Faubourg Saint-Honoré) created a geographic concentration of noble families without precedent in French history. This upsurge of a Parisian aristocratic society reflected new French economic realities: greater national affluence, relative decline of the power of landowners, and concomitant rise of the power of urban bankers. More importantly, it reflected the ascendancy of monarchic absolutism. In the new political order, centered on the king and his ministers, the ancient military and judicial powers of the nobility collapsed. Especially after the defeat of the Fronde (1648–1653), aristocrats found themselves transformed into courtiers in a pacified, centralized France. Salon receptions emerged as a key venue for the socialization of this newly leisured aristocratic class.

The artistic and intellectual ambitions of the salon also reflect the changed cultural ideals of the aristocracy. Stripped of its ancient military rights, the aristocracy abandoned the old ideal of *gloire* by arms as its highest honor. A new ideal of cultural refinement now became the goal of the noble family. In fostering this new politeness, the salon gave itself the literal mission of polishing the manners and the language of an aristocracy at one remove from provincial barbarism.

The coveted refinement of the Parisian aristocrat involved more than the proper use of the fork or of correct formulae of address. It required the capacity to conduct witty conversation, to engage in systematic meditation, to comment knowledgeably on the political and religious issues of the day (with enough artifice to avoid royal suspicion), to critique the latest philosophical theory. Cultural prestige suddenly became the preoccupation of every noble family. Salon hostesses vied for the honor of debuting a new play by Molière, showcasing the miraculous counting machine of Pascal, or staging a debate between proponents and opponents of Descartes.

As Linda Timmermans argues,[27] participation in Parisian salon culture demanded a certain minimum of literary and philosophical skill. The *salonnière* was expected to show a command of French in her conversation and her correspondence. She should be able to discuss the latest concerts, shows, and exhibitions as a connoisseur. The popular parlor games were often literary in nature, presupposing an acquaintance with classical and contemporary literature. An avid reader of novels and of essays by the *moralistes,* she was expected to discuss the movements of the heart in witty detail. She would wield the *distinguo* to perceive and comment on the slightest differences in the phenomenon of human love.

She was also expected to be a master writer. The vogue for correspondence became so marked that many Parisian aristocratic women wrote to their neighbors on a daily basis.[28] Madame de Sévigné[29] was only the most celebrated of the epistolers who established a literary reputation through the quality of their letters. Mme de Sablé revolutionized letter-writing through the invention of the *billet,* a brief note that simplified the conventions of the letter. Many *salonnières,* like Mlle de Montpensier,[30] cousin of Louis XIV, also composed extensive memoirs. Although technically private works, the letter and the memoir were routinely circulated in manuscript form among salon habitués.

Guided by the rules of polite conversation, salon culture soon produced a canon of published works by women. The novels of Mlle de Scudéry and of Mme de Lafayette, the poetry of Mme Deshoulières, the dramas of Mme de Villedieu, the devotional works of Mlle de Montpensier, the maxims of Mme de Sablé and of Mme de la Sablière, and the tales of Mme d'Aulnoy constitute the most visible part of the salon's literary production. Although much of the literary production confined itself to fiction and verse, an important portion of this new canon consisted in nonfiction works exploring philosophical issues. Reflecting the educational curriculum for women and the dominant concerns of salon debate, these works focused on moral philosophy, especially questions of moral psychology: the problem of moral freedom, the virtues, the will.

At mid-century, chroniclers of Parisian society cited hundreds of erudite *salonnières* in various compendia: *Dictionnaire des précieuses* (1661),[31] *Cercle des femmes savantes* (1662),[32] *Éloges des illustres savantes* (1668).[33] The chroniclers underlined the taste for philosophical argument, especially the allegiance to Cartesianism, that characterized many a new *savante.* In 1690, Gilles Ménage published the first modern history of women philosophers, *Historia mulierum philosopharum.*[34]

Most Parisian salons were modeled on the pioneering *chambre bleue* of Catherine de Vivonne's Hôtel de Rambouillet[35] and followed a similar pattern. An aristocratic woman invited guests to receptions in the evening or afternoon in the drawing-room or *ruelle* of her apartment. The primary activity of the salon was conversation itself, stimulated by parlor games. The salon routine was punctuated by more formal occasions: the public reading of a work in progress, the debut of a musical composition, poetry contests, scientific experiments, debates on literary and philosophical issues. Although politeness encouraged participants to avoid public controversies, the religious and political disputes of the day were never far from the salon surface. At the paradigmatic Hôtel de Rambouillet, Bossuet delivered his first sermon, scientists demonstrated how chameleons change color, and Chapelain presided over debates on proper usage and the latest literary vogue. More intellectually ambitious salons adopted the machinery of the scientific academy: official secretary, formal program, minutes, proceedings, archives.

Despite a certain similarity of structure, the Parisian neoclassical salons developed distinctive intellectual identities. Mlle de Scudéry's salon *Samedis* focused on literature. Mme de Sablé's emphasized theology. Mme de la Sablière's stressed experimental science.

The salons also acquired a distinctive ideological color. Deshoulières's was libertine and Gassendian. Montpensier's harbored the dissidents of the Fronde. Sablé's was Jansenist with a marked sympathy for Descartes. Housed in private residences rather than in the court, the salons aroused royal suspicion as dens of religious dissent and of political intrigue. Cardinal Mazarin, the prime minister of France in the middle of the century, attempted to recruit informers to infiltrate the salon of Madame de Sablé.[36]

Each salon also specialized in a particular literary genre. Under the direction of Voiture, Rambouillet encouraged elegant letter writing. Montpensier's salon produced a series of literary *portraits*. Sablé's pioneered the emergence of the *maxime*. Part of the originality of the moral philosophy produced by these women resides in the novel genres they devised to present a sustained argument on issues of moral psychology.

If the authors studied in this volume participated in salon society, each ultimately rejected certain conventions and values of the salon. Mlle de la Vallière and Mme de la Sablière broke completely with salon culture through dramatic religious conversions. Becoming respectively a Carmelite nun and a pious laywoman devoted to incurables, each composed works that denounced the hollowness of salon culture and the vices of the *salonnière*. Both illustrated the retreat to religious solitude undertaken by many aristocratic women in the later part of the seventeenth century.[37] Mme de Maintenon reformed the academy at Saint-Cyr by stamping out the last traces of *préciosité*. Mme de Sablé transformed the literary salon into an oxymoron: the Jansenist salon. Gourmet dinners and witty debates on love alternated with austere conferences on grace and letter-writing campaigns to save the nuns at Port-Royal.

If these philosophers transcended the limits of salon culture, they never abandoned the arms of the salon. Even as they defended a more religious or a more ascetical concept of happiness, they made their case through the *salonnière*'s arsenal of epigrams and dialogues. Their rhetoric used the conventions of polite conversation as its norm. Even in mystical passages, irony and concision retained their place of distinction. A critique of the intellectual and moral superficiality of the salon, the mature philosophy sketched by these five authors still bore the stamp of the salon, where moral philosophy remained tightly yoked to aristocratic manners.

A CANON SUPPRESSED

The canon of works in moral theory produced by salon women in early modern France raises an obvious question: why did the works disappear?[38] The disparity between the extensive list of women philosophers in Marguerite Buffet's 1668 study and their complete absence in standard histories of modern philosophy is striking. One cannot argue that these authors were simply unknown. As I argue in subsequent chapters, the publication of these works (in numerous editions), their acclaim by leading male philosophers of the modern period, and the recognition of these authors' philosophical acumen in literary chronicles rule out such an explanation. Other factors must be sought to explain the suppression of these philosophical voices.

First, the conventions of the period militated against an aristocratic woman publishing a work under her own name. Not only was such authorship considered a violation of feminine humility; it transgressed the aristocratic strictures against remunerated work. Private correspondence and manuscript works circulated among salon intimates were one thing; works published by a bookseller and sold on the public market were quite another. Mlle de Scudéry, a prolific novelist and essayist from the commercial classes, was seen as typically *bourgeoise* because of her public authorship and her energetic efforts to make a livelihood as a commercial author.

This disdain for public authorship meant that many philosophical works by women were published anonymously or posthumously. As a result, the identity of the actual author was often lost or contested. The anonymous authorship of a work by Louise de la Vallière permitted a later literary critic to ascribe it erroneously to a male author. The posthumous and anonymous publication of Sablière's *maximes* led to occasional confusion between her own work and that of La Rochefoucauld. The posthumous edition of Maintenon's works permitted her editor, La Beaumelle, to alter her style and theories along the lines of the editor's taste. The editor of the posthumous publication of Sablé's *maximes* used the occasion to add his own maxims to the work and to frame the work with a self-flattering introduction.

A persistent misogynist editorial prejudice compounded the risks of anonymous or posthumous publication. On more than one occasion, an editor has ascribed passages or entire works by early modern women authors to prominent male authors (Pascal, La Rochefoucauld, Fénelon) on the argument that women of the period could not have written with such style or with such philosophical insight—this despite massive internal and external evidence to the contrary.

Second, women philosophers of the period rarely wrote in the form of the treatise. If the norm for inclusion in the canon is Malebranche's massive *Recherche de la vérité,* the women studied in this volume need not apply. The dialogues, the maxim collections, and the essays do not pursue philosophical argument in the same way that the treatise does. However, the canon of modern philosophy has never excluded Montaigne's *Essais* or Pascal's *Pensées,* although neither of these works operates as a treatise. Given the elasticity of the criteria for male authors, the exclusion of women philosophers on the simple grounds of non-treatise literary form appears arbitrary. If the dialogues of Berkeley may be considered philosophical works, why not those of Maintenon? If the prayers of Pascal, why not the meditations of La Vallière?

The issue of the proper genre of philosophy presents obvious dangers. Opening the canon of philosophy to every work dealing with a philosophical theme simply abolishes the frontier between philosophy and non-philosophy. Novels, plays, sermons, even greeting cards would seem to fit. The works by women included as philosophical in this book qualify on more than thematic grounds. They are public, systematic works attempting to treat issues in moral philosophy. Memoirs and novels are excluded. The terms employed and the history of the author reveal an explicit knowledge of philosophical debates.

Most importantly, the works develop an argument on why the positions they defend are in fact true. Sablé's argument that friendship can be a site of authentic virtue is more than a subjective report on her own happy friendships. La Vallière attempts to demonstrate why a conventional or a rationalistic version of faith is fraudulent. To exclude these works because they do not follow the conventions of the treatise is to suppress a key chapter in the modern critique of virtue. It also contradicts the practice of the modern canon, which has not only included, but celebrated numerous works by male authors in genres other than that of the academic treatise.

Related to the problem of genre is the status of these women authors as *moralistes*. Unique to modern French culture, the *moraliste* dissected the movements of the human heart: the pretension of virtue, the empire of the will, the contradictory desires. A psychological and social critic, the *moraliste* charted the human propensity to deceive oneself and others. The *moraliste* preferred the brief literary genres that facilitated a rapier-like dissection: the maxim, the portrait, the fable. The works of the *moraliste* do not clearly fall into the disciplines of either philosophy, theology, or literature. In fact, the very inadequacy of the translation of *moraliste* as "moralist" indicates how awkwardly the world of the *moraliste*, the introspective aristocracy of early modern France, enters into the categories of contemporary Anglophone academe.

If studied at all, *moralistes* have been confined to departments of French literature. Mme de Sévigné has served as a significant female representative. In fact, the philosophy canon has long imported several male representatives of this tradition of moral analysis. Montaigne, Charron, Pascal, Arnauld, and Nicole are typical. No women, however, have figured as standard modern French *moralistes*. Without a greater incorporation of the canon of the *moralistes* into the philosophical as well as the literary canon of French modernity, the philosophical voice of the *salonnière* will remain suppressed.

Third, a secularist bias in the construction of the canon of modern philosophy tends to discount works written within a religious framework. "Rationalism" often functions as a normative rather than a descriptive criterion.[39] The critique of virtue by La Vallière or by Sablière emerges within works primarily concerned with religious salvation. To ignore or to dismiss the theological structure of such writings is to distort the moral theory of these philosophers. The persistent tendency to conceive modernity itself as the emergence of a philosophy liberated from religion inevitably reduces the religious works of the period to an enigmatic footnote. Within such a secularist grid, the moral arguments of the devout are easily dismissed as mysticism or poetry. And because of this dismissal, the philosophical contributions of works by militantly Catholic or Huguenot women are ignored.

Fourth, the current retrieval of the salon authors of French neoclassicism has often paradoxically marginalized them. Literary history has increasingly noted these women, but often in an auxiliary role. Thus, Sablé emerges as the editor of La Rochefoucauld, Sablière as the patron of La

Fontaine, Maintenon as the disciple of Fénelon, Deshoulières as the student of Gassendi. But their own works go largely unread and their own theories go largely unstudied.

Louise de la Vallière and Madame de Maintenon figure prominently in the melodrama of Louis XIV as, respectively, mistress and wife. Did La Vallière still love the king once she entered the convent? Did Maintenon push him to revoke the Edict of Nantes? But La Vallière's fiery critique of salon Cartesianism and Maintenon's elaborate apology for the virtue of temperance remain in the shadows.[40]

Once ignored, these authors now find themselves marginalized as maternal or marital ancillaries. It is their service to prominent men, not their own philosophical argument, that constitutes their alleged worth.

The philosophical retrieval of women thinkers of early modern France betrays a similar problem. Recent scholars have identified women as disciples of the dominant male philosophers of the period. We now possess a much more detailed map of the *Cartésiennes,* the *Malebranchiennes,* and the *Gassendiennes* who haunted the salons and even the convents.[41] The limitation of this style of retrieval is that women thinkers are once again pegged as auxiliaries to men. Women's works emerge as a subchapter in the long-standing story of the male modern canon. Such an approach minimizes the distinctively feminine sites of philosophy, like the salon and the convent. It ignores the genres of women's philosophy most removed from the male norm of the academic treatise.

Such an approach obscures the gender-specific nature of some of the philosophical works composed by women authors. Maintenon's theory of the virtue of politeness, for example, arises in the particular context of an aristocratic school with an all-female student body and an all-female faculty. To ignore the gendered nature of this philosophy is to suppress the specificity and the originality of her approach to virtue. Part of the purpose of this book is to explore the development of a philosophy that is an alternative to, and not only a derivation of, the philosophy produced by the canonical male theorists of the period.

Finally, raw misogyny has made its own contribution to the suppression of the philosophical works written by the women of the neoclassical salon. No one in the last half of the seventeenth century could ignore the sudden emergence of an aristocratic female society fascinated by philosophical issues to the point of writing about them. Numerous authors celebrated the new access of women to philosophical culture. Other authors, however, found the perfect weapon to dismiss the woman philosopher: ridicule. Molière's *Les précieuses ridicules* (1659) was the masterpiece of the skewering of the *salonnière* as a vain pedant tripping over Latin phrases and metaphysical arguments her sex would better ignore. Even more influential was

Boileau's *Satires: Book X*,[42] where he systematically ridiculed every prominent *savante* for daring to cultivate science and philosophy.

The successful caricature of the salon philosophers helped to bury their work as insignificant. Against this perduring stereotype, the first step in the retrieval of the moral philosophy of French neoclassical women is to take their work and their theory seriously.

HERMENEUTICAL METHOD

The method used in this book to interpret these philosophers draws from literary criticism, cultural history, philosophy, and theology. The primary focus, however, is philosophical. The texts are interrogated in the light of traditional philosophical categories and are related to the broader philosophical canon.

The point of departure for the analysis of these authors is the identification and presentation of their more philosophical works. Given the obscurity of these works, great attention has been paid to the translation of these works and a substantial citation of the works themselves. Only such ample documentation can acquaint the reader with this heretofore closed canon and indicate just how sophisticated its argument in moral philosophy is.

Drawn from literary criticism, considerations of genre highlight the global form in which these arguments operate. An understanding of the vogue of the *maxime* places the abrupt and paradoxical opinions of Sablé and Sablière in literary context. The overarching prayers of *Réflexions sur la miséricorde de Dieu* ground the second-person voice in which La Vallière studies the theological virtues. Maintenon's use of fictional and actual dialogue to present her pedagogical views accounts for the often unresolved character of her moral argument. To ignore the varied genres of these texts and to abstract propositions from these works as if they were academic treatises inevitably misinterprets the moral theory proposed by these works.

Philosophy provides the central tools for the analysis of the work's arguments. Thematically the analysis identifies how each work develops a position on one perennial issue in moral philosophy: the nature of virtue. It studies the particular virtues privileged by each author: friendship in Sablé; civility in Maintenon; the theological virtues in Sablière and in La Vallière.

The analysis also attempts to link the virtue theory of each author to wider philosophical concerns: the Jansenist theology of Sablé or the educational convictions of Maintenon. Focused on "the suspicion of virtue," the interpretation of these philosophies studies how each elaborates a critique of the claims of virtue in general or of particular virtues exalted by Christian humanism. Critical, the analysis offers a judgment on the originality of the contribution of each author to virtue theory and of the contradictions and inadequacies manifest therein.

Complementing the internalist critique, contextualist analysis places the works and theories of the women in a broader framework. The biographical sketch opening each chapter attempts to situate each woman's philosophy within her personal history, especially her intellectual history. Special attention is given to her philosophical formation. The mitigated skepticism of Sablé or the militant Augustinianism of Sablière emerge more clearly against the background of books read, lectures heard, circles attended, and letters received.

The religious genealogy of each author is crucial, since the theory of virtue argued by each woman closely follows the religious creed endorsed in maturity. The religious movements of the period (Jansenism, Gallicanism, Quietism, libertinism) and the Augustinian undertow of the entire French Catholic Reform illuminate the distinctive figure of virtue sketched by these *salonnières*. In each chapter the role of the salon in the formation of their philosophical and theological culture is underscored.

Several tools of social analysis also complement the literary-ideological study of these works. Gender analysis raises questions about the sex-specific nature of these arguments, questions that transcend simply noting the gender of the author. The study of La Valliére examines the carefully gendered "voice" of her book. Why does she present herself as Mary Magdalene in the prelude to her discussion of faith, hope, and charity? The examination of Maintenon underlines the gendered public (all-female student body and faculty) to which her dialogues are addressed.

Gender analysis not only identifies certain traits of tone or style as reflective of women's experience; it clarifies why certain virtues, such as fortitude or glory, recede in these author's works, and why other virtues, such as civility, are in the ascendant. It also explores sex-specific reasons why these authors criticize certain virtues esteemed by men (Maintenon) and why they distance themselves from a distinctively male critique of virtue (Sablé).

Finally, class analysis underscores the particular social milieu from which these concepts of virtue sprang. Although each author deals with a series of virtues concerning human nature as such, the account of virtue bears the traces of the concerns of the aristocracy of the *ancien régime*. The emphasis on politeness, the elaborate discussions of manners, the critique of ambition, the muffled references to politics, and the cautious irony express the anguish of the flight from the provincial manor by the noble turned courtier.

The analysis of these authors attempts to respect the social otherness in which the question of virtue emerges. The humanity dissected by this circle of philosophers bears a specific social rank and mourns a particular moment of social exile. The barbed elegies of civility spring from a chastened aristocratic class plunged into a court society where the possibility of an honest, let alone an evangelical, life of virtue was hardly gained in advance.

CHAPTER II

Madame de Sablé: A Jansenist Code of Moderation

Knowing how to discover the interior of another and to hide one's own is a clear mark of a superior mind.

— MME DE SABLÉ, Maxim no. 35

The model *précieuse* who became a *dévote,* Madeleine de Souvré, Marquise de Sablé (1598–1678) has survived as a footnote to modern French history. In literary chronicles, she appears as the patron of La Rochefoucauld. Hostess of a salon that perfected the genre of the *maxime,* she emerges as the inspiration of La Rochefoucauld's works. This ancillary literary role, however, obscures her own writings and ignores the original critique of virtue she proposes therein.

In religious history, Sablé survives as a faintly comical figure in the Jansenist controversy. Sainte-Beuve summarizes the perduring image of Sablé as a hypochondriac gourmet dabbling in religious controversy:

In lodging near Port-Royal of Paris, in a building she had constructed next to the convent, she created a novel position for herself. We can well represent her as she was during these years: one foot in the convent, the other in the street; hearing everything, fussing over everyone, interfering with everything; making herself the finest wit and the greatest theologian; avid for the smallest bit of gossip and for the most recent religious tome; interested from now on only in her salvation and in her new circle of monks, but still maintaining all her best friends from before; keeping close to her austere confessor, but not dismissing her cook; consulting both her physician and her moral theologian on her migraines and on her scruples; sponsoring lectures, colloquia, and debates in her salon, but feeling supported by the nuns on Communion day; helping the nuns by her marvelous potions and all-purpose elixirs, but putting into her jams and jellies only what is absolutely permitted. . . .[1]

20

This stereotype ignores Sablé's complex political role in the Jansenist movement. The sauces suppress the diplomatic soul of Sablé, who deliberately sought a compromise between the cloister and the salon in her personal life, and who attempted to construct a Jansenist ethic less astringent than that proposed by a Pascal.

The dismissal of Sablé as a self-indulgent amateur of Jansenism obscures the specificity of her contribution to the moral philosophy of the Jansenist circle. It is her moderation that distinguishes her account of the virtues from the more acerbic dissection of virtue carried out by her protegé, La Rochefoucauld. Like other Jansenists, she systematically unmasks the standard moral virtues as expressions of vice, especially the vice of pride. However, she exempts certain figures of love (friendship, affection, loyalty) from her critique. If she elaborates upon the hypocrisy animating salon gestures of virtue, she underlines the social benefits even feigned virtue can confer. This theoretical moderation reflects her own vocation as a reconciler in politics (between royalists and Frondeurs) and in religion (between Jansenists and Jesuits). Her characteristic moderation, however, does not prevent Sablé from composing a social critique of the hierarchy of rank that dominated the culture of the salon and of the court.

A DIPLOMAT'S LIFE

Born in 1598, Madeleine de Souvré belonged to an ancient aristocratic family in the region of Perche.[2] Her father, Gilles de Souvré, held numerous titles: marquis de Courtenvaux, baron de Lezines, chevalier des Ordres du Roi. He served as the governor of the young Louis XIII. Her mother was Françoise de Bailleul, dame de Renouard. Her family sided with the *parti dévot*[3] and supported Queen Marie de Médicis in the campaign for a more sectarian foreign policy. In 1610 Madeleine de Souvré was appointed lady-in-waiting to Marie de Médicis.

Little is known of Madeleine de Souvré's education. Clearly, however, she received an exceptional literary formation. Her letters were widely praised for their grammatical and stylistic purity. She early established herself as a sophisticated judge of works of poetry and fiction, although she had a marked aversion to historical works.

Her education also provided her with a fluency in Spanish language and literature. She studied Balthasar Gracián's *L'oraculo manual*[4] before its translation into French. She defended a heroic conception of love labeled by her contemporaries as distinctively "Spanish."

In her memoirs, the *salonnière* Mme de Motteville recalls this Hispanic outlook: "She [Sablé] was so convinced that men could have tender sentiments without committing a crime, that the desire to please women would move them to great and noble actions by inflaming them and by inspiring them with a sense of magnanimity and other sorts of virtue."[5] This Hispanophile conception of heroic love also announces one of the cardinal theses in Sablé's moral philosophy: the virtuous nature of friendship.

In January 1614, Madeleine de Souvré married the Marquis de Sablé. Mme de Sablé bore nine children, five of whom died in infancy. The four surviving children achieved some distinction: Urbain, marquis de Bois-Dauphin; Henri, Bishop of La Rochelle; Guy, a military officer killed at the battle of Dunkirk in 1646; and Marie, a cloistered nun. In an obvious marriage of political convenience, both spouses led separate and unfaithful lives. According to Tallemant des Réaux,[6] the young Mme de Sablé led a thoroughly coquettish existence in the salons of Paris. She conducted an open affair with the Maréchal de Montmorency, who was later executed for treason by Richelieu, and she may also have had an affair with the Chevalier d'Armentières.

Throughout her life, Sablé participated in the salon culture of Paris. Three salons in particular shaped her literary and philosophical sensibility: those conducted by Mme de Rambouillet, by Mlle de Scudéry, and by Mlle de Montpensier.

At the salon of Catherine de Vivonne, marquise de Rambouillet,[7] Sablé became acquainted with the social and literary elite of the period. She became a passionate reader of the works of Montaigne and of Voiture.[8] Chapelain praised the literary quality of her letters.[9] She developed a reputation as an apologist for Spanish literature. The salon's emphasis upon the various gradations of the sentiment of love influenced her later philosophical preoccupations.

During the Fronde (1648–1653), the uprising of a loose coalition of aristocrats and local parliaments against the growing absolutism of the French monarchy, Sablé managed to retain the loyalty of both sides. A partisan of the royalist cause, she maintained close contacts with the regent, Queen Anne d'Autriche, and her controversial prime minister, Cardinal Mazarin. She also nurtured close friendships with leaders of the Fronde (Mme de Longueville, Count and Countess de Maure), many of them habitués of the Hôtel de Rambouillet. Ever the diplomat, she engineered a political marriage between the Fronde's Prince de Conti and a niece of Mazarin; the two wed on February 22, 1654. In recognition of her diplomatic skill, Mazarin granted Sablé a state pension.

In the late 1640s and the early 1650s, Sablé frequented the famous "Saturdays" of Mlle de Scudéry.[10] This salon focused on contemporary literary matters. Among other literary genres, the salon habitués showed interest in light poetry, such as the satiric epigram. This literary taste clearly influenced the genesis of the *maximes* as the favored literary product of Sablé's later salon. Like most salons, Scudéry's "Saturdays" mixed social classes. Clerics like Bossuet and aristocrats like the Prince de Condé mingled with the bourgeois friends of Scudéry. Female authors like Mme de Villedieu and male authors like Pierre Corneille shared their latest compositions. The primary theme of this temple of the *précieuses,* the variations of love, would influence later debate in Sablé's salon.

Scudéry's salon exhibited the academic rigor the more intellectual salons were borrowing from the scientific academies of the period. Scudéry's salon stipulated a formal agenda for each session and produced a regular set of minutes, proceedings, and historical notices. Valentin Conrart,[11] a prominent member of the Académie française, served as the salon archivist.

In her roman à clef *Grand Cyrus,* Scudéry praised Sablé under the pseudonym Princess of Salamis:

> Never has anyone known so perfectly all the differences concerning love, as the Princess of Salamis knows them. I know of no activity as pleasant as listening to her make distinctions between pure love and worldly love; sincere love and feigned love; interested love and heroic love. She permits everyone to penetrate the depths of the heart. She depicts jealousy with words more horrifying than the image of serpents ripping apart the heart. She knows all the innocent joys, as well as all the sufferings, of love. Her knowledge of this passion is so perfect that Venus herself scarcely knows it better.[12]

The reputation of Sablé the moralist, specialized in questions of affectivity, is already established.

Later in the 1650s, Sablé participated in the salon of Mlle de Montpensier.[13] Habitués of the salon included aristocratic authors who would become close friends of Sablé: Mme de Sévigné, Mme de Lafayette, and La Rochefoucauld. In 1657 Mlle de Montpensier's circle invented a new literary genre: the *portrait.* The portrait consisted in a witty description of the physical, emotive, and moral composition of a particular person. The portrait focused on the distinctive vices and virtues that constituted the character of a person. Montpensier etched the portrait of Sablé under the pseudonym "Princess of Parthenia,"[14] and highlighted Sablé's signature vice: hypochondria.

The *portrait* quickly became a literary vogue throughout France. With the assistance of Jean Segrais, the secretary of Montpensier's salon, publication of the salon's portraits began in 1659.[15] The portrait's emphasis upon moral psychology, especially the subtle vices of the righteous, would shape the focus of the maxims later produced in Sablé's salon.

Sablé conducted her own salon, first at the fashionable Place Royale

(1648–1655) and then in her apartment adjacent to the convent of Port-Royal (1655–1678). A literary center from its inception, Sablé's salon pioneered a new genre of moral analysis: the *maxime*. It became a cenacle for the Jansenist movement and a center for debate on the philosophical and theological issues that engaged the Jansenists and their critics.

During the 1640s Sablé's life entered a somber phase. The death of her husband in 1640 led to serious financial difficulties. A bitter struggle over the family inheritance led to a lawsuit against her eldest son, Urbain. The death of her son Guy during the siege of Dunkirk plunged her into prolonged mourning.

This decade also marked Sablé's growing involvement with the Jansenist movement. In 1640 Mère Angélique, abbess of Port-Royal, noted Sablé's "conversion" in one of her letters.[16] In the same year, Sablé triggered one of the early controversies between the Jansenists and the Jesuits. Sablé shared with Anne de Rohan, Princesse de Guéméné, a text written by her Jesuit spiritual director, Père Sesmaisons, that justified frequent reception of Holy Communion, even after attendance at a ball, then considered a licentious activity. Already a partisan of the Jansenists, the scandalized Princesse de Guéméné presented the text to her spiritual director, Abbé de Saint-Cyran, the Jansenist chaplain of Port-Royal.

Saint-Cyran commissioned Antoine Arnauld, the movement's leading theologian, to refute the argument. Arnauld did so in *On Frequent Communion* (1643),[17] a literary success that defended the need of prolonged penance, even delayed absolution, before reception of Communion after the commission of serious sin. The book also launched the Jansenist attack against the alleged moral laxism of the Jesuits.

A retreat at Port-Royal in 1652 sealed Sablé's commitment to the Jansenist movement. In 1655 she constructed an apartment abutting the convent of Port-Royal in the Saint-Jacques neighborhood of Paris. One side of the apartment opened onto a balcony in the convent church, where Sablé attended religious services with the nuns. The other side opened onto the street, where guests arrived for the salon sessions hosted by Sablé. A gourmet noted for her fine cuisine and therapeutic recipes, Sablé attempted to balance a monastic liturgical life with an aristocratic salon life in her small apartment physically poised between the two worlds.

As the correspondence between Sablé and the abbesses (Mère Angélique, Mère Agnès) attests, the marquise was not an easy boarder.[18] Numerous conflicts erupted, especially when Sablé's pathological fear of contagion threatened to interfere with the life of the convent. Nonetheless, Sablé successfully maintained her status as a lay auxiliary to the convent for twenty years and effectively used her political connections to defend the Jansenist convent during the years of persecution.

The campaign against the convent of Port-Royal intensified at the very moment that Sablé opened her apartment there.[19] In 1653 Pope Innocent X promulgated the bull *Cum Occasione*, which condemned five theological propositions on grace and predestination. Subsequent papal declarations insisted that these propositions had been supported by Jansenius in his work *Augustinus* and that the Church was condemning these heretical propositions precisely in the sense that Jansenius had given them. The Jansenist party agreed that the propositions were indeed heretical. However, the Jansenists denied that Jansenius or his disciples had ever supported such theses.

A skilled lawyer, Antoine Arnauld devised a subtle distinction between *droit* (law) and *fait* (fact) to justify the Jansenists' mitigated acceptance of the Church's judgment. According to this theory, the Church had the authority to bind conscience in matters of *droit,* issues of faith and morals, since such questions directly touched salvation. The magisterium of the Church enjoyed the assistance of the Holy Spirit in these judgments. However, in judgments of empirical fact (*fait*), the Church could not bind the conscience of the faithful. The judgment that a particular individual had denied a doctrine of faith was based on fallible evidence. It was a purely human judgment, subject to subsequent revision or even reversal. While the Church could make such judgments and the faithful should respect them, these judgments of fact could never be an issue of divine faith.

The implication of this ingenious distinction for the Jansenist quarrel was clear. The Jansenists accepted the Church's condemnation of the disputed propositions. But they could not accept the empirical judgment that Jansenius had supported these heretical theses, because they saw no evidence for this in his works. The attitude before this apparently erroneous judgment by Church authorities would be one of "respectful silence."

Arnauld's *droit/fait* distinction resolved the problem of conscience for the majority of Jansenists, but it provoked opposition within and without Jansenist circles. A minority of Jansenists criticized this solution as an overly subtle casuistry that masked the serious problems in the Church's condemnation. Opponents of the Jansenists denounced the distinction as a radical assault upon the scope of the Church's religious authority.

In 1661 Louis XIV intensified the campaign against the Jansenists. With the support of the French episcopate, the throne drew up a formulary condemning the five propositions and stating that these propositions had been defended by Jansenius. The king specified that the formulary was to be signed by the clergy, members of religious orders, and lay teachers. Singled out for signature were the nuns at Port-Royal, the militant center of Jansenism in Paris.

Louis XIV's action precipitated the "Crisis of the Signature" at Port-

Royal. Could the nuns in good conscience sign the formulary? The majority of Jansenists, led by Arnauld, argued that one should sign, on condition that the qualified nature of the signature, based on the *droit/fait* distinction, was clear to all. A minority, led by Abbé Singlin, supported unconditional submission out of respect for Church authority. Another minority, led by Claude Lancelot, argued that one should refuse to sign, since even an equivocal signature appeared to condemn not only Jansenius, but also St. Augustine's doctrine on grace.

Throughout the crisis, Sablé urged the nuns to sign the formulary. She also pleaded with civil and ecclesiastical authorities to accept a qualified signature.

The two vicars of the Archdiocese of Paris handling the crisis added a codicil to the formulary that explicitly recognized the validity of the *fait/droit* distinction. Arnauld argued that this conciliatory gesture should remove any qualms of conscience about signing the document. Reluctantly the nuns of Port-Royal signed the amended formulary in June 1661.

Unsatisfied, the opponents of the Jansenists insisted that the vicars' irenic amendment be annulled and that the nuns sign a formulary without qualifications. Pope Alexander VI condemned the vicars' additions to the formulary on August 1, 1661. In November 1661, the Port-Royal nuns signed an unamended formulary. However, in front of their signatures they added their own declaration that their signature indicated only respect for, not total acceptance of, the document's findings of fact. Once again, the enraged critics of the Jansenists demanded total submission.

The controversy deteriorated in 1664 when Hardouin de Péréfixe, the new Archbishop of Paris, dispersed a dozen Port-Royal nuns to other convents, imposed a group of anti- Jansenist Visitation nuns on the convent, and posted an armed guard around the convent. In 1666 the Archbishop exiled the recalcitrant nuns to the older Port-Royal convent, located in the countryside, and placed them under interdict (exclusion from the sacraments) for disobedience.

He appointed Sister Flavie Passart the new superior of a small group of nuns at Port-Royal in Paris who had signed a new formulary without reservations. Throughout the crisis, Sablé maintained cordial relations with both groups of Port-Royal nuns and continued to seek a negotiated solution. The election of Clement IX to the papacy brought a temporary halt to the conflict. Worried by the possibility of schism and pressured by the opinion of a public appalled by the treatment of the nuns, Clement engineered a new, sinuous formulary repeating the Church's condemnations but softening the language of submission. The nuns' signature in January 1669 returned the convent to normalcy and inaugurated the "Clementine Peace."

Throughout the decade of crisis, Sablé played a central diplomatic role. In 1663 she hosted a committee headed by Gilbert de Choiseul, Bishop of Comminges, that sought to reconcile the quarreling parties. After the sanctions of 1666, she repeatedly intervened with royal and episcopal allies to soften the severity of the punishments and to devise a new compromise. She emerged as one of the architects of the Clementine Peace.

Correspondence from this period indicates the diplomatic skill of Sablé. In early 1664, a group of Jansenist theologians published a pamphlet on the *droit/fait* distinction that enraged the Bishop of Comminges, who had urged both parties to cease public debate on the controversy. In a letter, Sablé attempted to assuage the bishop's anger and to reignite the reconciliation committee he headed:

> You have found the way to make me happy and sad at the same time. Nothing is more pleasant than seeing your letter, but nothing is sadder for those who love these gentlemen than to see your complaints and your threats. . . . I must tell you that there is nothing in this world that disturbs me more than to see such a bright and good prelate as yourself and such teachers who have the same gifts from God, piety and intelligence, so opposed to each other. Although you roar like a lion in your letter, you have such a sweet soul that I do not fear sharing with you my feelings on the subject, although they differ from yours. Permit me, my lord, to tell you that I personally spoke out against the publication of these letters. However, by publishing these letters, these gentlemen in no way harmed you, because the letter you wrote to the king on this subject concedes more than these letters do. Further, these gentlemen have far more to fear than you do if they do something against their word. There is certainly much to criticize here, but nothing to punish.[20]

The letter's rhetoric accurately reflects the habitual diplomatic posture of Sablé. The tone mixes deference to the addressee (praise of the bishop's virtue, flattery of his hidden sanguine temperament) with a candid reproach of a vice (unjustified anger). The argument insists that both sides are closer than either would imagine: the virtues of the bishop and those of the Jansenist scholars are identical. The argument concedes that both sides have erred: the Jansenists by intemperate publication, the bishop by rash judgment. The letter shrewdly tries to bring the bishop back to a more irenic moment in the negotiating process (the redaction of a letter to the king that agreed with the Jansenist version of the *droit/fait* distinction) rather than freeze him in his current anger. By highlighting similarities in moral intention, in miscommunication, and in ecclesiastical theory, Sablé deftly indicates that a compromise between the two parties is closer than the current antagonism suggests.

In 1667, during the darkest moment of the campaign against Port-Royal, Sablé corresponded with Cardinal de Rospigliosi, a nephew of the pope and a prominent Curial official. In this letter, Sablé's diplomatic skills assume a legal precision:

> Being only a woman, I shouldn't dare even to speak to you about these things, but I happened to build a house for myself at Port-Royal in order to retreat from the world. It's true that these conflicts in the Church have caused and are still causing the greatest division. So you won't find it odd if I tell you that in the convent there were one-hundred-and-twenty nuns outstanding in piety. They took away eighty nuns who, because of their tender consciences, feared to offend the truth by saying that these propositions are in a book they haven't even read because it's in a different language than theirs. They were convinced that they could condemn these propositions wherever they might be found, even in Jansenius, if they aren't asked for anything else. . . .[21]

The letter's address shrewdly defers to the cardinal by an appeal to gender prejudice. It admits that theological controversies are not the concern of women. Sablé disingenuously presents herself as an onlooker who just happens to live near a convent where an unpleasant theological dispute has broken out. If her self-effacement scarcely matches the facts of her prominence in the controversy, it sets a tone of reverence that maximizes the power of the papacy to resolve the festering crisis.

The brief history of the controversy carefully avoids the substance of the quarrel. There is no discussion of grace. There is no attempt to defend the refusal of an unreserved signature. The issue is subjectivized as a matter of sympathy for the delicate conscience of pious nuns. Objectively, their conscience in this case might be distorted by scruples (fear of the least transgression) and by ignorance (inability to read the controversial text in Latin). But their moral sincerity deserves respect. Again, the argument is clearly disingenuous. No one ever accused the stubborn Port-Royal nuns of sentimentality and no one considered a convent renowned for its theological culture a cenacle of ignorance. Nonetheless, Sablé carefully transforms a dispute over doctrine and authority into a pastoral problem requiring the Church's compassionate solicitude.

Having set a reverential tone, Sablé the lawyer lays a carefully calibrated compromise on the table. Doctrinally, the nuns would agree to the condemnation of the five disputed propositions. (Neither party had disputed this part of the condemnation.) On the question of *fait*, the nuns would agree to a condemnation of the propositions wherever they might be found, even in the works of Jansenius. This subtle formula offered more than the "respectful silence" of Arnauld and less than the unconditional submission sought by the opponents of the Jansenists.

Sablé complemented her private crusade with a public campaign to support the proposed compromise. At her instigation, her son Henri, Bishop of La Rochelle, solicited a number of French bishops to sign a petition to the pope supporting this solution. In fact, the new formulary devised as part of the "Clementine Peace" uses language almost identical to the subtle recasting of the *droit/fait* distinction devised by Sablé.

In 1669 Sablé returned to her apartment in the Port-Royal convent, pacified by the terms of the Clementine truce. Her final years were tranquil, marked by a growing freedom from her longstanding fear of illness and of death.

Sablé died on January 16, 1678. At her request, she was buried in the common plot reserved for paupers in the parish of St. Jacques-du-Haut-Pas.

A JANSENIST SALON

In 1655, Sablé opened her apartment on the grounds of the convent of Port-Royal. Distinguished women of her salon included the authors Mme de Sévigné,[22] Mme de Lafayette,[23] the Abbess of Fontevrault,[24] the Abbess of Caen,[25] and Gilberte Pascal Périer.[26] Prominent men came largely from the Jansenist movement: the theologian Arnauld,[27] the moralist Nicole,[28] the jurist Domat,[29] Abbé Jacques Esprit,[30] and Blaise Pascal.[31] La Rochefoucauld,[32] although reticent concerning the Jansenist movement, elaborated a radical critique of virtue consistent with Jansenist anthropology.

Ever irenic, Sablé's salon also included opponents of the Jansenists: the Comte de Maure and the Marquis de Sourdis, who supported the more libertarian theology of Molina.[33] It even included the Jesuit literary critics Bouhours[34] and Rapin,[35] smuggled in as "contraband." Preoccupied by issues of health, Sablé frequently invited a group of medical doctors, headed by her personal physician, Valant.

Sablé's salon pursued a wide range of philosophical interests. Salon members debated the theses of Descartes through discussions of *Pensées sur les opinions de M. Descartes,* composed by Clausure.[36] The work explained and defended the dualism of Descartes. Marquis de Sourdis delivered a paper on physics: "Why Water Rises in a Small Tube."[37] Mme de Brégy,[38] a partisan of the Stoics, lecturéd on new translations of Epictetus. The paper "Thoughts on the Mind" sparked a metaphysical dispute among salon participants.[39] A conference on Calvinism (July 17, 1663) featured a debate between the Protestant pastor Gasche and the Catholic Père Desmares.[40]

The controversy inspired the work *Perpetuity of the Catholic Faith* by Arnauld and Nicole.[41]

The predominant philosophical issues of the salon were ethical in nature. "Thoughts on War"[42] offered a quasi-pacifist analysis of the ethics of warfare, complemented by Arnauld d'Andilly's provocative paper, "Why We Must Prefer our Friends to our Country."[43]

The bulk of the ethical discussions focused on the favorite salon topic: the variations of human love. Marquis de Sourdis's manuscript "Questions on Love" indicates the sort of questions that animated the salon's controversies and shaped the moralist literature produced by many salon members:

> Is it better to lose someone you love by death or by infidelity?
> Can one love something more than oneself?
> Is a greater jealousy a sign of greater love?[44]

As another Sourdis manuscript indicates, the questions on love often took a gendered form:

> Can a man loved by a woman in secret insult a rival who disturbs him?
> Must a man who received gifts from a woman give them back to her if she requests them before breaking up?
> Should a woman hate a man whom she loves but who does not court her because he is committed elsewhere?[45]

This preoccupation with moral issues, explored through epigrammatic analysis, provided the conditions for the emergence of the salon's distinctive literary genre: the *maxime*.

A written descendant of the "sentences" that structured the debates of Sablé's salon, the *maxime* may have begun as a type of literary salon game. Habitués of the salon would develop a sentence based upon the observation of manners. This sentence would usually take an ironic turn. Through successive criticism, offered in salon conversation and through epistolary exchange, salon members would polish the moral observation. The ideal was epigrammatic concision. The maxim's barbed judgments routinely incorporated the Jansenist suspicion of virtue that marked Sablé's circle.

Originally a collaborative enterprise, the production of maxims soon revealed a salon genius: La Rochefoucauld, whose *Maximes* (published in successive editions from 1665 to 1678) became the standard of achievement in the genre.[46] Sablé's intimate involvement in the genesis of La Rochefoucauld's maxims has never been disputed. In massive correspondence, Sablé criticized and proposed alternative phrasing for hundreds of maxims La Rochefoucauld had submitted for comment. In extreme cases, this process of editorial correction would submit the same maxim to more than thirty revisions.[47] La Rochefoucauld never hid his debt to Sablé: "You know that sentences are only sentences after you have approved them. I send to you what I took from you in part."[48]

Not confined to stylistic corrections, the editorial work of Sablé often revealed substantial philosophical differences with La Rochefoucauld. In a packet of fifteen draft *maximes* sent for comment, La Rochefoucauld had included a cynical sentence (no. 5) on friendship: "Most friends are disgusted by friendship and most of the devout are disgusted by devotion."[49] Sablé's response attempted to moderate the censure of friendship: "On the fifth. When friendships are not grounded in virtue, there are so many things that can destroy them that almost always we can find many causes for their destruction."[50] Sablé attempts to transform La Rochefoucauld's global critique of friendship into a partial critique of friendships founded upon vice. The presupposition, one rejected by La Rochefoucauld, is that other types of friendship, namely those founded upon virtue, escape such censure. Moreover, Sablé attempts to soften La Rochefoucauld's designation of disgust (*dégôut*) as the unique cause of friendship's collapse. She claims that a multiplicity of causes, many of them benign, account for the decline of affection.

In addition to her personal critiques of the *maximes,* Sablé abetted the genesis of La Rochefoucauld's collection by submitting drafts of his work to prominent literary acquaintances. More than a dozen critical responses indicated a gendered response to La Rochefoucauld's work. Male respondents tended to be positive, praising his acidic analysis of human pretensions to virtue as an excellent propadeutic to an Augustinian conception of human depravity and of the need for redemption. Female respondents, however, were uniformly critical, condemning the caustic dismissal of all virtue as an inaccurate reflection of the morally mixed nature of human experience, with its moments of authentic virtue as well as of counterfeit virtue masking the vice of pride.

Mme de Schomberg, Duchesse de Liancourt, criticized the *maximes* as morally dangerous inasmuch as they discouraged any effort at virtue. They also seemed to endorse a moral determinism that denied any authentic human freedom.[51]

Marie-Éléonore de Rohan, Abbess of Caen, attacked the misogyny of La Rochefoucauld in his treatment of female emotion:

> Sir, it seems to me that you have a greater understanding of the heart of men than of the heart of women. Despite my esteem for your ideas, I can't prevent myself from opposing your theory that women's emotions are responsible for

all their apparent virtue, because we'd have to conclude from that theory that reason is completely useless for them. Although it might well be true that sometimes they have stronger feelings than men, experience shows that they know how to surmount their emotions. When we've agreed that you've placed men and women on an equal footing, it would only be just to thank you. Ordinarily it's more common for women to hold their emotions in check than it is for men when they are bad-tempered, because convention and shame force them to do so when their virtue and their reason don't oblige them.[52]

At La Rochefoucauld's request, Sablé wrote a review of the book as part of a publicity campaign. Joined to a letter to La Rochefoucauld, the review diplomatically mixed positive and negative evaluations of the collection of *maximes:*

> Some believe that it's an outrage to humanity to make such a terrible portrait of it and that the author could only have found the model for this portrait in himself. They say that it is dangerous to publish such thoughts, and that, having shown that we only perform good acts out of bad reasons, we wouldn't try anymore to be virtuous, because all our virtue would be illusory. . . . Others, on the contrary, find the work very helpful because it reveals to people the false ideas that they have about themselves and makes them see that without religion they are incapable of doing any good.[53]

Unamused by the mixed review, La Rochefoucauld cut all negative criticism from the article and published the purely flattering section in the *Journal des Savants* in 1665.[54] The judicious Sablé found herself reduced to a blurb for the book's successful publication in the same year.

The extensive correspondence of Sablé during this period indicates how the philosophical interests of her salon served its predominant theological concerns. A letter from Blaise Pascal to Sablé (December 1660) thanks her for introducing him to Antoine Menjot, a Calvinist member of the salon. Menjot's medical and philosophical expertise helped Pascal to brook the problem of the immortality of the soul:

> A thousand thanks for having introduced me to M. Menjot. . . . Since I already admired him because of the things my sister [Gilberte] had told me about him, I can't tell you how delighted I was to meet him personally. You only have to read his work to know how much wit and judgment he has. Although I'm not capable of understanding all the matters he treats in his book, I can tell you, Madame, that I've learned a great deal from him. In a few words, he demonstrates the agreement between the immortality of the soul and the power of matter to alter its functions and to cause delirium. . . .[55]

Pascal's letter manifests the anguish that contemporary medical research on the brain had provoked in Christian philosophical circles. The moral freedom of the individual and the very spirituality of the soul seemed threatened by growing clinical evidence that physical causes could dramatically alter mental states.

In a letter to Sablé, the Marquis de Sourdis criticizes Pierre Charron's work *La sagesse*. Although some had praised the book as a propadeutic to faith, Sourdis condemns it as a subtle but thoroughgoing piece of skepticism:

> Throughout this work, we detect an intention to encourage people toward debauchery, irreligion, and libertinism, toward denying ourselves nothing nature asks for, as long as we are moderate. It praises just living for ourselves prudently and peacefully. That's in fact his motto. Finally, he encourages people to disguise their true life and to deceive the public, to ignore their country and to betray its good qualities by making them useless.[56]

Sourdis's letter attacks one of the *bêtes noires* of Sablé's salon: Neo-Epicureanism, vulgarized in the lives of the libertines. The critique is religious. Obedience to "nature alone" closes the subject to the recognition of and submission to the supernatural order. But the critique is also political. The designation of individual pleasure as the highest good destroys the social order by dulling the sense of one's sacrificial duties toward others.

CANON AND OBSCURITY

Unfortunately, Sablé's reputation as the patroness of La Rochefoucauld has obscured her own contribution to moral theory through a genre she virtually invented. After her death, Abbé d'Ailly[57] published Sablé's own maxims under the title *Maximes de Mme la Marquise de Sablé; suivies de Pensées diverses de M.L.D.* (1678).[58] These *Maximes* reveal Sablé's skill in using this tool of moral psychology, developed in her own salon. They manifest her distinctive moral outlook, a synthesis of social criticism and partial defense of virtue that differs sensibly from the bitter irony of La Rochefoucauld. They also indicate the key intellectual influences on her moral philosophy, in particular the influence of Montaigne, of Gracián, and of La Rochefoucauld himself.

The subsequent history of Sablé's maxims is a textbook case in the methods of suppression of the voice of women philosophers. Occasionally reprinted in new editions of La Rochefoucauld's maxims, the writings of Sablé were either published anonymously or misattributed to another author. Only in 1870 was a separate edition of Sablé's maxims republished under her own name.[59] Several Pascal scholars insisted that the most elaborate of the maxims, no. 81 on comedy, must have been composed by Pascal rather than by Sablé. The primary argument was that a minor writer would not have been capable of such moral analysis. The influential Brunschvicg, Lafuma, and Le Guern editions of Pascal's *Pensées* perpetuated this misattribution, until research in the 1960s decisively reattributed the maxim to Sablé.[60] Only at the end of the twentieth century, with the neofeminist expansion of the French literary canon, did complete editions of Sablé's maxims become widely accessible.[61]

The low literary opinion of Sablé's writings has also limited their dissemination. Literary critics have routinely dismissed Sablé's works as unoriginal, a simple pastiche of clichés from her sources. Oddly, even the editors of her work tend to discount her as an inferior version of La Rochefoucauld. Victor Cousin, the pioneering biographer of Sablé, informs the reader that he decided not to publish her maxims in their entirety because of their general mediocrity.[62] Jean Lafond, editor of a recent annotated edition of Sablé's maxims in a La Rochefoucauld volume, introduces Sablé's work with an apology: "If we present here the maxims of Sablé, it's not to suggest a comparison between the two, which would easily be to the disadvantage of the marquise."[63]

The critical dismissal of Sablé's work rests upon the longstanding interpretation of Sablé as a La Rochefoucauld *manqué,* a temporizer who lacks the courage and the acerbic wit of the master. In fact, however, Sablé simply disagrees with La Rochefoucauld on a number of central moral issues: concupiscence, freedom, friendship. It is a difference in belief, not timidity, that sustains her more moderate evaluation of human depravity in her own collection of maxims.

ANATOMY OF POWER

Certain of Sablé's maxims provide pragmatic counsels for success. Maxim 4 states that "It is sometimes useful to pretend that one is mistaken."[64] Sablé underlines the importance of style in achieving one's goals. Maxim 25: "There is a certain empire in the manner of speaking and acting that imposes and that wins, in advance, consideration and respect . . ." (23). Given the laboratory of the salon, Sablé pays particular attention to the proper conduct of speech. Maxim 36 praises the concise phrase: "Speaking too much is such a great fault, that in the area of conversation and business, if the good is the short, it is doubly good, because we win by brevity what we often lose by verbal excess" (28).

Sablé notes the link between power and knowledge, especially the knowledge of others gained through intimate dialogue. Maxim 37: "Practically always, we make ourselves master of those we know well, because the one who is perfectly known is in a way subordinated to the one who knows him" (28). Maxim 35 traces the strategy of this psychological empowerment: "Knowing how to discover the interior of another and to hide one's own is a clear mark of a superior mind" (27). Significantly, the more pragmatic maxims do not present success in terms of economic wealth or political power. Rather, reflecting the culture of the salon, they conceive success as psychological knowledge achieved through a careful discipline of interpersonal dialogue.

The capacity of the skillful to know and govern others carries its own moral danger. The esteem of style and manner can easily blind the observer to questions of substance. External grace can occult internal content. Maxim 48: "The exterior and the circumstances often elicit greater respect than the interior and the reality. A poor manner spoils everything, even justice and reason. The *how* is the most important part of things. The appearance we give gilds, trims, and softens even the most troubling things" (34). Typically, Sablé locates the source of the human fascination with form in the shadows of a darkened intellect and will. Rather than guiding the human person to truth, the engaging argument often leads the person to a misjudgment reflecting the weakness (*faiblesse*) and the bias (*prévention*) of the mind.

LEARNED IGNORANCE

Several of Sablé's maxims possess a more psychological cast, inasmuch as they present variations on Socratic ignorance. Maxim 38 argues: "The study of and search for truth often serve only to make us see, by experience, the ignorance which is naturally ours" (29). Sablé, however, adds her distinctive contours to the philosopher's confession of ignorance. More emotive, Sablean ignorance connotes madness. Maxim 8: "The greatest wisdom of humanity is to know its folly" (16).

Sablé moralizes the quest for authentic knowledge: "It is quite vain and useless to make an examination of everything which happens in the world, if that does not serve to correct oneself" (16). Conversely, moral vice often appears as the outward sign of the incapacity to grasp one's mental and moral infirmity. Maxim 7: "Mediocre minds, poorly formed minds, especially the semi-savants, are most subject to opinionated stubbornness" (15). While playing on the Socratic paradox of the ignorance of the wise and the vain knowledge of the fool, these maxims evoke the Jansenist portrait of depraved human nature, where the recognition of one's confusion constitutes a privileged moment in the personal itinerary of moral and religious conversion.

SOCIAL CRITIQUE

The majority of Sablé's maxims constitute a critique of aristocratic society. The critique focuses upon the vices typical of this milieu. Like La Rochefoucauld and Pascal, Sablé unmasks the self-interest, especially the pride, that disguises itself as virtue or necessity among the nobility.

Several maxims dissect the vanity that animates the salon's commerce: polite conversation. Instead of dialogue, such discourse normally consists of speeches strictly reducible to the speaker's partial interests. Maxim 29: "Everyone is so busy with her passions and her interests that she always wants to talk about them without ever entering into the passion and interests of those to whom she speaks, although they have the same need to be heard and helped" (24).

In a minute study of the psychology of conversation, Sablé describes the chasm between the social conventions of politeness and the empire of the will in defending oneself. Maxim 31: "One of the things which makes it difficult to find pleasant people, who seem reasonable in conversation, is that practically none of them think more about what they want to say than responding exactly to what one says to them. The most tolerant are happy to show an attentive expression, but at the same time, one sees, in their eyes and in their spirit, a removal and a precipitation to return to what they want to say . . ." (25). In this maxim, Sablé not only satirizes the desperate search for personal triumph that dominates the conversation of the salon; she also underscores the obstinacy of the human will in excluding the presence and interests of others, even in the anodyne exchange of everyday information.

Several maxims attack more directly the corruption of social power. Sablé contests the material wealth and the moral poverty of her peers. Maxim 67: "It is quite a common fault never to be happy with one's fortune and never unhappy with one's soul" (40). The link between economic prosperity and happiness reveals that virtue no longer motivates the leading members of society. Maxim 32 notes that "Good fortune almost always makes some change in the procedure, the tone, and the manner of conversation and action. It is a great weakness to want to adorn ourselves with that which is not ours: if we esteemed virtue more than any other thing, then neither any favor nor any promotion would ever change the heart or the face of people" (26).

For Sablé, the definition of self-worth in terms of material fortune is only one sign of a society closed to the pursuit of virtue. Upon closer scrutiny, even apparently altruistic actions manifest themselves as strategies of personal empowerment. Maxim 74: "Virtue is not always where one sees actions which appear virtuous; sometimes, one only recognizes a favor in order to establish one's reputation or to be even more firmly ungrateful toward favors one does not wish to recognize" (43). The courtly rules of politeness themselves become weighted markers in the game of political aggrandizement.

In her critique of aristocratic society, Sablé distinguishes between a physical aristocracy (defined by blood and rank) and a spiritual aristocracy (defined by possession of authentic virtue). The communion of the virtuous is more substantial than the communion of family members, who are united only by biological line. Maxim 30: "The ties of virtue must be deeper than those of blood, because one good man more clearly resembles another good man by morals than a son resembles his father by his face" (24). The maxim clearly discounts the value placed upon lineage in the society of the period. For Sablé moral identity supplants family descent as the key trait of the individual and of society.

Sablé does not hesitate to criticize the court itself. Courtly society under Louis XIV has created a type of aristocracy that prides itself uniquely upon political connections. The preoccupation with court affairs suppresses the intellectual as well as the moral virtues. Maxim 2: "True merit depends neither upon time nor upon fashion. Those whose only quality is having an air of the court promptly lose it when they are away from court. But good sense, knowledge, and wisdom are the source of happiness everywhere and anytime" (14). Courtly society not only corrodes the moral virtues by its exaltation of self-importance; it destroys the capacity of the intoxicated courtier to think with balance and clarity. Not without a primitivist touch, the maxim indicates that authentic intellectual virtue (*bon sens, le savoir, la sagesse*) resides outside the court gardens.

DRAMA AND MIMESIS

Sablé's severest critique of French society is presented in her most famous maxim, no. 81, "On Comedy." This paragraph-length meditation provides a categorical condemnation of theatrical performances. "All the great diversions are dangerous for the Christian life, but among all those which the world has invented, there is none greater to fear than the comedy" (46). This criticism of the theatre is hardly novel for a member of the Jansenist circle. The sympathizers of Port-Royal, led by the moralist Nicole,[65] had repeatedly condemned attendance at the theatre as incompatible with Christian righteousness. Both Catholic and Calvinist canons of the period banned Christian burial for members of the theatrical profession.[66] Sablé's criticism of the theatre as a dangerous "diversion" echoes the broader Jansenist critique, perfected by Pascal,[67] of a society that suppresses religious questions under a curtain of jaded entertainments.

Strikingly, however, Sablé does not employ the traditional Christian arguments against the theatre. The churches had habitually condemned the theatre because of the sexual license of comic pieces and the debauchery, even prostitution, for which many theatres had become notorious. Sablé, on the contrary, criticizes the comedy because it creates an illusion of authentic love and, through mimetic participation, manipulates the emotions of the public.

For Sablé, the danger is not obscenity or license. These can be rejected easily by the educated spectator. The danger lies in theatrical presentations of moral and reasonable love, illusions that subtly alter and destroy the authentic affections of the self. "It [comedy] is so natural and so delicate a representation of the passions that it makes them come alive and makes them arise in our heart. This is especially true of love, when one provides a fairly chaste and honest love, because the more it seems innocent to innocent souls, the more are those souls susceptible to comedy's effects" (46).

Exposure to such models of romantic love prods the spectators to engineer such artificial relationships in their everyday lives. "So, one goes away from the comedy with the heart so full of all the sweets of love and the mind so persuaded of its innocence that one is completely prepared to receive the same pleasures and the same sacrifices that one has seen so well depicted in the comedy" (46). For Sablé, the deleterious effect of theatre lies primarily in its power to imprison us in an imaginary society, where sacrifice and pleasure take root in manufactured emotions rather than in the struggle for virtue. Theatre promotes a false sense of "innocence" that precludes the realistic assessment of one's need for moral and religious conversion.

SOCIAL ILLUSION

Several maxims develop their social critique by examining the gap between appearance and reality, a gap nurtured by the rules of social esteem. Maxim 19 diagnoses the contradiction: "We are more worried to appear as we should be than to be in effect what we should be" (20). This desire to appear virtuous rather than to be virtuous fosters a distinctive web of social deception. Maxim 20: "If we had as much care to be what we should be as we have to deceive others by disguising what we are, we would be able to show ourselves just as we are, without having the trouble of disguising ourselves" (21).

Sablé detects a particularly virulent strain of appearance-reality conflict in the way in which her contemporaries execute their high offices of social trust. Maxim 23: "We often have a greater desire to pass for conscientious than to execute conscientiously our office, and often we prefer to be able to say to our friends that we have done well for them rather than having, in fact, done well" (22). For Sablé, the virtues and offices of the aristocrat are often nothing other than a slothful quest for social applause, artfully concealed under the polish of self-advertisement.

VIRTUE'S VIRTUE

Despite the severe social criticism presented in the preceding maxims, Sablé's moral reflections are distinguished by a refusal to adopt the thoroughgoing cynicism of other authors in her salon. Her correspondence with La Rochefoucauld frequently contains criticism of his extreme dismissal of all "virtues" as masks of interest. Several maxims develop this positive moral theory, which attempts to defend the veracity of certain virtues and even, paradoxically, the social value of certain vices.

Sablé insists that, despite its perversions, virtue still constitutes the soul of authentic aristocracy. Maxim 72: "Those who are stupid enough to esteem themselves only by their nobility despise, in some way, that which makes them noble, since it is only the virtue of their ancestors which has made the nobility of their blood" (42).

Sablé explicitly condemns the tendency of her peers to detect a hidden vice behind every virtue. Maxim 61: "There is nothing which doesn't have some perfection. Happily, good taste finds it in everything. However, natural malignity often discovers a vice hidden among several virtues, in order to highlight and publish it. This is more a trait of congenital evil than a sign of discernment, and it is quite wrong to pass one's life in the single-minded delight in another's imperfections" (38).

In her theory of virtue and vice, as well as in her political and religious *praxis*, Sablé exhibits her characteristic moderation. The critique of the social counterfeits of virtue cannot obscure the preeminent value of virtue itself and the authentic, if rare, instances of its exercise.

Sablé even argues that in the daily struggle between the virtuous and the vicious, the virtuous often win. Maxim 9: "Honesty and sincerity in action shake those who are cruel and make them lose the way by which they plot to arrive at their ends, because the cruel usually believe that one never does anything without artifice" (16).

Not content with the defense of virtue, Sablé contends that even aristocratic vice is not without social utility. Maxim 71: "It is almost better that the great of this world seek glory and even vanity in good actions, rather than not being touched by it at all, because, although they do not act by principles of virtue, there is at least this advantage: that vanity makes them do what they otherwise would not" (42). Sablé's critique of human duplicity takes place in a universe notably more optimistic than that of La

Rochefoucauld, one where even vice can paradoxically serve the goals of virtue.

In one area, Sablé is particularly adamant on immunity from deceit: the personal experience of love. Maxim 80 encapsulates Sablé's position: "Love has a character so particular that one can neither hide where it is nor pretend where it is not" (46). The particular veracity of the sentiment of love is rooted in the unitive knowledge that is characteristic of it. Maxim 79: "Love is to the soul of the one who loves what the soul is to the body of the one it animates" (45). Sablé's insistence on the veracity of the sentiment of love clarifies her disdain for the theatre, which threatens to distort the one area where authentic interpersonal knowledge might emerge.

Sablé's defense of the value of human love emerges even more clearly in her small treatise, "Of Friendship." First published in the nineteenth century by Victor Cousin,[68] this treatise defends friendship as the most common example of virtuous relationships.

Sablé argues that friendship represents a synthesis of the fundamental virtues of social intercourse. "Friendship is a species of virtue which can only be founded upon the esteem of the persons loved, that is, upon the qualities of the soul, such as fidelity, generosity and discretion, and on the good qualities of mind" (79). Sablé insists that authentic friendship requires equality, a basic reciprocity between the partners. "It is also necessary that friendship be reciprocal, because in friendship one cannot, as in romantic love, love without being loved" (79).

Another characteristic of authentic friendship is freedom. Friendship can only arise from an act of the will, not from affective inclinations. "One must not give the name 'friendship' to natural inclinations, because they depend neither on our will nor on our choice. Although they may make our friendships more pleasant, they must not be the foundation" (79). Sablé admits that certain "friendships" seem to be constructed upon mutual calculation, but she dismisses such unions as counterfeits of authentic friendship. Silent on the merits of family hierarchy, Sablé lauds friendship as a privileged locus for the mutual, egalitarian pursuit of virtue.

Sablé's positive evaluation of friendship is clearly a riposte to her protegé, La Rochefoucauld. In his own maxims, La Rochefoucauld argues that all friendship is but a mask for egoistic interests. His Maxim 83 is typical: "What humanity has named friendship is only a business, a reciprocal arrangement of interests, only an exchange of services; finally, it is only a commerce where self-love always proposes something to win."[69] Sablé's

Maxim 77 closely parallels La Rochefoucauld's: "Society and even friendship for most people is only a business that lasts as long as there is a need" (45).

Obviously both authors draw upon the same primitive phrase. The differences between the maxims, however, are striking. La Rochefoucauld's condemnation of all friendship as a pact of self-interest becomes Sablé's mitigated condemnation of most friendships (*la plupart des hommes*) as commercial enterprises. Some friendships clearly escape censure. La Rochefoucauld's designation of self-love (*amour-propre*) as the cause of friendship yields to Sablé's softer designation of need (*besoin*) as the cause. Even when their vocabularies coincide, Sablé's moderation guides her to conclusions that clearly diverge from the global cynicism of La Rochefoucauld.

Sablé's defense of the moral value of friendship may also reflect a gendered difference with La Rochefoucauld. For aristocratic men of the period friendship was in fact often an alliance founded upon mutual military, political, and economic interests. The advancement of the prestige and the welfare of one's family line demanded such calculated acquaintanceships. Barred from most public exercises of power, however, aristocratic women often experienced a more disinterested type of friendship. Mutual esteem and affection without the calculation of social advancement were more likely to arise. From her early defense of love *à l'espagnol,* Sablé had insisted upon the possibility and the moral value of such a disinterested friendship between men and women, as well as among women themselves.

TOWARD GOD

Few of Sablé's maxims deal explicitly with religious issues. This reticence reflects the implicit rules of the genre, which tended to limit itself to questions of moral psychology. It also reflects salon etiquette, which considered passionate political and religious debate impolite. In several maxims, however, Sablé does broach specifically theological questions.

The opening maxim of the collection deals with religious epistemology. Sablé praises the act of faith, whereby the believer submits himself or herself to God's revelation. Maxim 1: "As nothing is weaker and less reasonable than submitting your judgment to that of someone else, rather than using you own, nothing is greater and more intelligent than blindly submitting your judgment to God, by believing on His word everything that He says" (14).

This argument has an unmistakably Jansenist turn. The reasonableness of the act of faith, defended by mainstream Catholic theology, disappears. On the philosophical level, one must suspend judgment. Descartes's methodic doubt clearly finds an echo. However, on the theological level, one must accept God's revelation solely upon the authority of God's word. Philosophical skepticism and theological fideism embrace.

Religious virtue does not escape Sablé's censure. The piety of the devout habitually masks self-interest. The charity inspired by piety rarely reaches the evangelical norm of self-sacrifice. Maxim 64: "There is always enough self-love hiding behind the greatest piety to place clear limits on one's charity" (39). The sentence wryly suggests that the true temper of the religious soul emerges in the contradiction between the caritative rhetoric of piety (*dévotion*) and the prim determination to maintain one's interests against sacrificial altruism. Rather than dilating the charity of the devout, pious exercises often serve as an indictment of the grasping, self-enclosed soul.

A MODERATE'S CREED

Sablé's voice as a moralist transcends the particular positions she takes on any given virtue or vice. Her moral judgments are tempered by a moderation that systematically prefers nuanced critique to categoric condemnation. Her characteristic moderation detects the distortions of intellect and will, including the distortion of alleged virtues, engineered by human concupiscence. However, it prefers to interpret these distortions as salutary lessons to those seeking the narrow path of righteousness rather than as signs of utter human depravity.

The distinctive moderation of Sablé's critique of virtue governs her treatment of both intellectual and moral virtue. Her critical treatment of science illustrates the temperance of her censure. Maxim 21: "There is no one who can't draw some assistance from and benefit from the sciences. But there are few people who don't take away some presumption from the information and the knowledge they have received from the sciences, if they don't use them as is proper and natural" (22). The maxim clearly criticizes the tendency of science to provoke pride among its practitioners. But the critique is measured. Whereas all people benefit from science, not all suffer from its characteristic vices. A minority appears to escape completely. Moreover, the moral vice derives from the misuse of science. The proper use of science, marked by respect for its natural purposes, can reduce the moral dangers substantially.

Sablé's moderation also influences her treatment of vice in the ethical domain. The moral tares of others should serve as cautionary tales for our own conduct rather than as trophies of a human fragility we gleefully denounce. Maxim 49: "The stupidities of other people should be a lesson for us rather than an occasion for us to mock those who do them" (34).

Part of authentic wisdom consists in the power to recognize the moral defects of others with a certain magnanimity. Maxim 34: "Truly great understanding embraces everything. There is as much character in enduring the faults of others as in recognizing their good qualities" (28). Moderation here constitutes something more than a trait of temperament or a hesitation to make a definitive judgment. It is a moral stance that paradoxically brandishes the virtues of patience and tolerance upon the debris of virtues unmasked.

Sablé's characteristic moderation does not represent a halfway house between the optimism of Renaissance humanists and the pessimism of Port-Royal. It only softens a clearly Jansenist anthropology. Several maxims underscore the concupiscence that has gravely distorted human nature. Maxim 18: "We love novelties and extraordinary things so much that we even have a secret delight in seeing the most tragic and horrifying events, both because of their novelty and because of the natural malignity within us" (20). In Sablé's perspective, this natural malignity may not poison every friendship or corrode every virtue, but it tarnishes most relationships and is the secret guest of most virtues. Even moderated, human concupiscence twists human perception and human action.

CONCLUSION

The literary success of La Rochefoucauld has long obscured Sablé's distinctive contribution to moral philosophy. In effect, Sablé pioneered an alternative to the academic philosopher's approach to ethics through the treatise. The maxim permitted Sablé and her colleagues to evoke issues of moral psychology through an ironic sentence. Whereas La Rochefoucauld simply asserts certain theses on the illusion of virtue, Sablé often develops an argument to defend her theses. She attempts to convince us that theatrical performances are dangerous, that pride taints public service, and that friendship is a sure *locus* of virtue. Often dismissed by literary critics as pedantic, Sablé's efforts to justify her positions enhance the philosophical quality of her maxims.

Sablé's contribution to moral theory is not limited to the creation of a new genre of moral analysis. She uses the standard tools of the moralists to develop a critique of social hierarchy. Whereas other moralists focus on universal issues of moral psychology, Sablé often fastens on class-specific distortions of virtue. She studies the gap between appearance and reality as the chasm between the alleged altruism of public service and the bitter pride that actually drives it. She dismisses the nobility of blood as a caricature of the true nobility of virtue. It is the courtier, not the servant, she presents repeatedly as the model of duplicitous virtue. By conjoining the analysis of virtue with the critique of aristocracy, Sablé transforms the maxim into an arm of social criticism.

Sablé's characteristic moderation also constitutes an original note in the circle of Augustinian moralists. Her moderation is more than a matter of tone. It reflects her diplomatic creed. While human nature is fallen and much alleged virtue is only disguised vice, the fall is not as radical as her Jansenist colleagues assert. While the mission of the moralist is to unmask human illusion, the honest execution of the mission cannot lead to a dismissal of every virtuous act or to despair over human moral agency. The suspicion of virtue must be balanced by a suspicion of the suspicion.

Finally, Sablé's work manifests the specific contours of the salon philosophy of the period. In her writings, the salon becomes the subject, not simply the milieu, of moral reflection. The evidence of human duplicity is the carefully observed script of salon conversation: the gap between word and gesture, the refusal to listen, the minute strategies of political conquest. Conversely, Sablé locates virtue in one specific place: in the egalitarian friendship of *salonnières* pursuing moral and religious reform. In other words, Sablé designates as "virtue" none other than the devout fellowship that constitutes the *telos* of her Jansenist salon.

CHAPTER III

Madame Deshoulières: A Naturalist Creed

Of reason, one must expect nothing:
Too much unhappiness teaches us
That it counts for nothing once the heart begins to act.
— MME DESHOULIÈRES, "Rondeau"

Literary historians have long recognized Antoinette du Ligier de la Garde, Mme Deshoulières (1638–1694),[1] as a leading poet during the reign of Louis XIV.[2] Starting in 1672, Deshoulières published a series of poems that earned her contemporary acclaim as "the tenth muse"[3] and "the French Calliope."[4] Her verse covered a wide range of genres: odes, idylls, sonnets, rondeaux, maxims, portraits, biblical paraphrases, and translations from Latin. Her poetry alternated between light satire, in the disguise of dog-and-cat epistles, and solemn panegyrics, in the form of odes on the triumphs of Louis XIV. In the field of drama, Deshoulières composed a comedy (*Eaux de Bourbon*), tragedies (*Genséric, Jules-Antoine*), even an opera libretto (*Zoroastre*).

In recognition of her literary achievements, Deshoulières was elected a member of the Academy at Arles, of the Academy of the Ricovrati at Padua, and of the Abbé d'Aubignac's Académie des belles-lettres in the Parisian Hôtel Matignon. Although ineligible for election to the Académie française, which officially banned women from membership, Deshoulières received formal recognition from the Académie. In 1691, during the inauguration of Fontenelle, Académie officials declaimed one of Deshoulières's poems on Louis XIV as part of the official proceedings.

If literary history has accorded Deshoulières a modest niche in its account of neoclassicism, philosophical history has ignored her. This is paradoxical, since Deshoulières brought unusual philosophical credentials to her literary work. In fact, her poetic canon constitutes an important chapter in the Renaissance naturalism that perdured in France throughout the seventeenth century. This omission of Deshoulières is even odder given her contemporaries' judgment that she was dangerously *philosophe*—that is, too clearly attached to the skeptical and libertine creed of her associates.

Deshoulières's works also provide an original contribution to virtue theory. Convinced that the human person is an integral part of the material cosmos, Deshoulières transforms the virtue of humility into a reverence before the physical environment that constitutes the origin and the term of human existence. She similarly recasts the cardinal vice of pride as an arrogance that destroys the material environment in the name of reason and of ontological hierarchy.

FORMATION OF A NATURALIST

Born in 1637, Antoinette du Ligier-de-la-Garde was baptized on January 2, 1638 in the Parisian church of Saint-Germain-l'Auxerrois.[5] Her father was a *chevalier de l'ordre du roi* and the *maître d'hôtel* for the queen Anne d'Autriche. He also performed a number of services for the queen mother and regent, Marie de Médicis.

Conducted by a series of tutors, Antoinette's education was unusually extensive for a woman of the period. She learned Latin, Italian, and Spanish. She became an accomplished musician, dancer, and equestrian. She avidly read the novels of Urfé, La Calprenède, and Mlle de Scudéry, although she later condemned the novel as a superficial literary genre.

Among her tutors, the poet Jean Hesnault[6] proved the most influential. A disciple of the philosopher Gassendi,[7] Hesnault introduced Deshoulières to a naturalism that explains the activities of all creatures, including human beings, in terms of material causation. Reputedly a libertine, Hesnault also transmitted to Deshoulières a thoroughgoing skepticism regarding the religious and ethical mores of baroque France. Like Hesnault, Deshoulières adopted Lucretius, the Latin disciple of Epicurus, as her mentor in metaphysics. In her mature poetry, especially the nature idylls that established her reputation, Deshoulières systematically developed the naturalist metaphysics and anthropology she had inherited from Hesnault.

In 1651 she married Guillaume de la Fon-de-Boisguérin, seigneur Deshoulières. A military officer, M. Deshoulières was attached to the service of the Prince de Condé, a leader of the Fronde. The marriage of convenience permitted both parties to pursue their divergent interests. M.

Deshoulières left France with Condé at the height of the civil wars of the Fronde. Mme Deshoulières returned to her parents' home, where she continued her studies. The enthusiastic reading of the works of Gassendi sealed her naturalist convictions and introduced her to contemporary disputes in French philosophy.

In 1656 Mme Deshoulières attempted to bring her husband back from exile in the Lowlands. After a flattering reception at the court in Brussels, she was arrested in February 1657 and imprisoned. Suspicions of espionage or spite on the part of court rivals probably motivated the arrest. In October 1657 her husband masterminded a daring rescue of his wife and both escaped to the French border. A personal interview with Louis XIV in the presence of the queen-regent, Anne d'Autriche, and the prime minister, Cardinal Mazarin, reintegrated the disgraced couple into French court society.

Always fragile, the marriage now collapsed. In 1658 M. Deshoulières petitioned for a legal separation of goods and persons. Bankrupt, he assigned his remaining assets to his creditors. Abandoned and impoverished, Mme Deshoulières began her literary ascent. Her modest salon in the Rue de l'Homme Armé hosted a circle of writers of a decidedly libertine bent: Fléchier,[8] Des Barreaux,[9] Mascaron,[10] Benserade,[11] Quinault,[12] Pellisson,[13] Ménage,[14] and La Monnoye.[15] As Eugène Asse[16] argues, her salon constituted the link between the libertinism of the Fronde and that of the Régence in the early eighteenth century.

In 1662 she published her first work: a portrait of the skeptical thinker Linières. She in turn is the subject of a literary portrait under the title "Amarylis." She imposed herself as an arbiter in the literary disputes of the period. She took the side of the moderns in the quarrel over whether an inscription on a triumphal arch should be written in Latin or in French. In 1667 she committed a celebrated literary gaffe when she published a sonnet mocking Racine's *Phèdre*. A partisan of Corneille, she championed the worthless *Phèdre* of another playwright, Pradon. In 1684 she fought a literary duel with the Duc de Saint-Aignan over the nature of gallantry.

It is as a poet that Deshoulières established her literary reputation. In 1672 *Le Mercure galant* published the first of her nature idylls. Acclaimed for their style, her poems propagated her naturalistic creed. For two decades, she used her poetry to demonstrate the material causes of human behavior, especially those traits commonly interpreted as more "spiritual." She repeatedly criticized the claims to human transcendence based upon pretensions of reason, love, or immortality. In the moral domain, she condemned the destruction of self and environment justified by rationalist anthropology.

In recognition of her literary distinction, the Academy of Padua (1684) and the Academy of Arles (1689) elected her to membership. In 1688 Louis XIV granted her a modest pension.

In 1682 Deshoulières began to suffer from breast cancer. Her poetry became more austere. The pastoral verse of the 1670s ceded to a more abstract, philosophical poetry. As the illness progressed, she composed *Réflexions morales,* a series of maxim-like meditations on death and human illusion. She underwent a religious conversion, abandoning her naturalist creed in favor of a renewed Catholic orthodoxy. Her final poetic works, paraphrases of the psalms, indicted her former skepticism. The youthful translator of Lucretius, enchanted by the material cosmos, had become the commentator of the Vulgate, celebrating the hope of immortality and mocking the religious skepticism of the libertines.

Toward the end of her life, Deshoulières's reputation as a poet began to decline. Following the lead of Boileau,[17] contemporary critics increasingly reduced her literary career to her risible role as leader of the anti-Racine claque. Deshoulières herself recognized the oblivion to which her canon seemed destined. In her poem, "To Reverend Father Bouhours, on his book, *The Art of Thinking Well Concerning Literary Works*" (1687), Deshoulières tweaks the famous Jesuit critic for having ignored her in his discussion of contemporary French literature:

> In a triumphant list
> Of famous authors which your book praises,
>   I don't see a place for my name.
> About me—isn't it true?—You haven't given a thought.
>   But also in the same vein
>   You have forgotten Pascal,
>   Who nonetheless didn't do such a bad job thinking.
>   Such company consoles me.
>
>   (*D* I:203)

Madame Deshoulières died in Paris on February 17, 1694.

CANON OBSCURED

For more than a century, the works of Mme Deshoulières remained popular. The first edition of her collected poetry appeared in 1687.[18] The last complete edition appeared in 1803.[19] The collapse of the pastoral as a popular genre consigned her work to obscurity, although several of her idylls have survived as standard anthology pieces.

In the eighteenth century the *lumières* recognized Deshoulières's contribution to philosophy. In his celebrated dictionary, Pierre Bayle praised her skepticism. In the article on Hesnault, Bayle treated her apparent denial of human immortality:

> It is certain that anyone who spoke this way literally would be denying the immortality of the soul. But to save the honor of Madame des Houlières, let's just say that she was following some poetical conventions that we are not supposed to take too seriously . . . not that one can't hide a good bit of libertinage under the privilege of versifying.[20]

In the article on Ovid, Bayle lauded her naturalist subordination of the human species to nonrational animals: "One of the most lucid and of the most brilliant minds of the seventeenth century preferred the condition of sheep to that of humans."[21] Both Voltaire[22] and Rousseau[23] cited her contribution to metaphysical poetry of the period.

As Deshoulières's canon disappeared from circulation, her role in neoclassical naturalism vanished from philosophy texts. Literary critics, however, continued to point out that Deshoulières's works contributed more than innovations in the pastoral genre. They constituted a central chapter in the libertine skepticism of the neoclassical era. Antoine Adam summarizes the common literary portrait of Deshoulières the salon skeptic: "She had the reputation of being foreign to all religious belief and her poetry seems in fact to carry the reflection of this incredulity."[24] The literary image of Deshoulières as skeptic nonetheless often ignores the naturalist metaphysics that drives her so far from religious orthodoxy.

The philosophical retrieval of Deshoulières should focus on the naturalism that undergirds her distinctive moral and theological theory. Indebted to Lucretius and to Gassendi, this metaphysics permitted Deshoulières to develop an original ethics that contests anthropocentrism and that defends the material environment against human manipulation. It also shaped her original contributions to virtue theory. The religious virtue of humility is recast as an ecological reverence for the material world, which is the origin and the end of the human person. The naturalist creed of Deshoulières emerges with particular clarity in several poetic genres. These include the portrait, the imitation of Lucretius, the idyll, the lyric, and the maxim.

PORTRAIT

In her early poetry, Deshoulières specialized in the genre of the moral portrait. First developed in the salon of Mlle Montpensier,[25] the portrait provided a thorough sketch of the physical, emotional, intellectual, and moral character of a particular person. Deshoulières's portraits follow the conventions of the genre. They gently mock the temperamental foibles of their subjects. They fulsomely praise the subjects' intellectual qualities and social contribution. In these routine portraits, however, Deshoulières's distinctive philosophical preoccupations emerge.

In the "Portrait of Mademoiselle de Vilenne" (1658), Deshoulières lauds her subject's intellectual accomplishments. The greatest achievement of Mlle de Vilenne is her judgment, buttressed by her classical education:

> Pride suits her well; and, as her greatest glory,
> She has sound judgment and excellent memory.
> Her writings are charming; they are composed with fine wit.
> She speaks at least as well as she writes.
> Happily, tender verses strongly please her;
> And, if I didn't fear to anger her,
> I would say that she has made some admirably well.
> She does not need any translation
> Of what we have from Tasso or Virgil.
>
> (*D* I:3)

In this praise of the woman poet-scholar, the portrait of Vilenne becomes self-portrait. For Deshoulières, the preeminent qualities of a woman are artistic achievement, especially the capacity to write poetry, and erudition, specifically the mastery of classical Latin and of Renaissance Italian. These literary skills surpass the physical and emotional qualities analyzed earlier in the poem. The quality of religious piety, a commonplace of the portrait literature, is noticeably absent from the poem. In this portrait the intellectual virtues trump the moral and the theological.

Deshoulières's metaphysical concerns emerge more clearly in another poem, the "Portrait of Monsieur de Linières" (1658). In her analysis of Linières, a suspected libertine, Deshoulières treats the question of his Epicurean naturalism:

> Some believe him irreligious; but, whatever one may think,
> I believe that at bottom Tircis is not impious.
> Although he often mocks certain articles of faith,
> I believe that he is as Catholic as I am.
> By blindly following the opinions of Epicurus,
> And believing too much in nature alone,
> By wanting to interfere by making judgments
> On everything contained in the New Testament,
> One easily wanders from the path of grace.

Tircis will return to it; it's only with a smile
That he says that one cannot go against destiny.
He will change his view at the hour of death.

(*D* I:8)

This defense of Linières against the charge of religious skepticism is scarcely convincing. It is difficult to see what is left of orthodox religious faith in a writer who explicitly endorses Epicurus's materialist account of existence and who satirically dismisses central claims of the Catholic faith, such as the Trinity and the Incarnation. Linières's dismissal of supernatural revelation, as epitomized in the New Testament, is wholly consistent with his affirmation of "nature" as the sole explanation of all phenomena. Deshoulières's evocation of a possible deathbed conversion as an earnest of religious faith defies the logic of Linières's thoroughgoing naturalism.

Deshoulières's presentation of Linières's controversial views manifests the anxiety concerning her own naturalistic creed. Like the priest Gassendi, she sought to fuse classical materialism with certain theistic beliefs. However, her unconvincing effort to ally materialist metaphysics with religious faith in her fellow Epicurean, Linières, suggests the strain of such a synthesis.

IMITATION

The most systematic presentation of Deshoulières's naturalist philosophy emerges in her "Imitation of Lucretius." This poem follows *De Rerum Natura* by providing a versified analysis of the nature of the cosmos. It also closely follows the theses of Lucretius: that matter is the fundamental principle of existence; that all beings represent variations of the material principle; that material objects cohere through an atomic structure. Although Deshoulières abandons the hexameter of Lucretius in favor of a more complicated stanza form, she carefully follows certain formal components of *De Rerum Natura,* such as the opening invocation of Venus.

The poem's cosmology is informed by a materialist metaphysics. Although God (Venus) provides the ultimate cause of the genesis of the cosmos, a material principle differentiates the cosmos into a series of discrete bodies:

The order of an extrinsic cause
Makes, by invisible moves,
Enter into the form of various bodies
All the sympathy described by academics.

(*D* I:101)

The distinctive form of each body and the interrelationship between bodies and between body parts ("sympathy") can be explained by a sole material cause. Although this material principle is not self-explanatory (and, hence, is dependent upon divine causation), it provides a comprehensive explanation for all empirical phenomena. A major part of the Imitation's polemic is to demonstrate that spiritual and mental phenomena, as well as corporeal movement, can be explained by material causation.

Throughout history, matter causes a variety of corporeal forms to appear:

> Immediately, narrow and vegetative spirits
>   Through undulating movements
>   Make desires come alive;
>   And these unextinguishable forces
> From which nature derives both its force and its fire,
>   Are transformed into other sources.
>   They render eternally inflamed
>   All the fleshly principles.
>   (*D* I:102)

This dynamic principle of matter animates all variations of nature. The rise and decline of various bodies indicates the constancy of a principle of life that shapes discrete material entities without sacrificing its own vitality. The various manifestations of life, whether vegetative or animal, represent variations in degree, not in kind, of a perduring material principle.

Deshoulières clarifies this principle of material causation by reference to the atomic structure of the various bodies:

> These atoms conjoined with the light,
>   By their extreme fluidity,
>   Are always in society
>   With the regulating essence.
>   (*D* I:102)

Each body echoes the hidden dynamism of the principle structuring the cosmos. Despite the appearance of solidity, each body is composed of material atoms attracted to each other in the shifting structuring of discrete bodies. Each body becomes a mini-society where growth and decline occur according to the laws of the omnipresent material "essence."

Deshoulières insists in particular upon the origin of humanity in this dynamic dance of matter:

> And, in a cyclone of subtle matter
> Placing them everywhere in inequality,
> All the human race is the blessed offspring.
> Its multiplicity rises to infinity.
>
> (*D* I:102)

The dynamism of matter not only explains the appearance of human beings in the differentiation of discrete bodies; it also explains the intrahuman differences and hierarchies that characterize society. For Deshoulières, special divine intervention in the creation of the human soul is no longer required.

Deshoulières emphasizes the capacity of the hypothesis of material causality to explain all metaphysical questions in a systematic manner:

> The more one examines, the more one digs
> Into the chaos of the true, where move in every way
> The particular individuals,
> And where our organs, rather than reason, figure things out:
> The various facts arising
> Indicate that in this system one can easily grasp
> All the obedient beings,
> And that one can finally specify what envelops them.
>
> (*D* I:102)

For Deshoulières, the elusive envelope that contains all beings is matter itself, construed along the line of atomistic vitalism. Significantly, it is attention to our "organs" (especially, but not uniquely, our brains) that will reveal the omnipresent causality of matter. "Reason," construed as a nonmaterial faculty of analysis, can only divert us from the actual structure of nature and our complete submersion within nature. The recognition of the material matrix of nature illuminates the "obedience" to the atomic laws of nature that radically unite all existents.

"Imitation" manifests Deshoulières's allegiance to the Epicurean materialism of Lucretius. It also indicates her position in the philosophical controversies of mid-seventeenth-century France. She decisively sides with the naturalists against the rationalism of Descartes and the scholasticism of the Sorbonne and of the Church. She firmly places human nature within the confines of the material cosmos. She derides the exaltation of reason, a key trait of human transcendence in rationalist and scholastic anthropology. If, in the footsteps of Gassendi, she affirms God's existence, she banishes divine intervention from intracosmic and intrahuman history.

The strict materialism of "Imitation" also reveals Deshoulières's aesthetic perspective upon the cosmos. Nature is not simply the locus of the history of material causation, it is the site of the mysterious love that characterizes the universe, this "attraction" that typifies being from the simple atomic composition of a rock to the complex romantic dramas of human persons. In her numerous animal poems and romantic sonnets, Deshoulières explores the various specifications of this omnipresent affection. In several nature poems, she criticizes the Cartesian abolition of the amatory structure of the cosmos, reduced to the mathematical attributes of extension and movement.

IDYLL

Deshoulières's naturalism receives its fullest exposition in the series of pastoral idylls that established her poetic reputation. In these pieces, Deshoulières repeatedly places humanity within the confines of material nature. She contests the division between animal and human. She challenges the exaltation of reason as a sign of human transcendence over nature. The materialist anthropology of the idylls grounds a moral critique of human pretension. Animal innocence is contrasted favorably with human intellection. Animal serenity trumps human inquietude. The moral virtues are discounted as illusory and as inferior to animal instinct. The idylls contest the concept of the human person as *imago Dei* as they sketch the incertitude of reason and celebrate the primacy of sentiment.

In "The Sheep," an idyll of 1674, Deshoulières contrasts the happiness of animals with the inquietude of humans trapped by illusory desires and faulty reason. The happiness of the grazing sheep derives from their perfect conformity to nature:

> One does not force you to shed tears;
> You never form useless desires.
> In your tranquil hearts love follows nature:
> Without feeling its evils, you have its pleasures.
>   (*D* I:24)

The animal's existence perfectly follows the material laws of cause and effect that rule nature. Its serenity springs from its incapacity to theorize— to theorize falsely—and, thus, to imagine an illusory future.

Human beings, on the other hand, destroy themselves by "ambition, honor, interest and imposture" (*D* I:24). This catalogue of vices indicates the source of human anxiety and self-destruction. Human beings characteristically seek to place themselves in a future that is superior to the present they currently enjoy. The ambitious hope of imminent reward plunges humans into constant inquietude, often tainted by the deception of self and others. For Deshoulières, this agitation concerning the future is especially pitiable because human calculations can change nothing in a cosmos ruled by material fate:

> Of the things here below fortune decides
>> According to its different caprices.
>> All the efforts of our prudence
>> Cannot shield us from the least of its blows.
>>> (*D* I:25)

The mute animal, serenely inscribed within the present, contrasts favorably with the nervous human, perpetually plunged into illusions concerning his or her future in a cosmos ruled by material laws that elude human control.

Deshoulières vehemently criticizes the pretension of reason to bolster human happiness. She evokes the radical fragility of reason:

> This proud reason about which they make so much noise
> Is not a sure remedy against the passions.
> A bit of wine disturbs it, a child charms it;
> And ripping apart a heart which calls it for help
>> Is the only effect it produces.
>> Always impotent and severe,
> It opposes everything, but resolves nothing.
>>> (*D* I:25)

Reason is alternately weak and pernicious. It fails to provide the certitude rationalists claim for it. "There is in this universe / Nothing certain, nothing solid" (*D* I:25). Although uncertain as a guide, the phantom of reason entices human beings to pursue such treasures as "riches" and "beauty." This calculating reason, in the service of rapacious dreams, can easily lead its captives to "criminal concerns" (*D* I:25). It also blinds humans to the brevity of their existence and their inevitable death.

In the perspective of "The Sheep," reason emerges as the tool of human illusion rather than the means of human transcendence. Rationality becomes the fabricator of vain desires by a species that cannot in fact avoid the laws of nature and the inevitability of death. The distinctive faculty of humans, reason, achieves neither its cherished theoretical goal of certitude nor its practical goal of ensuring human happiness. On the contrary, it plays a tragic role in human existence by shoving the human person into an illusory future, by ceaselessly provoking anxiety concerning that future, and by obscuring the order of existence determined by nature, an order serenely followed by animal instinct.

In "The Birds" (1678), Deshoulières focuses the animal/human contrast upon the figure of birds returning to a landscape emerging from winter into spring. The idyll continues Deshoulières's critique of human vice and praise of animal serenity. It clarifies the animal/human difference through an analysis of freedom. The idyll also provides a broad sketch of Deshoulières's Epicurean metaphysics.

In describing the landscape, Deshoulières dwells upon the marvel of the metamorphosis of winter into spring. The seasonal transformations manifest the glorious "love" or sympathy that guides nature through its various changes:

> If Love were not mixed into this change,
> We would see all things perish.
> Love is the soul of the universe.
> As it triumphs over the winters
> Which desolate our fields by a rude war,
> It banishes the chill from an indifferent heart.
>
> (*D* I:46)

Deshoulières's account of nature is nonmechanistic. The cycle of the seasons reveals a loving vitalism at the center of material change. The idyll celebrates the sensuous richness ("the liveliest and most brilliant colors"—*D* I:46) of the changes wrought by nature's amatory causation.

The poem also indicates Deshoulières's explanation of human phenomena by material causation. Nature's sympathetic synthesis of atoms determines human emotion, such as the transition from chilly indifference to passionate love, as surely as it effects seasonal change. The use of a common vocabulary to describe such transitions in both the cosmic and the psychological domains is more than metaphorical.

In distinguishing the animal from the human, Deshoulières praises the freedom of the birds. In her naturalist perspective, freedom becomes fidelity to instinct rather than election of alternative goods:

> Little birds which charm me!
> You want to love? You love.
> You dislike some place? You go to another.
> You are known neither for virtues nor for faults. . . .
> There is no sincere language,
> There is no freedom, except among animals.
>
> (*D* I:47)

The only brake upon this freedom, construed as instinctual action, is physical restraint: in this case, the hunter's net. This account of freedom as instinctual fidelity carries the mark of Deshoulières's libertine background and associations. Authentic freedom emerges as the power to follow one's material-emotive instincts, emancipated from the restraints of a chimeric reason. The frank, instinctual freedom of animals contrasts favorably with the pale freedom typical of humans, subject to "attack by everyone / By deceptive exterior they try to overcome us" (D I:47).

The human/animal difference regarding freedom reflects a broader difference concerning the human/animal relationship to nature itself. Whereas the birds live in a blind conformity to nature, humans have established a state of war against nature:

> Every year nature renews her lessons in vain.
> Far from believing them, scarcely are we born
> Before we learn to fight against her.
> We prefer, by a bizarre choice,
>   Ungrateful, enslaved as we are,
> To follow what human caprice has invented,
> Rather than obeying our first laws.
>
> (*D* I:47)

The fundamental human error is the refusal to recognize our dependence upon nature and, thus, to comprehend our own nature and actions through reference to our source. In defiance of nature, we follow theories of human identity based upon a reason that is only "caprice." We pride ourselves on a freedom that is "bizarre," since it devises a war against the very principle, nature, that is our origin and our measure. At the poem's conclusion, Deshoulières emphasizes the practical difficulties embedded in our work, such as our cumbersome agriculture and viticulture, engendered by the systematic contempt of nature.

The idyll of "The Birds" indicates Deshoulières's skill in transforming anthropological into cosmological categories. The treatment of freedom and love is exemplary. Negatively, freedom is defined as immunity from physical restraint. In this sense, a bird or a human being is free insofar as it is not blocked by external constraint. Positively, freedom is the capacity of a being to follow its instinct. The bird flying toward food and the woman drinking a glass of water are both freely acting inasmuch as they successfully follow their drives of hunger and thirst. Human freedom of choice represents a difference only of degree, not of kind, with the other variations of freedom that characterize all members of the cosmos. In fact, this

"rational" freedom is comparatively fragile, given its tendency to miscon-
strue our relationship to nature and to elect imaginary futures.

Similarly, the idyll refuses to limit love to the intentional activities of rational beings. Love emerges as the attraction among atomic particles that
structures the cosmos and causes material change. In this perspective, romantic human love constitutes only one variation among the combinations
of attraction and repulsion that govern the entire chain of being. Rather
than manifesting a human specificity, which would differentiate human beings from the material cosmos, phenomena such as freedom and love only
reveal the radical similarity between humans and the rest of nature. Upon
closer inspection, those activities ascribed to a superior intellect and will
reveal themselves as variations, often quite pale, of qualities common to
the very stuff of matter.

In "The Flowers" (1677), Deshoulières shifts from the human/animal
relationship to the human/plant relationship. She praises the serenity of
the flowers, limited to a brief existence free of anguish. The repeated contrast between the brief but colorful life of the garden flowers and the long,
painful life of humans becomes the locus for a meditation on the burden
of human life itself:

> Console yourselves, jonquils and vines;
> You live a few days, but you live happily.
> Neither liars nor the jealous
> Disturb the innocent tenderness
> Which springs beings to life between Zephyr and you.
>   (*D* I: 44)

The "innocence" of the flower consists in its blind participation in the laws
of nature. The human vice evoked by the idyll resides in the human tendency to defy nature both through the lie, the denial of what exists, and
through the jealous coveting of another's status.

In heightening the contrast between plant and human life, Deshoulières
underscores the emotional toll of human existence. Romantic experience,
in particular, tends to destroy the human quest for happiness:

> You [the flowers] do not feel the mortal sadness
> Which devours tender hearts
> When, full of extreme passion,
> We see that the ungrateful object we love
> Lacks all interest or is otherwise committed.
>   (*D* I:44)

Human consciousness is the realm of desire, rarely fulfilled in its illusory hopes. The innocence of plant life consists, in part, in its exemption from desire, the motor of human destruction.

Deshoulières emphasizes the different relationship to death posed by plant life and human life. The flower participates in a cycle of painless death and rebirth: "You die in order to relive" (*D* I:45). Human beings, on the other hand, do not enjoy such an organic cycle. Their deaths constitute a radical annihilation:

> Sad reflections! Useless wishes!
> > When once we cease to be,
> > Lovely flowers, it's forever.
> One fearful instant destroys us without exception;
> We only see an unclear future beyond death:
> At most a faint memory of our names
> > Conserved by society.
> We enter forever into the profound rest
> > From which nature has pulled us.
> > > > (*D* I:45)

Despite the reference to an "uncertain future," the treatment of death clearly contests the possibility of human immortality. The greatest hope vis-à-vis death concerns the survival of one's reputation in human history. Such metaphorical immortality, a commonplace of Renaissance literature, does not diminish the annihilation of each human being operated by death.

In highlighting the radicality of death, Deshoulières emphasizes the moral indifference of death: "This frightening night which confuses the hero/ With the coward and the perjurer" (*D* I:45). This account of death differs decisively from the Christian account, which conceives the moment of death precisely as the moment of divine judgment of one's moral actions.

The idyll's meditation upon the radicality of human death concludes with a bleak evaluation of the merits of human life itself. The anguish of this existence indicates that death may be a welcome deliverance:

> Life, is it such a sweet good?
> Whenever we love it so much, do we consider
> How many are the anxieties from which its loss delivers us?
> Is it only a pile of fears, of suffering,
> > Of works, of worries, of pain?

> For everyone who truly knows human misery,
> Death is not the greatest of misfortunes.

(D I:45)

In Deshoulières's perspective, the tare of human existence does not reside primarily in physical misfortune, such as illness. Rather, it consists primarily in the web of "fears" and "worries" humans construct in their own anxious relationship to the future.

"The Flowers" constitutes an acerbic attack upon the premises of rationalist anthropology. Self-consciousness, the ground of human dignity in Cartesian theory, becomes the motor of tragedy in Deshoulières's. The human capacity for self-reflection imprisons the human subject in constant regret regarding the past and apprehension regarding an uncertain future. The imminent destruction of the self by death only radicalizes the pathos of the human mind tormented by useless desires.

"The Flowers" also manifests the strict naturalism of Deshoulières. The severe treatment of human immortality, in particular, underscores the complete immersion of the human being within the confines of the material cosmos. The refusal of human beings to recognize this actual dependence, accompanied by their flight into illusions of the future, is precisely what renders human existence inferior to vegetative existence, serenely embedded in the course of nature.

The idyll of "The Stream" (1684) develops Deshoulières's customary contrast between the serenity of nature and the tragedy of human pretension. It provides a concerted attack upon the human claims of superiority through reason. It presents a moral critique of the violent domination of nature, especially of the animal world, operated by such rationalist anthropology.

In detailing the happiness of the stream, the poem focuses upon the stream's lack of fear of death:

> You abandon yourself, without remorse, without terror,
> To your natural inclination.
> No law among you makes it criminal.
> Old age for you has nothing horrifying.
> Near the end of your course,
> You are stronger and more beautiful
> Than you were at your source.

(D I:150)

The stream is exempt from the anxieties that destroy human existence. In particular, it is free from the anguish concerning aging and death that reduce many human beings to emotional slavery.

Deshoulières underscores the emotional burden that easily incapacitates humans. The passions tend to remove the person from the possibility of internal peace:

> Concerning so many passions which nourish our heart,
>> Learn that there is not one
> Which does not drag after itself trouble, pain,
>> Repentance or misfortune:
>> Day and night, they rip apart
>> The hearts of which they are mistresses.
>
> (*D* I:151)

The affective thicket surrounding humanity plunges human beings into emotional inconsistency. Love, praised as the highest of human passions, is in fact the one "most to be feared" (*D* I:151), since its disappointments are especially brutal. The human condition involves a bitter relationship to time, with the past subsumed in regret and the future colored by fear.

The emotive inconstancy of the human person is matched by a moral instability. In "The Stream," human vice is epitomized by infidelity:

> From all sorts of unions,
> How our life is removed!
> Of treasons, of horrors and of dissensions,
> It is always accompanied.
>
> (*D* I:151)

Human existence characterizes itself by its betrayal of commitments. In its refusal to fulfill promises, humanity contrasts poorly with the serenity of the rest of nature, such as the stream, constant in its fidelity to itself.

Despite its affective slavery and its mendacious relationship to the future, humanity tends to exalt itself as a creature of reason and the unique subject of rights. Deshoulières criticizes the illusion of this rationalist anthropology:

> Don't brag to me about these imaginary goods,
>> These prerogatives, these rights
> Invented by our pride in order to mask our miseries.
>
> (*D* I:152)

Rather than manifesting human nobility, the claims concerning reason only reveal the human vice of pride. Rights do not reside in the structure of the human person. Rather, humans invent rights to justify the oppression of others.

This exaltation of human reason and right legitimizes the human domination, indeed destruction, of nature:

> It is humanity itself which tells us that, by a just choice,
>   Heaven placed, in forming human beings,
>   The other beings under its laws.
>   Let's not flatter ourselves. We are
>   Their tyrants rather than their kings.
>   Why do we torture you?
> Why do we shut you up in a hundred canals?
> And why do we reverse the order of nature
>   By forcing you to spring into the air?
>
> (*D* I:152)

Humanity's manipulation of nature, symbolized by the canal and the fountain, is grounded upon "rights" and "prerogatives" humanity has itself invented. The idyll suggests that religious tradition, such as the creation narratives, has intensified the human tendency to envision nature as an object submissive to human desire. Rather than recognizing its dependence upon nature and measuring its action to conform with nature, humanity has disfigured nature under the empire of a "reason" that is only a rationalization of domination through a fiction of rights.

The evidence of human self-delusion and domination leads Deshoulières to contest the ancient conception of the human person, refurbished by the Cartesians, as *imago Dei:*

> Finally, in this horrible pit
> Of misery and vanity,
> I lose myself; and the more I see
> The weakness and malignity of humanity,
> The less of the divinity
> I recognize in its image.
>
> (*D* I:153)

Rather than revealing our likeness to God, reason only accentuates our distance from nature and nature's God. The exercise of reason, by which we reduce nature to the object of our covetous passions, indicates the rapaciousness of the human subject. Human technology rests upon a rationality that disguises its will to dominate under a veil of self-fabricated rights. The pretension of divine sanction and even divine resemblance only intensifies humanity's blindness concerning the motives and consequences of its manipulation of nature.

"The Stream" highlights Deshoulières's capacity as a moralist. Her naturalist metaphysics grounds a distinctive moral code. The recognition of one's dependence upon material nature is not simply an epistemological principle; it implies a moral responsibility to the well-being of this nature. A posture of sympathetic solidarity replaces the rationalist posture of domination. Similarly, Deshoulières's critique of the exaltation of reason as a sign of human transcendence is not confined to a theoretical dissent from an implausible anthropology. It is a critique of the practical consequences of this error, of the destruction of the material cosmos in the name of an illusory reason and right.

Deshoulières's nature-idylls manifest the distinctive contours of her naturalism. They indicate her relatively strict allegiance to the Epicurean atomism studied in her tutelage under Gassendi. Her materialism rests upon a theory of atomic sympathy imported whole from her classical sources. Her neoclassical conventions, such as the repeated invocation of the goddess Iris, maintain the classical cast of her argumentation. The treatment of the elements owes far more to the Greco-Roman sources than to the new cosmology of Galileo or Copernicus. For Deshoulières, all phenomena may be explained by their participation in the material cosmos. This cosmos, however, remains the classical universe of sympathetic causation, easily personified by the gods and goddesses of Greek antiquity. This naturalism remains an authentic revival of classical atomism, foreign to the new cosmology of extension and movement.

The naturalism of the idylls, nonetheless, is not a simple reprise of Epicurean metaphysics. Deshoulières transforms classical naturalism by her anthropological focus. The poetry not only situates humanity within the framework of nature; it analyzes the vice and emotive confusion that flow from human misconceptions regarding nature. In the development of her moral psychology, Deshoulières employs the tools of the neoclassical *moraliste*. Faithful to the traditions of the genre, Deshoulières dissects the illusions of the human heart. She repeatedly analyzes the human refusal to face and accept one's mortality. She treats this refusal as the symptom of a broader refusal to acknowledge the roots and rule of humanity in material nature. Human pride, the major vice of the *moralistes,* is specified by Deshoulières as the human denial of its dependence upon nature and its vain fabrication of a quasi-divine reason as the proof of human superiority. Affectively, this illusionary rationalism plunges human beings into exaggerated fears and hopes concerning an imaginary future, unconformed to the facts of nature. Ethically, this spiritualization of the human self justifies an attack upon nature as an object destined for domination. Humanity inaugurates a civil war against the very source of its existence.

Finally, the literary form of the nature-idylls reinforces the naturalistic theses they defend. Deshoulières does not simply describe the landscape, the seasons, or the animals; she addresses them as the audience of her poetry. Written predominantly in the second person, the idylls' repeated use of personification places the human narrator and the nonhuman addressee on terms of ontological equality. Even more radically, several of the idylls transform the human-nonhuman dialogue into a pedagogical relationship where the stream or the sheep becomes the instructor of the human narrator concerning the structure of the real and the proper path to happiness. The human superiority fabricated by a vain rationalism is decisively reversed by the invocation of nonhuman nature as supreme teacher. In the very form of the poetry, naturalistic solidarity supplants the dualistic fable of dominating difference.

LYRIC

Several lyrical poems clarify the naturalistic anthropology presented by Deshoulières in the idylls. These poems do not simply situate humanity within the milieu of nature; they sketch a normative anthropology in which sentiment, rather than the chimera of reason, rules humanity.

In "To Madame xxx. Dream," Deshoulières contrasts reason with the emotion of love. Having lost the faculty of reason in her dream, the narrator faces the greater power of love:

> Having lost the sense of all my reason,
> I believed myself to be, Iris, in a dark swamp,
> > Where the nightingales, one after the other,
> > Seem to tell me, in their language:
> 'You resist in vain the power of Love;
> > Sooner or later this god will possess you.'
> > > (*D* I:35–36)

Enchanted by the song of the nightingale, the narrator pursues the bird in an effort to entrap it. The "infinite pleasure" of love, expressed by the song of the birds, overwhelms the earlier exercise of reason.

In "Rondeau" (1677), Deshoulières sharpens the distinction between love and reason. The efforts of reason to combat the arousal of love are useless:

> Of reason, one must expect nothing:
> Too much unhappiness only teaches us
> That it counts for nothing once the heart begins to act.
> Only flight, Iris, can save us;

It is the path the most useful to take
  Against love.

(D I:43)

Romantic experience reveals the impotence of reason against the power of emotion. Love, the structuring principle of natural history, inevitably destroys the defenses of reason, the frail construct of human pride.

In another "Rondeau," Deshoulières intensifies the quarrel between reason and sentiment. Reason routinely rebukes the narrator for her abandonment to passion:

> What use do these sentiments serve?
> In my slightest abandonment to feeling,
> My reason always arrives to tell me:
>   'Be quiet.'

(D I:20)

Immediate romantic experience (in this case, the arrival of the shepherd-lover), however, manifests the superiority of the passions in this struggle:

> But what doubling of passion
> Do I feel during my martyrdom to love?
> My shepherd appears, he sighs;
> There he is: 'Vain reasonings,
>   Be quiet.'

(D I:20)

Reason, reduced to useless rationalization ("vain reasonings"), collapses under the weight of emotion. The human experience of attraction and repulsion, epitomized in the drama of romantic love, manifests the primacy of affectivity, rather than reason, in the human person.

Deshoulières's systematic valorization of sentiment over reason grounds a primitivistic theory of human history. In "Ode to M. de la Rochefoucauld, author of *Moral Reflections*" (1678), Deshoulières praises early human societies in which members followed their primitive instincts in fulfillment of basic physical needs:

> In the happy country when without prejudice
> One let morals go freely,
> Humanity was not avid
> Of riches or honors:
> It lived on wild fruit,

> Slept under open-air covers,
> Drank in a clear stream;
> Without goods, without rank, without envy.
> As it entered life,
> It entered the tomb.
>
> (*D* I:50)

This idyll of egalitarian society, not without its libertine tint ("morals go freely"), praises a human life based uniquely upon instinct. The simple life, literally in conformity with nature, banishes the vices (greed and envy) that ravage hierarchical societies built upon social ambition and contempt. Rather than improving the human lot, the rise of technological societies based upon the prerogatives of reason has destroyed the entente with nature maintained by a more emotive race of humans.

The "Ode to la Rochefoucauld" also provides the occasion for Deshoulières's most severe condemnation of dualistic anthropology. Examining the body-soul relationship, Deshoulières insists upon the intimate connection, if not the actual identity, between the two principles:

> Invisible connections,
> Although the soul is divine,
> Unite it to the body.
> Does the soul have some bitterness?
> The body beats itself and consumes itself,
> And shares its anguish.
> Is the body captive of pain?
> The soul no longer feels joy,
> It itself weakens as does the body.
>
> (*D* I:49)

Somatic and psychic experiences are neither distinct nor parallel phenomena in the history of the individual. Psychological bitterness and physiological contortion arise simultaneously. Physical pain and spiritual anguish constitute twin effects from the same cause. The identity of somatic and psychic history in the sequence of causality manifests the inadequacy of dualistic accounts of a separate psychic-somatic history or the Cartesian effort to theorize an interaction between two opposed principles. Despite the pious bow to the "divinity" of the soul, the ode clearly designates body-soul activity as a single response to material causation.

Deshoulières's praise of sentiment and critique of reason indicate the normative status of "nature" in her philosophy. The natural life of human beings consists in fidelity to instinct in fulfillment of physical and emotive needs. It entails a pacific appropriation of nature for basic needs, modeled by the gentle gathering societies of antiquity. Conversely, it demands a renunciation of rationalistic society, built upon the violent conquest of nature. Humanity's immersion within material nature emerges as an ethical goal, not simply as a metaphysical fact of the human constitution. In her systematic exaltation of sentiment over reason and her praise of rural simplicity over urban sophistication, Deshoulières contributes to the French primitivism that will mature in the noble savage of Rousseau.

MAXIM

Deshoulières presents the most pointed expression of her philosophical creed in a series of poems she labels "reflections." Modeled after the period's *maxime* literature, popularized by the Jansenist salon of Madame de Sablé,[26] these reflections are proverb-like exercises in moral psychology. "Réflexions diverses" (1686), the most elaborate of this genre, is a series of rhymed stanzas (8–12 lines) focused upon one of the commonplaces of *moraliste* essays: human vanity. Deshoulières explores the standard subsets of the theme: the illusion of virtue; the vice of flattery; the futility of learning; the incapacity to face death. She transforms these common objects of moral critique, however, into theses at the service of her militant naturalism and of her critique of rationalist anthropology.

In several reflections, she underscores the radical limits of human knowledge:

> The human mind is so limited!
> However much time we give to study,
>   However intelligent we may have been born,
> We know nothing deeply, nothing with certitude:
> For us, everything is burdened with shadows.
> The light which comes from the rarest knowledge
> Is only a fatal lightning bolt, an ardor which misleads us.
> We should fear it more than ignorance.
>   It gives birth to so many great errors;
> You can't stress enough that the pursuit of knowledge
>   Is usually nothing other than learning to doubt.
>   (*D* I:204–205)

Not only does this maxim underscore the vanity of human knowledge, it specifically attacks the twin pretensions of rationalist knowledge, with its claims of certitude (*avec certitude*), and noetic foundations (*à fond*). In Deshoulières's perspective, the skeptical opponents of Descartes clearly have the stronger case.

The weakness of human reason indicates the fragility of the entire human constitution. In Reflection XIII, Deshoulières depicts this fragility in the narrator's address to an ancient palace. The negative comparison reveals the inferiority of human nature to inanimate, let alone animal or vegetable, being:

> Palace, we last less than you,
> Although your components have sustained the effects of war,
>   And although, like you,
>   We were pulled from the womb of the earth.
>   What frail machines we are!
> Barely do we manage to live more than half a century.
> A little nothing can destroy us; And the work of a God
>   Lasts less than a work of humans.
>
> (*D* I:203)

The mechanistic metaphor for human nature ("frail machines") suggests the materialistic framework of the maxim's metaphysics. The maxim also suggests a certain religious skepticism. The human constitution, supposedly "the work of a God," proves far less durable than the battle-worn construction of humans.

Humanity's pretensions concerning the power of its reason and the nobility of its spiritual transcendence nurture certain disorders within the human psyche. In Reflection VI, Deshoulières diagnoses the refusal to accept mortality as the most glaring of these psychic tares:

> Miserable toy of blind fortune,
>   Victim of evils and of law,
>   Humanity, you who, in a thousand places,
>   Must find life inhospitable,
> Why is it that you so fear the power of death?
> Coward, look at death without changing your expression;
>   Imagine that, if it is an outrage,
>   It is the last you will have to endure.
>
> (*D* I:200–201)

The refusal to accept death plunges humanity into prolonged anguish concerning hypothetical futures and prevents humanity from discovering its rightful place within, rather than above, nature. The maxim's opening description of "blind fortune" evokes the physical laws of nature that determine the human constitution—especially the mortal nature of that constitution, which the fantasies of human reason refuse to accept.

According to Deshoulières, the spiritual pretensions of humanity have distorted the moral constitution of the human person. Nowhere is this moral distortion clearer than in the pretension of virtues as signs of human superiority. This critique of virtue as vain illusion is a commonplace of the period's *maxime* literature. In Deshoulières's reflections, however, the critique of virtue is rooted in her effort to explain all human behavior in terms of material causality.

Reflection IX dissects the virtue of wisdom. It acidly criticizes the sentimental title of wisdom pinned by society upon the elderly:

> We believe we've become wise,
> When, after having seen more than fifty times
> The autumnal fall of leaves,
> We abandon the dangerous use of certain pleasures.
> We're deluded. Such a change
> Is not the work of a free choice.
> And it is only the pride cloaking humanity
> Which, using every pretext,
> Gives to the cause of virtue
> What we owe to the cause of aging.
>
> (*D* I:202)

It is biology, not intentionality, that explains the human person's gradual abandonment of dangerous habits as health declines and death approaches. Not only does the claim of wisdom rest upon a common vice, vanity; it rests upon the illusion of human freedom ("a free choice"). This critique of the claims of free will reflects the maxim's broader determinism. Human knowledge emerges only under the guidance of the physical environment, which shapes humanity under a strict pedagogy of cause and effect.

Deshoulières delivers a similar critique of the virtue of prudence. This key moral virtue, pretending to make the human person master of destiny, only plunges the moral agent into a destiny controlled by nature:

> The incense we give to prudence
> Leads my mood to despair.
> What is its purpose? To see in advance
> The evils that we must endure—
> Is it such a benefit to predict them?
> If this cruel virtue had some certain rule
> Which could remove them from us,

> I'd find the worries it gives bearable enough;
>   But nothing is so misleading as human prudence.
> Alas! nearly always the detour it takes
> In order to help us avoid an awaiting misfortune
>   Is the path which takes us right to it.
>
> (*D* I:202)

Prudence not only rests upon an overevaluation of human reason cruelly contradicted by experience, it blithely ignores the limitations of human existence set by nature and nature's laws. The successful prediction of one's future is quite different from the successful creation of one's future, the illusion sustained by the prudent in their vanity.

In Reflection X, Deshoulières attacks the neoclassical form of virtue celebrated by the Renaissance. She dissects in particular the claims of courage that surround certain figures of antiquity:

> We scarcely recognize ourselves in discussions of courage
> When we elevate to the rank of the generous
> Those Greeks and Romans whose suicidal deaths
>   Have made the name of courage so famous.
> What have they done that is so great? They left life
>   When, after crushing disgrace,
> Life didn't have anything pleasant left for them.
>   By one single death they spared themselves a thousand.
>
> (*D* I:202)

The putative virtue of courage only masks a flight from pain, perfectly comprehensible under the amoral rubric of stimulus and response. In the balance of pain and pleasure, it is hardly surprising that a disgraced aristocrat would choose suicide over a probable future of poverty, exile, and social opprobrium.

This maxim closely echoes the Jansenist critique of virtue. It is the humanist retrieval of virtue, with its apotheosis of the noble pagan, that is the object of Deshoulières's criticism. However, unlike the Jansenists, Deshoulières criticizes claims of virtue as a refusal to recognize material causation rather than libertarian self-determination as the matrix of human action.

The moral corruption operated by the erroneous estimate of human reason extends to the social sphere. Self-love, the fruit of exaggerated rationalism, easily opens the human person to the deceit of flattery:

> What poison for the soul are false praises!
> Happy are those who don't believe flattering speeches!

> Thinking too well of oneself makes one fall every day
>> Into humiliating mistakes.
> Self-love is, alas, the most stupid of loves;
> Nonetheless, it is the most common of errors.
>> (*D* I:201)

Intoxicated by one's self-importance, based upon a false account of one's reason and virtue, the human person constructs a society based upon deceit. Mutual flattery leads humanity to confusion rather than to serene cooperation within the network of nature.

In Reflection II, Deshoulières summarizes her global estimate of human nature. She reverses the hierarchy of being by demonstrating the superiority of inanimate objects over human nature. Typically, the problem of death and aging provides the occasion for the comparison:

> Inanimate beings, outcasts of nature,
>> Oh! You make many envious;
>> Time, far from injuring you,
>> Only renders you more precious.
> We seek with ardor an antique model;
> Time raises the price of a bust or painting;
> The voyager stops to gaze at the awesome ruins
> Of a circus, of a tomb, of a magnificent temple;
> And, for our own old age, we have only contempt.
>> (*D* I:199)

The maxim notes the irony of the human condition: the human person constructs artifacts that far outlast in time and esteem the person who made them. The naturalism of Deshoulières controls the comparison. In a temporal, rather than spiritual, framework, inanimate artifacts prove the more impressive. The history of human art, rather than demonstrating the superiority of humanity, only underscores its fragile duration.

Deshoulières's corpus of "reflections" indicates her transformation of a literary genre, namely the maxim, according to the imperatives of her naturalistic metaphysics. She borrows the proverb-like form and the moral psychology from the Jansenist milieu that engineered the maxim. Unlike the Jansenists, however, Deshoulières does not employ the maxim to unmask the sinfulness of the human condition and to prod the reader toward acceptance of graced redemption. For Deshoulières, the ignorance and confusion unveiled through the maxim's commentary reveals the danger of a human nature conceived as transcending and mastering nature. The maxim uncovers humanity's patent roots within nature and urges a more radical solidarity with the material cosmos than that proposed by the rationalist.

CONCLUSION

The literary corpus of Deshoulières indicates the close relationship between philosophical reflection and poetic creation in seventeenth-century France. In Deshoulières's hands, the nature idyll becomes an apology for the material causes of human action. The lyric becomes a weapon in the exaltation of the value of sentiment over that of reason. The maxim becomes a catalogue of arguments against the claims of rationalism. The literary portrait becomes a mirror of the skeptical, scholarly woman Deshoulières epitomized as the head of her salon. Deshoulières presses a wide variety of neoclassical literary genres into polemical service of her naturalistic creed, rooted in the tutelage of Gassendi and in the careful study of Lucretius.

Recent interpretations of Deshoulières have tended to distort the nature of her contribution to philosophy. Frequently, literary critics have assimilated Deshoulières to the Jansenist movement on the basis of her mastery of the *maxime,* her friendship with La Rochefoucauld, and the consonance between her low estimate of human reason and the pessimistic anthropology of Port-Royal. Vincenza Guidarelli offers a typical interpretation of Deshoulières in the Jansenizing vein. "The basic concept of the nature of man held by Madame Deshoulières, like that of La Rochefoucauld, was related to the image of man which resulted from the influence of Jansenist dogma. . . . The image of man drawn by the poetess conforms to the Jansenist concept of fallen humanity."[27] This quick assimilation of Deshoulières to the Jansenist movement suppresses key tenets of the poet's philosophy. The persistent critique of immortality and the effort to demonstrate the omnipresence of material causation are ignored. The dominant perspective of Deshoulières's poetry, a militant naturalism, simply disappears.

A comparison between the approaches to virtue developed respectively by Madame de Sablé and by Madame Deshoulières casts the specificity of Deshoulières's approach into greater relief. The two concur in considering virtue as the mask of vice, specifically the vice of pride. Both contest the claims of reason by the Cartesian or the Aristotelian as damaging illusions nurtured by pride. For Sablé, however, the illusions of reason and virtue reflect human concupiscence: the sinful ensemble of ignorance, prejudice, and passion that has marked humanity since the fall. It is this radical sinfulness that taints the apparent virtues as well as the obvious vices of humanity. For Deshoulières, on the other hand, the violent vanity of humanity is without theological roots. The fundamental pride of the human person, manifest in exaggerated claims of reason and the related claims of dominion over nature, springs from a refusal to recognize humanity's actual place in the circle of material nature. From Deshoulières's perspective, not only is human virtue a mask of vice; the entire concept of virtue and vice is illusory. Animal instinct, itself ruled by material causation, is the actual origin of the "virtue" and the "vice" philosophers erect on their erroneous account of free will.

The implausible assimilation of Deshoulières's philosophy to Jansenist theology does underline one of the central problems in interpreting Deshoulières: the question of her actual religious convictions. Throughout her life, she was ostensibly a Catholic. However, the materialist theories in her writings, her salon's free-thinking reputation, and her lifelong alliance with libertine aristocrats indicate her religious skepticism, which appears to have persisted until her conversion in the 1680s. Her neglect of the baptism of her son Jean Alexandre (born in 1666) until he was an adult (in 1685) was considered a shocking provocation by her contemporaries.[28]

Internal and external evidence indicate that her religious creed encompassed, at most, a thin deism. Such a naturalistic creed recognized a divine force as the necessary cause of the network of nature in which all material beings operate. However, the actual operation of this network, including the action of human agents, can be explained by the autonomous laws of nature. There is no further need for the hypothesis of divine intervention or of the miraculous.

Deshoulières's bold and repeated denials of human immortality constitute the most striking trait of her skepticism. As Henri Busson argues,[29] the division between the devout and the skeptical in the seventeenth century did not concern the existence of God. The village atheist was indeed rare in a society in which practically everyone admitted the existence of some supreme being who created the cosmos. Rather, the question of personal immortality was the pivot of the quarrel between the orthodox and the libertine. Deshoulières clearly attacks the belief in personal human immortality as an illusion with dangerous consequences. Psychologically, it throws the human agent into a pointless anguish concerning a nonexistent future. Morally, it ignites the *hubris* of the human agent, who mistreats supposedly inferior animal orders and assaults the material environment.

Finally, the major problem in interpreting the work of Deshoulières lies in its virtual suppression as philosophically significant. Marginalized as the author of charming pastorals, Deshoulières the metaphysician and moralist has virtually disappeared. In fact, her poetic canon systematically elaborates a comprehensive naturalism that reduces all phenomena to material causation. Her analysis of human nature unmasks the material determinants of personal behavior and does not hesitate to challenge the reality of free will and of personal immortality. Using nature as a normative and not only a descriptive category, she develops an ecological ethics in which reverence for the material cosmos emerges as a new cardinal virtue.

Deshoulières's naturalism is not unproblematic. The origin of the alleged human illusion concerning the soul, freedom, and immortality is never specified. The mechanism by which purely material causes create such spiritual concepts is never unveiled. Nonetheless, Deshoulières's naturalist metaphysics and ethics remain a sophisticated philosophical argument, an argument still buried beneath the sighs of the shepherd.

CHAPTER IV

Madame de la Sablière: The Ethics of the Desert

It is difficult to vanquish our passions, but it is impossible to satisfy
them.
— MADAME DE LA SABLIÈRE, *Christian Maxims*

Marguerite Hessein, Madame de la Sablière (1640–1693) has
survived in literary history as wife and patron. She married the poet Antoine de Rambouillet de la Sablière. She cultivated the career of the fabu-
list Jean de la Fontaine. She directed a literary salon featuring prominent
artists. The standard portrait of Sablière as benefactress, however, ignores
her own contribution to moral philosophy. In two works, *Christian Maxims*
and *Christian Thoughts,* Sablière critiques the moral virtues from the stand-
point of an Augustinian theology of sin and redemption. Her writings reflect the classical culture and the "Cartesianism" that earned her renown
in philosophical circles of the period. More importantly, they express her
rejection of salon humanism during her last years of religious retreat. Austere in form and apocalyptic in tone, Sablière's meditations sketch a moral
code of monastic rigor.

BANK, SALON, DESERT

Born in Paris in 1640, Marguerite Hessein was the eldest child of
Gilbert Hessein and Marguerite Menjot Hessein.[1]
A successful financier, her father had made his fortune through commerce and through the foundation of his own bank. Her mother was the
daughter of Jean Menjot, a treasury official, and Anne Mallard, widow of
Guillaume Le Just, a military officer. Devout Protestants, both parents typified a particular social milieu: the Huguenot high bourgeoisie of Paris.

Pastor Mestrezat baptized the infant on March 18, 1640, in the Calvinist church at Charenton.

Marguerite's maternal uncle, Antoine Menjot, played the central role in her intellectual development. A physician and a militant Protestant polemicist, Menjot avidly participated in the philosophical salons of Paris, where he befriended Blaise Pascal. He guided his niece through the Huguenot culture that embraced her until the establishment of her own irenic salon.

Marguerite's education was conducted in her domicile by a series of private tutors. After her mother's death in 1649, Marguerite's uncle, Antoine Menjot, and her cousin, Madeleine Gaudon de la Raillière, marquise de Saint-Aignan, took primary responsibility for guiding the tutorials. The curriculum was unusual for a woman of the period. Extensive study of Greek and Latin developed Marguerite's talents as a serious classicist. Later, in her salon years, the epistoler Corbinelli would write about her: "She understands Homer as well as we understand Virgil."[2] Thorough instruction in mathematics nurtured Marguerite's lifelong interest in scientific experimentation, especially in astronomy. Her uncle personally instructed her in Calvinist doctrine. He also introduced her to the principles of contemporary philosophical systems, in particular those of Descartes and of Gassendi.

On March 15, 1654, Marguerite Hessein married Antoine de Rambouillet de la Sablière,[3] son of a celebrated financier. Another member of the Parisian Huguenot elite, M. de la Sablière had already acquired a reputation as a leading poet, specializing in the genre of the madrigal. A youthful stay in Italy had given him the opportunity to master the Italian language and to study Renaissance poetry. Marguerite's father had arranged the marriage in the obvious hope of mutual social and economic advantage for the two Protestant commercial dynasties. However, the gap in the ages of the spouses (he was sixteen years her senior) and the groom's libertine morals presaged marital problems to come.

Despite the relative tranquility of its first decade, in which Mme de la Sablière gave birth to three children,[4] the marriage deteriorated dramatically in 1667. M. de la Sablière began to harangue his wife on their incompatibility in the evident hope of pressuring her to leave their home. His campaign reached a paroxysm on March 1, 1667, when he ordered his wife to enter the convent-run hospice of Charonne. Despite multiple efforts at reconciliation, Mme de la Sablière acknowledged the collapse of the marriage in 1668. On April 29, 1668, she filed suit for a legal separation of goods and persons. On May 18, 1668, the Court of Châtelet granted the separation and condemned M. de la Sablière as the culprit in the marriage's collapse. The court ordered him to restore his wife's dowry with interest and to pay her substantial alimony. It also placed a restraining order upon him in virtue of his irrational treatment of his wife. Following the custom of the period, however, M. de la Sablière retained custody of their three children.

Economically independent through a financial settlement with her estranged husband and through the donations of relatives appalled at her mistreatment, Mme de la Sablière opened her new Parisian home on July 19, 1669. The house on the Rue Neuve-des-Petits-Champs quickly became one of Paris's most distinguished salons. Habitués of the salon included the political, religious, and literary elite of the capital. Leading French aristocrats mixed with such foreign dignitaries as Queen Christina of Sweden[5] and Jean Sobiesky,[6] the future King of Poland. Eminent writers included Perrault,[7] Pellisson,[8] Benserade,[9] Fontenelle,[10] Mme de Sévigné,[11] Marquise de Lambert,[12] Racine,[13] and Molière.[14] The salon even blended Sablière's Protestant relatives and friends with a circle of erudite Catholic clergy: the ecumenical Bishop Huet of Avranches,[15] the academician Abbé Testu,[16] and the Jesuit literary critic Père Bouhours.[17]

The salon years also marked a revival of Sablière's scientific interests. A series of tutors guided her personal research and made scientific presentations at her salon sessions. Barthélemy d'Herbelot instructed her in anatomy and natural history. François Bernier[18] updated her on recent scientific discoveries and cultivated her passionate interest in astronomy. The young mathematician Sauveur,[19] who would later serve as a professor at the Collège Royal, taught her advanced geometry. The mathematician Roberval[20] explained developments in the new field of calculus.

Sablière complemented her tutorials with outside instruction at major scientific venues in the capital. She frequented d'Alencé's courses on physics, Verney's[21] lectures on anatomy at the Jardin du Roi, and Cassini's[22] astronomical experiments at the Parisian Observatory. Several histories of science cite Mme de la Sablière's pioneering role as a woman astronomer.[23]

The salon period also witnessed Sablière's growing philosophical interests. Her tutor, Bernier, instructed her in a variety of philosophical systems, with special emphasis placed upon the theories of Descartes. In 1675 he composed a philosophical work for her: *Abrégé de la philosophie de Gassendi*.[24] An opponent of Descartes, he explained the common critiques of the then dominant Cartesian system. He dedicated his skeptical *Doutes* (1682)[25] to her. In an essay on the diversity of the human race (1684), Bernier recalled Sablière's thesis that the discovery of new peoples may force a redefinition of the salient traits of human nature.[26]

In a letter from the period, Antoine Menjot praised Sablière for the eclecticism he detected in her current philosophical theories: "I admire the judicious synthesis you have made between Epicureanism and Pyrrhonism. The first will help you taste the most satisfying pleasures of the heart and, if you still have some scruples remaining, the second will immediately heal you by making you doubt the pleasures just tasted."[27] However, other evidence indicates that Sablière defended the theories of Descartes in the salon's philosophical discussions. Both Bayle[28] and Voltaire[29] attest to the intellectual prominence of Mme de la Sablière in the philosophical debates of the era.

One member of the salon became a protegé of Sablière: Jean de la Fontaine.[30] Already celebrated for his first volume of *Fables,* La Fontaine joined Sablière's circle as an impoverished author in 1670. In 1673, La Fontaine became a permanent house guest of Sablière.

In his celebrated *Discours à Mme de la Sablière,* La Fontaine presented and then criticized the Cartesian philosophy upheld by the associates of Sablière. He particularly criticized its mechanistic theory of animals:

> That the beast is a machine:
> That everything is done in it without choice and by springs;
> That there is neither feeling nor soul;
>   In it everything is flesh.
>   Such is the watch that moves
> In eternally identical paths, blind and without destiny.
>   Open it, read its internal life:
> All these wheels take the place of mind;
>   The first moves the second;
> A third follows; it rings at the end.
> To believe these people, the beast is nothing but this.
> This is how Descartes explains it—
> Descartes, this mortal we would make a god.[31]

On May 2, 1684, during his inaugural speech as a member of the Académie française, La Fontaine praised Sablière under the title of "Iris."[32]

Toward the end of the 1670s, Sablière's career as a salonnière visibly ebbed. An ardent affair (1676–1680) with a military officer, Charles de la Fare, embittered Sablière, as evidence of the officer's multiple infidelities flooded the salons. The death of her estranged husband in 1679 permitted Sablière to reconcile herself with her children but placed her in new economic peril. Sablière underwent a religious crisis that culminated in her conversion to Catholicism. She abandoned her house on the Rue Neuve-des-Petits-Champs in 1680 for a more modest residence on the Rue Saint-Honoré, where she again lodged La Fontaine.

Madame de Sévigné, a close friend of Sablière, discussed Sablière's conversion in her correspondence. Sévigné insists on interpreting this sensational conversion of a *savante* as the work of God alone:

> Mme de la Sablière is now in the Hospital of the Incurables, fully recovered from an illness they long thought was incurable. No one is more delighted at her recovery than I. She is now in the blessed state of being devout and being really devout. She's made good use of her free will, but isn't it God who made her do it? Isn't it God who made her want to do it? Isn't God the one who delivered her from the empire of the demon? Didn't God transform her heart? Doesn't God make her walk upright? Isn't it God who gives her the vision and the desire of being united to Him? That's exactly what's happening here. God is crowning her with all of His gifts. If that's what you want to call free will, so be it. But I'd rather stand with Saint Augustine on these issues.[33]

Clearly influenced by the Augustinian theology of her Jansenist allies, Sévigné underscores the role of divine initiative in the conversion, at the expense of any human agency. For Parisian salon society, the conversion of Sablière to Catholicism represented more than a change of religious allegiance. Intellectually it indicated a reversal of philosophical creed by a woman previously allied with the more skeptical disciples of Descartes and of Gassendi. Morally it signaled a public renunciation of the licentious life she had previously led.[34]

From the time of her conversion, Sablière adopted a more solitary life as a devout penitent. Under the spiritual direction of the Jesuit Père Rapin,[35] she undertook a rigorous program of meditation and mortification. She began charitable work with patients at the Hospice des Incurables, a hospital dedicated to the care of Catholics suffering from incurable diseases. So committed did Sablière become to this demanding apostolate that she rented a small apartment on the hospital grounds and began to spend more time there than at her home. Literary friends, especially La Fontaine, lamented her growing aloofness. In correspondence from the period, her uncle Antoine Menjot decried her growing attraction to monasticism.[36]

Although withdrawn from the world, Sablière's hospital apartment was not a monastic cell. Her library contained numerous philosophical works: Descartes's *The Passions of the Soul,* Malebranche's *The Search for Truth,* Epictetus's *Enchiridion,* Marcus Aurelius's *Meditations,* and the works of St. Augustine. She maintained her telescope and, according to Boileau,[37] continued her astronomical research. Fine china surrounded her beloved red teapot.[38] The relics of salon culture, however, barely mitigated the ardor of Sablière's final quest: a spiritual abandonment of mystical intensity to God.

After the death of her spiritual director, Père Rapin, in 1687, Sablière placed herself under the direction of Abbé de Rancé,[39] the austere reformer of the Cistercian abbey of La Trappe. In Rancé, Sablière discovered a soul analogous to her own. Rancé was an aristocrat who had developed a brilliant literary reputation in the salons and then, in a moment of religious conversion, had abandoned this life for the cloister of the Cistercian order. Already the celebrated director of several aristocratic women, he understood instinctively the spiritual itinerary of a salon intellectual who had renounced Parisian society and who now sought solitary union with God.

In her earlier correspondence with Père Rapin, Sablière had flooded the priest, himself a habitué of salon society, with questions of conscience: the lingering bitterness over the romance with La Fare; the marriages of her children; her economic worries (*MDS*, 152–157). In the new correspondence with Rancé, however, the psychological anguish and the social preoccupations ebb. A spiritually mature Sablière and a more ascetical director explore the path of a complete abandonment to God in the state proper to a cultured laywoman.

Sablière's letters to Rancé present the spiritual life as a *via negativa* focused upon the abandonment of the will to God. The heart of union with God is strict surrender of one's personal inclinations to the divine will, with a concomitant silencing of the faculties of the intellect and of the imagination. "For our part, we must always let ourselves fall under His [God's] hand with the greatest abandonment and the least amount of reflection that we can" (*L* 33: July 30, 1688; *MDS*, 285). The goal is movement from the active life of discursive meditation and good works to a more passive surrender to divine providence.

As Sablière advanced in this path of abandonment, she experienced a painful darkening of the senses and, especially, of the intellect:

> What I've clearly learnt through suffering and what I am still clearly learning is that I must not have the slightest attachment to anything whatsoever in the world. Thus, I can form no other desire on earth than to ask that God accomplish His holy will, which I do not know. If I were able to know it, there is absolutely nothing I could do to accomplish it. But it seems to me that I am in such obscurity and such ignorance concerning everything I do, that I do not know whether in any action or thought I please God and act as I should. (*L* 21: December 1, 1688; *MDS*, 293)

Not without Quietist echoes, the correspondence with Rancé repeatedly depicts the spiritual life in the vocabulary of the desert: dryness of soul (*la sécheresse*), the void (*le vide*), nothingness (*le néant*).

Primarily centered upon her personal spiritual struggle, Sablière's letters to Rancé also manifest her extensive biblical and patristic culture. The Psalms, centerpiece of the monastic breviary, and the Epistles of St. Paul are the most frequently cited biblical books. Her library at the Incurables contained several Latin Bibles, a French *New Testament,* and a Latin breviary from Cluny. Under Rancé's direction, Sablière studied a series of patristic and monastic authors. St. Gregory the Great, St. Dorotheus,[40] and St. Bernard are the most frequently cited Church Fathers. All three focus on one of the favorite themes in Sablière's correspondence and moral treatises: the virtue of humility. In addition to these works, Sablière's library contained the writings of St. John Chrysostom, St. Cyprian, Tertullian, and Cassian.

In the last two years of her life, the tone of Sablière's spiritual voice changed. A new joy replaced the previous aridity. Seriously ill, she finally tasted a peaceful union with God. "I am in complete solitude, which is what I always wanted, as you know. I am happier than I could possibly tell you. I am with God and with suffering, which I consider the constant tokens of His goodness toward me" (*L* 56: September 7, 1692; *MDS,* 331). The suffering that had previously created an obstacle to complete abandonment has now become the means for a trusting union with God.

Shortly before her death, Sablière explained to Rancé this serene acceptance of her imminent demise:

> I am so happy! I see nothing but eternity before me! When we have given our heart to God, everything is done. We only have to continue to make whatever sacrifices to Him we can. Every day I see the place where I will be buried and I find the sight so tranquil that I like it completely. But it seems to me that on this occasion, as on any other, we should desire nothing. (*L* 59: 1692; *MDS,* 333–334)

The years of purification undertaken in a quest of abandonment have ended in an ecstatic embrace of mortality.

Madame de la Sablière died on January 6, 1693.

WANDERING CANON

Madame de la Sablière composed two works in moral theory: *Christian Maxims* and *Christian Thoughts*. However, she did not know that she had actually written two treatises for public circulation. Therein lies a curious literary tale.

During the final years of her religious retreat under the direction of Rancé (1687–1693), Sablière composed a series of maxims. Her aphorisms followed the conventions of the *maxime*, the literary genre popularized by the salon of Mme de Sablé. They are brief sentences or paragraphs, written with maximum concision. They employ paradox and irony to score their moral point. They examine issues in moral psychology: the nature of the will, of reason, of imagination, of the passions. They concentrate upon the status of the virtues, routinely decrying virtue as the subterfuge of vice, especially of pride.

Sablière transformed the genre by theologizing it. Her maxims explicitly cite Christ, sin, grace, the sacraments, and the gospel. She focuses in detail on issues of prayer. In Sablière's work, the psychological and ethical concerns of the *moraliste* are integrated into a mystical theology rooted in complete abnegation of the will.

Sablière did not publish her maxims during her lifetime. Over the centuries, a series of fortuitous circumstances resurrected the maxims in two collections shaped by posthumous editors.

In 1705, an Amsterdam edition of the *Maximes* of La Rochefoucauld added a new collection of aphorisms by another author. Entitled *Les maximes Chrétiennes de M*****,[41] the new work appeared without further attribution. A Parisian edition of La Rochefoucauld in 1725[42] reprinted the *Maximes Chrétiennes*, with the author still anonymous. A new edition of 1743, from the same publisher and under the same title, quoting the royal permission to publish given the editor, Etienne Ganeau, in 1736, cites Mme de la Sablière as the author of the work. In the edition of 1777,[43] Mme de la Sablière's name is added to the title: *Maximes Chrétiennes par Mme. de la Sablière.*

Numerous external factors confirm Sablière's authorship of the maxim collection. The opinions of three centuries of editors, of specialists in French literature,[44] of the biographer Menjot d'Elbenne (*MDS*, 249–251), and of Sablière's immediate descendants (*MDS*, 251) concur in attributing the work to Sablière. Internal evidence as well points to Sablière as the author. The vocabulary, the style, the themes, and the references in the work closely follow the same traits in the letters written by Sablière to Rancé during this period.

The genesis of Sablière's second work, *Pensées Chrétiennes*, is even more convoluted (*MDS*, 269–271). Menjot d'Elbenne, Sablière's scholarly biographer, gained access in 1878 to a manuscript collection of letters possessed by the Duke d'Aumale in the Bibliothèque de Chantilly. Erroneously titled *Lettres de Madame de Sablé*, the manuscript consisted of late-seventeenth-century letters to Rancé, transcribed in the eighteenth century. Both d'Aumale and Menjot d'Elbenne recognized that the letters, dated from 1687 to 1693, could not possibly have been written by Mme de Sablé, who died in 1678. Moreover, the internal references to economic problems, three adult children, daily life at the Incurables, and details of her apartment designate Sablière as their author. The "M.D.L.S." cited by the manuscript as the author is clearly Madame de la Sablière, not Madame de Sablé.

Independent corroboration for this attribution is found in two other collections of Sablière's letters. One is the manuscript *Lettres de Madame de la Sablière à Monsieur l'Abbé de la Trappe* (see *MDS*, 270), personally transcribed by Mlle de la Jonchapt, secretary to Madame de Maintenon. This manuscript, containing material nearly identical to that in the Chantilly manuscript, has the advantages of being written shortly after Sablière's death and of providing explicit attribution to Sablière. Another extant manuscript transcribed by Jonchapt, *Lettres de Madame de la Sablière à Monsieur de Rancé, abbé de la Trape* (*sic*—see *MDS*, 271), attests to the same authorship.

Embedded in the manuscript collection of letters is a brief work, *Pensées Chrétiennes D.M.D.L.S.* Obviously, the author is the same as that of the letters ascribed to M.D.L.S.: Madame de la Sablière. *Pensées Chrétiennes* consists of twenty maxim-like sentences containing spiritual counsels. Similar to *Maximes Chrétiennes* in language and theme, *Pensées Chrétiennes* is more fragmentary in nature. Possibly the maxims were originally Sablière's jottings on fundamental attitudes in the spiritual life, influenced by the teaching of Rancé.[45] Compared with *Maximes Chrétiennes*, *Pensées Chrétiennes* focuses even more intensely on the central attitudes of the Christian in a spiritual itinerary of strict surrender to the divine will. The instructions on prayer, detachment, and abnegation constitute a miniature treatise in ascetical theology.

Pensées Chrétiennes was published for the first time in 1923, as an annex to Menjot d'Elbenne's biography of Sablière (see *MDS*, 263–266). Menjot d'Elbenne's judicious editorial work has provided subsequent students of Sablière with a scholarly triptych of the three extant works of Sablière: *Maximes Chrétiennes*, *Pensées Chrétiennes,* and *Lettres à l'Abbé de Rancé*, all composed in the last years of Sablière's life.

VIRTUE AND ITS COUNTERFEIT

Christian Maxims provides a systematic sketch of Sablière's moral philosophy. The work analyzes the central virtues and vices. It critiques the moral virtues, especially in their neoclassical form, as the products of pride. It privileges the theological virtues as the only sure foundation of the ethical life. It complements the account of the virtues with a rigorist moral code echoing certain Jansenist positions. Rooted in a theological anthropology underscoring the primacy of grace, Sablière's moral theory emphasizes the necessity of contemplative solitude for the disciple called to witness the gospel in a corrupt society.

VIRTUE'S MAP

Numerous maxims detail the anatomy of virtues and vices, the habits at the center of the moral agent. Several passages praise the acquisition of the moral virtues. "To the degree that one advances in virtue, one loses all taste for the pleasures of the world. Similarly, to the degree that one advances in age, one disdains the amusements of childhood" (*MC* 85; *MDS,* 260). Sablière praises particular virtues, such as piety. "There are pious actions that appear contemptible to human eyes but that hold great worth before God" (*MC* 89; *MDS,* 260). She condemns specific vices, such as sloth. "The soul of the lazy resembles unplowed land. It produces only bramble and thistle" (*MC* 86; *MDS,* 260). The virtues and vices here cited indicate the religious cast of Sablière's analysis. Maxims 85 and 89 also illustrate one of Sablière's procedures in moral argument: the use of metaphor, especially biological analogies, to demonstrate an ethical point.

Humility and pride occupy the antipodes of Sablière's geography of virtue and vice. Humility is the central disposition of the ethical life. "The true glory of a Christian does not consist in elevating oneself above others, but in humbling oneself in order to be more conformed to Jesus-Christ" (*MC* 59; *MDS,* 258). Typically, Sablière theologizes the virtue by rooting it directly in the person and example of Christ. Pride causes psychological confusion as well as moral corruption. "Pride is the source of all our commotions and all our disturbances" (*MC* 75; *MDS,* 259). Several maxims develop variations on the humility-pride opposition that determines the moral temper of the soul.

Sablière argues that the vice of pride does not cover all personal idiosyncrasy. The Christian rightly manifests stubbornness in resistance to the wisdom of the world. It is Christ who reveals the distinction between the illegitimate exaltation of the self and the legitimate opposition of the self to public opinion:

> There is a vicious individualism inspired by pride. This is what the Son of God condemns so frequently in the Pharisees. But there is an evangelical individualism that stoutly opposes the trends of the world, both in thought and in action. This difference sharply distinguishes the just from the sinful and the worldly. (*MC* 5; *MDS,* 252)

Pharisaical pride, the vain reliance upon oneself for one's own salvation and for one's own indulgent interpretation of the law, is the object of Christ's condemnation.

In many passages Sablière undercuts this simple portrait of the psychological war between virtue and vice. Numerous apparent instances of virtue are only masks of vice. Our poses of humility are rarely humble. "The sentiments of humility apparent in our words are insincere if we angrily try to convince others to accept what we say about ourselves" (*MC* 24; *MDS,* 254). Pride animates many of our allegedly righteous actions. "We often lay down severe principles out of haughtiness. We like to decorate ourselves with the appearance of virtue and it costs us nothing to give others an insupportable yoke that we would never impose on ourselves" (*MC* 23; *MDS,* 254). In several maxims, Sablière details the hypocrisy that taints our putative virtue in word and gesture. She isolates the self-interest, often brutal in its conquest of others, that governs the exercise of virtue.

More broadly, Sablière questions the value of the moral virtues in general. The transitory nature of the moral virtues indicates that their acquisition cannot be the end of the human quest for happiness. "If we recognized that virtues acquired with so much effort can quickly disappear in the commotion of the world, we would not seek our happiness in them. Rather, we would flee them as an enemy who only thinks about stealing our most precious treasures" (*MC* 51; *MDS,* 257). The thirst for growth in virtue can easily impede, rather than advance, our salvation. "We must be suspicious of all brilliant virtues. It is only the love of humiliation that the demon cannot turn into a trap" (*MC* 49; *MDS,* 257). Again, humility alone retains some claim to authentic virtue.

Even the cardinal virtues earn Sablière's censure. Prudence, which functions as both an intellectual and a moral virtue in the Aristotelian-Thomistic tradition, contains little that is virtuous in and of itself. "Prudence is cowardly and timid, if it is not animated by the zeal of charity" (*MC* 72; *MDS,* 257). In itself, prudence only masks a vice, cowardice, for the self-interested. It is a cautious calculation of one's interests that systematically removes the risk of self-sacrifice. Typically for Sablière, prudence has moral value only when it is subsumed under the power of a theological virtue: namely, charity.

Sablière criticizes with particular severity the neoclassical version of virtue. Classical antiquity provides an inadequate model of virtue for the Christian. "The virtue of the pagans has occasionally led them to scorn the world, but only Christian virtue can make desirable being scorned by the world" (*MC* 48; *MDS,* 257). The cultivation of virtue divorced from the influence of grace vitiates the moral life and paradoxically plants the moral agent in the heart of vice: pride.

CHARITY SOVEREIGN

Sablière's treatment of the theological virtues differs dramatically from her criticism of the standard moral virtues. The theological virtues, a sovereign gift of God, free the Christian to lead an authentic moral life. Their depth and constancy contrast starkly with the ephemeral and often illusory moral habits fabricated by the efforts of the self.

The theological virtue of faith not only effects personal assent to the truths revealed by God; it provides the person with a moral vision opposed to that of the world. "Faith makes us regard as goods what the world regards as evils, and as evils, what the world calls goods. And it is from the difference between these ideas that is born the different conduct of the just and of the sinful" (*MC* 11; *MDS,* 253). Rather than supplementing the moral vision proper to all human beings due to their common nature, faith inspires a moral vision opposed to that carried by a corrupted nature prone to moral error. Faith thus becomes a necessity, not an auxiliary, for correct moral perception and for the right action guided by that perception.

The theological virtue of hope is essential to perseverance in the moral life. The desire for eternal union with God steels the soul in adhesion to the good through its moral conflicts. Sablière underscores the specifically theological nature of this hope. "If the hopes that we develop for our salvation are not grounded in God's Word, they are false and misleading. In vain do we promise ourselves what God does not promise" (*MC* 80; *MDS,* 259). The virtue of hope is a gift permitting us to endure moral combat. It is not a reward for our own moral merits. "We must place all our hope in God when we have recourse to Him, no matter how unworthy we are of His graces" (*MC* 99; *MDS,* 261).

Primary among the theological virtues is charity. Charity unites and vivifies the various actions of the moral life. Sablière underlines that authentic charity, inspired by the Holy Spirit, is strictly an operation of the will, not of the passions. "The love that God demands of us is not a sensate love, but a preferential love, which commits us to sacrifice everything rather than displease Him" (*MC* 46; *MDS,* 256–257). Theocentric, Sablière's concept of charity reduces all moral obligations to the single obligation of fidelity to God. Ascetical, it reduces the traits of the righteous life to the unique trait of self-sacrifice.

In Sablière's perspective, charity not only emerges as the greatest of virtues; it becomes the very criterion of morality, inasmuch as its presence or absence determines the moral character of a particular act. "Charity sanctifies the most ordinary actions, pride corrupts the most sublime virtues"(*MC* 9; *MDS,* 253). This opposition underscores the thesis that motive, rather than the act itself or its consequences, is the primary determinant of an act's ethical value. Only charity, a divine gift, can provide the proper motive for moral actions. Rather than crowning the standard moral virtues, charity often opposes them, since they are easily tainted by the motives of pride.

Despite their primacy, the theological virtues admit of counterfeits in Christian culture. Hope can easily disguise itself as presumption, a confidence in salvation that suffocates moral responsibility. "We have a shameful mistrust of divine providence in our temporal business, but for the business of our salvation, we have a reckless confidence in His mercy" (*MC* 20; *MDS*, 254). Rather than strengthening the moral life, such a bogus hope only destroys it through trust in a divine mercy shorn of justice and reduced to puerile sentimentality.

Charity can distort itself, becoming merely a busy service to neighbors. Even spiritual service, decorated in the rhetoric and works of piety, can become an illusion of charity if the agent has abandoned his or her personal work of conversion in the economy of salvation. "When we neglect our own salvation, it is not charity that compels us to work at the salvation of others" (*MC* 13; *MDS*, 253). The supreme matrix of the moral life, the theological virtues maintain their fecundity only in their pristine state, that is, as gifts of God humbly received in the order of redemption and of sanctification.

ANATOMY OF PASSIONS

Sablière complements her critique of the moral virtues with a severe treatment of the passions. The passions often prevent moral conversion by immobilizing the will. "In general, we easily accept the resolution to reform ourselves. We happily toy with the idea of virtue. But as soon as we must combat some passion, the resolution weakens. We no longer feel capable of executing an intention that we had formed without difficulty but that we cannot execute without doing violence to ourselves" (*MC* 26; *MDS*, 254–255). In Sablière, the passions always emerge as morally negative forces. They lead to personal self-destruction by plunging the moral agent into insatiable fantasies. "The desires inspired by the passions are the wishes of the sick, which we cannot satisfy without destroying ourselves and without making ourselves miserable" (*MC* 84; *MDS*, 260). For Sablière, hell is literally a personal state of unrestrained passion. "There is no more deplorable state than that of sinners who find no obstacle to their desires and whom God abandons to the caprice of their passions" (*MC* 34; *MDS*, 255).

Sablière's critical assessment of the passions manifests the voluntarist cast of her moral philosophy. The passions are neither useful nor neutral accompaniments to the will's adherence to the good. On the contrary, they routinely vitiate the will in its operations. Even passions tinged by moral sentiment often contain a hidden link to vice. In her study of regret, Sablière demonstrates how apparently ethical feelings of compunction can fail to be moral at all. "Only the sadness of penance is a reasonable sadness. All the others are marks of weakness or of the corruption of nature" (*MC* 54; *MDS*, 257). The moral determinant here is volitional: whether the agent wants to repent. At best, the passion of sadness is incidental to the will; at worst, it reflects a hidden vice.

Feelings of moral guilt manifest the same problem. "When we are distressed about our faults without correcting them, it is a sign that the sadness springs, not from grace, but from pride and self-importance" (*MC* 78; *MDS*, 259). The moral issue is whether the agent has chosen to correct his or her faults. It is a question of the will. If the will has chosen the path of reform, the state of anxiety is irrelevant. If the will has not so chosen, the sentiments of compunction are the noisy accessories of vice.

Sablière's voluntarism influences her theology as well as her anthropology. Her concept of God emphasizes the omnipotent will as one of God's central attributes. The divine will animates all cosmic and personal action. "We cannot resist God's will. It is always fulfilled in us, either by obedience, if we conform oursevles to it, or by our punishment, if we revolt against it" (*MC* 61; *MDS*, 256). In this passage, Sablière suggests her solution to the problem of moral evil. On one level, the sinner defies God's will by violating God's moral laws. On another level, the sinner implicitly affirms God's will, inasmuch as the temporal and eschatological punishment visited upon the sinner reflects God's eternal law of justice.

MORAL RIGORISM

Sablière's critique of virtue and of passion reflects the moral rigorism informing her entire ethical work. This rigorism manifests itself in her treatment of mitigating factors affecting moral responsibility. The standard teaching of the Catholic Church, especially as propounded by Jesuit casuists of the period, claimed that a variety of factors limited the culpability of those who performed immoral actions.[46] Common extenuating factors included ignorance, passion, prejudice, and habit. Sablière, however, systematically minimizes these mitigating factors by a rigorist interpretation of personal responsibility for moral action.

Sablière discounts the ignorance the powerful often claim as an excuse for immoral or negligent conduct. "When the great, by appearing to desire flattery, prevent someone from telling them truths which might enlighten them, their ignorance is in some way voluntary and does not exempt them from sin" (*MC* 6; *MDS*, 252–253). She warns of the dangers of vicious habits in the elderly. "Habits in old age are not less of an obstacle for salvation than are the passions in youth" (*MC* 21; *MDS*, 254). This judgment of the habits in the elderly is comparatively severe inasmuch as the casuists routinely counseled confessors to treat obdurate sinful habits, especially those of the elderly, with leniency. The censure of the passions of youth echoes her more global suspicion of the passions as morally destructive and her concomitant refusal to accept the passions as an excuse for evil behavior.

Sablière also dismisses the appeal to prejudice, the social conventions opposed to the moral order, as an excuse for moral failure. The moral life of the Christian involves a spiritual combat against cultural traditions opposed to the authentic good. "Custom may never serve as an excuse or pretext for sin. As it is the world that establishes custom, it must always be considered suspect by Christians, who swore at baptism to renounce the world and its wisdom" (*MC* 18; *MDS*, 254). The sacraments seal the struggle against moral conventionalism. Grace mandates and sustains the courage to resist social prejudice.

Sablière's rigorism governs her concept of moral knowledge. She insists that moral deliberation, in its specific applications as well as in its basic principles, must achieve crystalline certitude. Typically, the path to this certitude involves the removal of the influence of the passions. "There would be no incertitude in Christian morality if people, who almost always agree on general rules and principles, would draw the consequences without consulting their passions" (*MC* 8; *MDS*, 253). This insistence upon certitude in moral matters closely parallels the Jansenist system of tutiorism, which argued that the moral agent should seek unshakable certainty before undertaking a particular course of action.[47] It contrasts with casuist systems of morality (probabilism, probabiliorism, equiprobabilism), which claimed that some degree of probability in moral knowledge is acceptable when complete certitude is either impossible or undesirable.[48] The emphasis upon certitude also reflects the Cartesian cast of Sablière's epistemology.

PRAYER AS MORAL MATRIX

The moral combat of the Christian requires a spiritual life rooted in profound prayer. "It is no more possible for the soul to maintain itself in grace without prayer than it is for a body to survive without food" (*MC* 32; *MDS*, 255). The spiritual life requires a serious, though not absolute, solitude on the part of the Christian. "We must separate ourselves from the world and in a certain manner from ourselves, in order to hear God in retreat. The tumult of the world and of the passions often prevents us from hearing Him" (*MC* 76; *MDS*, 259).

This social and psychological solitude does not simply provide the focus to maintain one's moral integrity; it is a necessary condition for the genesis of mature moral knowledge. Only the prayerful soul can grasp its actual moral duties. "Only those to whom God speaks in the bottom of the heart can understand the whole extent of their obligations" (*MC* 98; *MDS,* 261). If the moral life is rooted in the theological virtues, the virtues flourish only in a life of contemplative prayer ardently pursued. Sablière's maxims repeatedly evoke the mystical root of the ethical righteousness ignited by God's sovereign work within the soul.

Grounded in spiritual solitude, the ethical struggle against the world is also ecclesial. The sacramental life of the Church initiates the Christian into a moral drama substantially different from that of unredeemed nature. "The birth that we receive in baptism and that makes us Christians elevates us far above everything we are, both by nature and by fortune" (*MC* 1; *MDS,* 252). For Sablière, the opposition between the mystic and the institutional Church is illusory, inasmuch as the spiritual progress of the soul depends intimately upon the acceptance of the gospel as proclaimed by the Church and as celebrated in the sacraments of the Church.

Adherence to the Church does not entail admiration of the allegedly Christian society in which the contemporaries of Sablière live. The majority of Christians contradict the teaching of the gospel by the sinful lives they lead. "If we made an idea of the gospel based on the lives of the majority of Christians, we would believe a host of things directly contrary to those established by Jesus Christ Himself" (*MC* 29; *MDS,* 255). The spiritual combat against the world includes a struggle against a culture formally baptized as Christian but in fact animated by the raw pursuit of self-interest.

Sablière's mystical horizon is simultaneously an eschatological one. Numerous maxims underscore the death that awaits each person and the overture to eternity that death represents. The purpose of our spiritual life and the moral combat sustained by it is the Beatific Vision: eternal happiness with God. "There is no moment in which we cannot merit eternal happiness. Thus, time is something so precious that the world does not have anything valuable enough to pay back the one who gave it to us" (*MC* 15; *MDS,* 253). Unfortunately, anxiety diverts the person from the absolute future, an eternity united with or separated from God, to a temporal future of material gain or loss. "Without ceasing, we are busy about our uncertain future, which does not concern us. We do not think about the future that cannot fail to happen and upon which our eternal happiness or unhappiness depends" (*MC* 12; *MDS,* 253). Only a constant focus upon the certitude of death and divine judgment, tempered by the hope of eternity, can unveil the true stakes in our moral struggle.

MORALIST AS THEOLOGIAN

Christian Maxims indicates the distinctive voice of Sablière in the concert of seventeenth-century *moralistes*. Like other moralists, she sketches an ironic chart of the virtues, the vices, and the passions. She wryly names the vice behind the virtue and the power behind the altruism. She maps the chasm between appearance and reality that troubles the psyche and the court. Sablière's theological transformation of the genre, however, is not the pious decoration of a skeptical moral code. The corrosive treatment of the virtues halts with the entry of the theological virtues. Faith, hope, and charity impose themselves as the necessary stimulants and guarantors of the vacillating moral virtues. The order of grace supplants the order of self-cultivation as the framework of the moral life. Sablière provides a radically Augustinian account of the moral enterprise, an account emphasizing human depravity and utter dependence upon God's grace. In Sablière's theological perspective, authentic morality entails a religious conversion one cannot effect through the power of one's disordered passions and illusory virtues.

Moreover, the distinctiveness of Sablière's voice is heightened by the mystical tone of her moral theology. The virtues cannot flourish simply because the person acknowledges Christ as redeemer and is nourished by Word and sacrament in the communion of the Church. A vital moral life requires a serious contemplative life pursued with vigor. Only in contemplative prayer can the soul taste the source and goal of the moral life: God. Only in the purgations of the spiritual life can the disparate desires of the soul find their integration in a single, fundamental desire to love God alone. In prayer of the heart, charity predominates and the moral constellation of duties finally takes its true shape. In this mystical vein of her moral philosophy, Sablière's personal contemplative experience clearly finds an echo. But her insistence on the primacy of prayer and solitude is more than autobiographical. It represents a democratization of mysticism. In her account, contemplative vision is neither the privilege of an elite nor the vocational duty of the cloistered religious alone. It is a state necessary to every person serious about choosing the good and avoiding evil.

GOD ALONE

Christian Thoughts provides a less elaborate moral theory than that developed in *Christian Maxims*. In fact, the brief treatise focuses uniquely upon the soul's union with God. This collection of spiritual counsels describes the conditions necessary for total abandonment to God. The *via negativa* sketched by Sablière is austere, an absolute detachment from the world and from the self in absorption with God alone.

The point of departure for this religious abandonment is complete detachment. "Detach yourself from every creature, no matter how perfect it may be" (*PC* 1; *MDS,* 265). So extreme is this detachment that the liberated soul treats the cosmos as if it simply did not exist. "Consider everything created as if it did not exist and as if it had already returned to the nothingness toward which it runs" (*PC* 6; *MDS,* 265). The earlier emphasis upon the appropriation of one's death now expands to a recognition of the utter contingency and mortality of the world itself. Only in this stark relativization of creation can the supreme worth of the immortal soul and the absolute value of God emerge with proper force.

Psychological detachment from self is even more crucial than disengagement from the external world. Sablière methodically catalogues the human faculties that must be silenced in order to rest in God alone. The intellect must limit itself to considerations of God and of one's personal vocation. "Empty our understanding, only using its operations for God and for the state where He has placed us" (*PC* 3; *MDS,* 265). Similarly, the memory must be purified and centered upon uniquely religious concerns. "Forget everything that the memory has retained, using it only for God and for our state in life" (*PC* 4; *MDS,* 265). The will, as well as reason, must simplify its attachments by adhering to God alone. "We must keep our mind for considering God alone and our heart for loving Him alone" (*PC* 15; *MDS,* 266). The purification of the faculties of intellect, memory, and will serves a radical theocentrism. Sablière's pointed vocabulary underscores the absolutism of this psychological detachment. It is only (*ne . . . que*) God who is the proper object of these faculties. The purgation of these faculties must eliminate all (*tout . . . ce*) other objects.

Even in their purified state, the faculties do not operate autonomously. It is God's activity, not the intellect's reflections upon this activity, that engages the enlightened soul. "Only consider God working in our soul and do not add any of our own reflections" (*PC* 10; *MDS,* 266). Paradoxically, the supreme knowledge of God resembles a state of forgetfulness in which the soul's particular identity has vanished. "Hold your state of being lost in God, considering Him as our only principle" (*PC* 11; *MDS,* 266).

The state of abandonment brings the contemplative to incomparable peace, although it is God, not serenity itself, that is the end of the abandonment. The major source of human anxiety, concern over the future, disappears in the soul's act of complete trust in divine providence. "With neither hope of compensation nor fear about the future, abandoning ourselves completely to God, we should do everything that will please Him" (*PC* 8; *MDS,* 265). Despite the tranquillity of the state, Sablière describes it in dark colors. The bleak vocabulary of the void (*vide*), of nothingness (*néant*), of forgetfulness (*oubli*), and of loss (*perdu*) dominates the treatise. The rhetoric of the *via negativa* can only evoke, and not define, a mystical union that transcends temporal action.

This religious abandonment requires profound solitude. In an extended paragraph, *Christian Thoughts* develops an apology for strict solitude and a critique of the temptation to social intercourse:

> We should stay in solitude as much as possible, because it is there that God communicates with the soul. Let us not flatter ourselves by saying that we learn more from conversation, because we learn more alone. By union with God, we obtain more graces to live with our neighbors than we would by speaking with them. Let us not flatter ourselves by saying that we are only speaking about God. We should only speak to Him, unless He inspires us to do otherwise or our state in life obliges us to do so. (*PC* 12; *MDS*, 266)

This maxim is a virtual charter for the superiority of the eremitical life, where contemplative adoration becomes the supreme good. This solitude, however, does not suppress moral outreach to the neighbor. On the contrary, it is only in prayerful solitude that one can hear the divine summons to a particular vocation, the state of life where each Christian must love and serve the neighbor. Moreover, the inspiration granted by God in this solitude guides us to love the neighbor in ways we would not devise by ourselves. Rather than eluding moral duty, contemplative solitude draws the person to the heart of moral duty where God speaks to and strengthens the docile conscience through grace.

QUIETISM MITIGATED

The ascetical theology limned by *Christian Thoughts* bears unmistakable traces of Quietism, the mystical movement then influential in French Catholicism.[49] The Quietists stressed the primacy of complete abandonment to God, with a concomitant stilling of mental faculties and suppression of the passions. Similarly, they discounted the acquisition of moral virtues and the use of discursive thought and imagination in acts of prayer. Sablière's affinity with Quietism involves more than her Quietistic vocabulary of abandonment and self-abnegation. One maxim echoes one of the more controversial Quietist theses: "Those who place all their might and all their glory in the Lord can no more fall than can the Lord Himself" (*PC* 17; *MDS*, 266). This aphorism appears to argue that complete abandonment to God can result in impeccability in the Christian. The parallel with Christ ("the Lord Himself") even suggests a certain divinization.

Church authorities condemned such theses as fostering presumption and as destructive of the moral labor necessary for every Christian until the moment of death.[50]

Despite its Quietist resonances, *Christian Thoughts* actually unites the mystical and moral orders in a manner opposed to Quietism. For Sablière, authentic abandonment to God does not free the Christian for antinomian license. On the contrary, mystical union places the Christian before a more stringent set of moral duties and fortifies the Christian with a greater zeal than does the routine moral experience of the conventionally religious. Part of the originality of Sablière's moral philosophy resides in this junction between a mystical ascent of eremitical purity and a rigoristic set of moral obligations rooted in one's personal vocation.

CRITICAL EVALUATION

Sablière's maxims constitute a minor chapter in the Augustinian moral philosophy of the seventeenth century. They subordinate the moral virtues, unstable and illusory, to the theological virtues, sovereign gifts of grace. Illuminist, they center the moral enterprise within the soul's mystical ascent to God, an ascent rooted in divine initiative rather than in the agent's works. In Sablière, the theological order invades the moral order, vitiated by sin and its offspring, ignorance and passion.

Despite its consistent Augustinian slant, Sablière's moral philosophy manifests certain inconsistencies. The greatest is the inability to reconcile freedom and necessity, construed in a theological key. On the one hand, Sablière insists upon personal moral responsibility. Excuses for moral mediocrity, such as ignorance and prejudice, are firmly discounted. On the other hand, Sablière underscores the utter dependence of the human person upon God's action. An authentic moral life depends completely upon the theological virtues, infused by the Holy Spirit. The apex of spiritual ascent, essential for mature moral discernment, is one of complete passivity before God. While the union between moral rigorism and a spirituality of abandonment constitutes one of the originalities of Sablière's ethics, the principles of the union remain unclear. Human freedom and divine necessity are juxtaposed rather than synthesized.

Even with its internal contradictions, Sablière's account of the moral life makes a distinctive contribution to moral philosophy. It sketches a prophetic ethics, a code of the moral agent opposed to the world and its corrosive wisdom. The ethical person is not the *honnête homme*, the prudent moral ideal of genteel culture in the seventeenth century. It is the redeemed saint, the sinner freed to a life of charity by the sovereign action of God and summoned to a particular set of moral duties in the midst of austere prayer. Like the biblical prophets, the moral agent undergoes purgation in a growing abnegation of the will. And like the biblical ancestors, the modern prophet faces a stony social destiny: exclusion, ostracism, persecution. Authentic moral witness entails an ethics of resistance.

Sablière's moral theory also develops a distinctive voluntarism. The moral worth of an act resides uniquely in the posture of the will of the agent who performs the act. Questions of consequence, of circumstance, and of the intrinsic quality of the object of the act are ignored. Theoretically and practically, the intellect and imagination are discounted in favor of the will alone. The passions are firmly dismissed. In Sablière's voluntarism, however, the faculty of the will is not the autonomous architect of its own destiny. The will here is a creaturely agent, intelligible only in the itinerary of sin and redemption. The will's capacity to choose and to adhere to the good does not manifest the will's independent merit; it reflects the grace operative in the soul due to God's sovereign work of redemption. If the will stands at the center of Sablière's account of the moral act, it is a finite, concupiscent will witnessing to a salvation not of its own fabrication.

Informed by a mysticism of abnegation, Sablière's ethics also operates an original junction between moral theology and ascetical-mystical theology. In her perspective, questions of actions toward others (moral theology) and of the ascent of the soul to God (ascetical-mystical theology) cannot be so neatly separated. All moral questions touch upon the posture of the will of the moral agent, turned either away from God in concupiscence or toward God through grace. The moral quality of every action invariably reflects the degree to which the moral agent has united himself or herself with God. The contemplative solitude ardently defended by Sablière is not a vocational necessity for a vowed or lay elite. It is a necessity for the moral maturation and for the moral discernment of every human agent. The study of the soul in its ascent toward God, focused upon the traits of apophatic prayer, manifests the hidden infrastructure of moral endeavor.

Like Sablé and Deshoulières, Sablière uses the tools of the maxim to unmask the pretensions of moral virtue. Prudence, courage, and justice are systematically deflated as the expressions of human pride. Like the two previously studied philosophers, Sablière takes particular aim at the virtues epitomized by pagan antiquity and prized by neoclassical authors, especially in their veneration of Stoicism. Sablière's critique of virtue, however, differs in several major respects from that operated by Sablé and Deshoulières. Her dismissal of the cardinal moral virtues is rooted in an exaltation of the theological virtues implanted by grace. Faith, hope, and charity are treated with reverence, indeed with a certain awe. This Augustinian celebration of the theological virtues contrasts with Sablé's critique of virtue (the theological virtues are only obliquely affirmed) and Deshoulières's frank dismissal of all virtues, moral or theological, as illusory. Sablière's account of society also contrasts with that proposed by Sablé and Deshoulières. Although the latter philosophers critique the vices and illusory virtues of society, specifically aristocratic society, the value of society as such remains unquestioned. Sablière, on the other hand, designates social interaction itself as a central block to the reception of and the exercise of the theological virtues. Her eremitical anthropology insists upon substantial solitude as the necessary condition for the exercise of the theological virtues in a contemplative intensity proper to their divine source and end.

Finally, Sablière's moral philosophy provides an answer to a perennial theological question: the specificity of Christian ethics. For Sablière, Christian ethics is neither a complement to nor a completion of an ethics constructed upon simple human nature. Christian ethics contradicts naturalist ethical systems, which are rooted in a corrupt nature. Only in the light of faith can the heart of the moral life, the ecstatic love of God and neighbor, surface. Only in the center of contemplative prayer, guided by grace, can the person's true vocation and moral obligations impose themselves. The Church's narrative, proclaimed in Scripture and sacrament, and the Christian contemplative's vision, nourished by prayerful abandonment, are essential to the very disclosure of the moral life, as well as to the successful execution of its imperatives.

To a naturalist ethics, inevitably canonizing human passion and prejudice, Sablière opposes a strictly theological ethics, grounded in the redemptive grace of Christ. Sablière's quarrel with ethical naturalism transcends the critique of the cardinal virtues. It questions the very possibility of a purely philosophical ethics divorced from a theological framework. The fideist edge of Sablière's ethics suppresses the halfway house of Christian humanism.

CHAPTER V

Mademoiselle de la Vallière: The Logic of Mercy

O Lord, glorious God of mercy, change my inconstancy into firmness, change all my disordered passions into a burning thirst for Your charity.

— MLLE DE LA VALLIÈRE, *Reflections on the Mercy of God*

A celebrity of the seventeenth century, Louise-Françoise de la Baume Le Blanc, Mademoiselle de la Vallière (1644–1710) was a mistress of Louis XIV. Having borne the king four children, Mlle de la Vallière caused a sensation with her religious conversion and her entry into the Carmelite order. Known in religion as Soeur Louise de la Miséricorde, La Vallière emerged as the "Magdalene" of neoclassical France, the model of the penitent who had abandoned the court in favor of the convent.

La Vallière's life has never lost its fascination for biographers. Dozens of books recount the story of the limping provincial adolescent who conquered Versailles court society only to renounce its pomps in the dark cloister of Carmel. Artists have fictionalized her in novels and dramas—not without a prurient wink at the tale of the courtesan turned nun.[1]

Largely ignored in the romantic portrait of La Vallière is her status as an author. In 1671 she composed *Reflections on the Mercy of God*,[2] a devotional work written as the tribute of a penitent to a compassionate God. An immediate success at its first publication in 1680, the book underwent five editions before the end of the decade and remained a devotional staple of Francophone Catholicism for centuries.

Primarily a work of piety, *Reflections on the Mercy of God* holds unusual philosophical interest. The book is an elaborate exercise in moral theory. La Vallière provides an extended analysis of the theological virtues of faith, hope, and charity. She studies common counterfeits of the theological virtues in the society of the period. She develops a critique of the alleged value of moral virtues, with a pointed dismissal of the cardinal virtue of prudence. And she sympathetically sketches how religious virtue can transform the passions into sentiments of reverence.

La Vallière's moral philosophy also offers a distinctively gendered account of ethics. The narrator of *Reflections* is not La Vallière alone; it is the composite persona of every redeemed woman who witnesses to God's mercy *qua* woman. The moral ideal celebrated by the treatise is not the universal virtuous agent. It is the gendered saint, related to God through irreducible sexual difference, who supplants the equally gendered types of the *salonnière* and the courtesan.

The sentimentalized portrait of La Vallière masks the philosophical background she brings to her analysis of virtue. Her mature theological culture, rooted in the study of the works of St. Teresa of Avila, replaced and contested the Aristotelian and Cartesian culture she had developed through private reading and salon debate. Her personal and theoretical knowledge of the libertine mentality grounds her excavation of the practical atheism that suffocates the virtues in the aristocratic elite. Her early artistic and literary formation exposed her to the *préciosité* she condemns as the enemy of substantial virtue.

CONSTRUCTING THE MAGDALENE

Louise Françoise de la Baume le Blanc was born in Tours on August 6, 1644.[3] Her father, Laurent, Seigneur de la Vallière and gouverneur du chateau d'Amboise, had distinguished himself as a military leader devoted to the royal cause. Her mother, Françoise Le Prévost, was the wealthy widow of a member of the Parisian parliament. After the death of Seigneur de la Vallière in 1651, Louise's mother married Jacques de Courtavel, marquis de Saint Rémy.

Militantly Catholic, Mlle de la Vallière's family raised her in an intensely religious milieu. Four close relatives followed ecclesiastical vocations: uncle Gilles de la Vallière, bishop of Nantes; uncle Jacques de la Vallière, Jesuit priest; and paternal aunts Elizabeth and Charlotte, both Ursuline nuns in Tours. Louise's great aunt, Marie Guyard, known in religion as Soeur Marie de l'Incarnation, was an Ursuline mystic and writer who exerted a palpable influence upon the piety of the family. Conducted by her aunt Elizabeth and other Ursuline nuns, Louise's early education introduced her to Tridentine piety and to the mastery of letters. According to contemporaries, the young Louise excelled in literary studies: reading, grammar, penmanship, composition, and public speaking. She began early to show evidence of her personal literary style, which was respected throughout her lifetime for its clarity and concision.

In 1655, Mlle de la Vallière moved to the chateau of Blois, the residence of Gaston, duc d'Orléans and brother of Louis XIII. Louise's stepfather served as the chateau's *maître d'hôtel*. She shared in the education offered to the three daughters of Orléans, supervised by Abbé de Rancé,[4] chaplain to the duke. Predominantly literary, the royal education also initiated Louise into the aristocratic arts of etiquette, elocution, painting, music, and equitation. La Vallière shared the Orléans family's passion for the latest literary vogue: the *roman d'épopée*. With the royal nieces, Louise read the novels of Honoré d'Urfé,[5] La Calpranède,[6] Gomberville,[7] and Mlle de Scudéry.[8]

In 1661, La Vallière officially entered court society as maid of honor to the Duchesse d'Orléans. After a secret exchange of letters, ghostwritten for both parties by Louis XIV's secretary, Dangeau, La Vallière and Louis XIV began an affair. At first carefully hidden, La Vallière's role as royal mistress gradually received official recognition. A series of royal balls and concerts were dedicated to her, including the festive inauguration of the palace at Versailles in 1664. She bore Louis XIV four children: Charles (1663–1665); Philippe (1665–1666); Marie Anne de Bourbon (1666–1739); and Louis de Bourbon (1667–1683). In 1667, Louis XIV legitimized Anne and ennobled her under the title of Mademoiselle de Blois. In 1669, he legitimized Louis and ennobled him under the title of the Comte de Vermandois, Amiral de France.

La Vallière continued her artistic and philosophical formation during her court years. She followed courses in painting and sculpture at the Académie Royale. She attended premieres of the dramatic works of Racine and of Molière. She studied philosophical works, in particular those of Aristotle and of Descartes. Contemporaries cite her discussions of the *Nicomachean Ethics* and of the *Discours de la méthode* in the Parisian salon debates of the period.[9] In the 1660s, she cultivated a circle of salon intellectuals of a pronounced libertine bent: Lauzun,[10] Bussy-Rabutin,[11] Benserade,[12] and Dangeau.[13]

In 1667, the rise of a new royal mistress, Mme de Montespan, signaled the eclipse of La Vallière's influence. For several years, Louis XIV awkwardly shared his affection among La Vallière, Montespan, and his wife, Queen Marie-Thérèse d'Autriche. In 1667, he granted La Vallière the domain of Vaujours and the title of Duchesse de Vaujours. In 1669, he gave her a mansion at Saint-Germain-en-Laye. By the end of the decade, however, the affair had faded and La Vallière gradually retired from the social life of the court.

At the beginning of the 1670s, La Vallière underwent a dramatic religious conversion. In 1670, she succumbed to a serious illness, possibly smallpox. After recovering from the illness, she confessed her sins, renounced her life as a courtesan, and began a life of penitential prayer. She emerged from seclusion as a member of the pious court circle led by Maréchal de Bellefonds. She started a serious life of meditation and spiritual reading under the direction of Père César du Saint-Sacrement, who attempted to moderate her desire for extravagant physical mortifications. Her new theological culture focused on the study of such mystical works as *The Imitation of Christ* and St. Teresa of Avila's *The Path of Perfection*. Bossuet, the court preacher and tutor to the dauphin at Versailles, counseled her almost daily throughout her religious crisis. Another court preacher, the Jesuit Bourdaloue, also influenced her spiritual development and her nascent monastic vocation.

Shortly after her recovery from her illness, apparently in early 1671, La Vallière wrote the essentials of the book *Reflections on the Mercy of God* in her notebook. She claims to have composed the work in three days, although the original draft of the text was probably enlarged and revised in the years that followed. The work expresses La Vallière's repentance for her sins and her reliance upon God's mercy. Although the philosophy of the work is influenced by the spiritual counsels of Bossuet, Père César, and Bellefonds, the style and argument of the text are clearly La Vallière's own.[14] A comparison between the book and the extensive set of letters from La Vallière to Bellefonds during this same period uncovers a close match between the two works in terms of vocabulary, style, reference, and ideology. Queen Marie-Thérèse later published the first edition of *Reflections* apparently as a wedding gift for La Vallière's daughter, Mlle de Blois, who married the Prince de Conti in 1680.

After her conversion, La Vallière's position at court became increasingly untenable. On Ash Wednesday, 1671, she fled Versailles and sought asylum at the Visitation convent at Chaillot. On Louis XIV's orders, however, Lauzun forced her to return to court. Bossuet and Bellefonds persuaded Mère Agnès, the superior of the Carmelite convent at Paris, to admit La Vallière to the Carmelite order. Reluctantly, Louis XIV agreed to permit La Vallière to test her vocation as a nun. In early April 1674, La Vallière took public leave of the king and the queen. The official court painter, Mignard, painted a farewell portrait of La Vallière. In the portrait, she clutches in her hands the *Imitation of Christ* and St. Teresa of Avila's *Rule,* the charter for Carmelite convents. At her feet lie the discarded bric-a-brac of court and salon: a mask, a globe, a purse, a string of pearls, a deck of cards.

Now acclaimed throughout France as the modern *Madeleine,* La Vallière had become a religious celebrity. Each step of her initiation into her Carmelite vocation became the occasion for public celebration of her conversion and for fervent attacks on the decadence of the court.

On April 19, 1674, a packed convent church witnessed La Vallière's entry into Carmel as a postulant. The cramped sanctuary contained a legion of priests and at least three bishops, including Harlay de Champvallon, Archbishop of Paris. The glittering nave included an army of aristocrats and a troop of salon intellectuals, grouped around the novelist Mlle de Scudéry. In his sermon, Jean-Louis de Fromentière, Bishop of Aires, denounced the moral atmosphere of the court:

> If it is difficult to achieve one's salvation in society, how much more difficult it must be to achieve it in what they call "high society," in what we call the court, where so many obstacles to salvation come together with so much force! The court—where all the vanities are on display, where all the pleasures are so intense, where all the arrogance reaches the heights! The court—where so many passions are unleashed, so many occasions of sin flaunted, so many pernicious examples given! Ah! Who could stay alive in a place where, as St. Ambrose says so well, death enters by all the senses, right down to the substance of the soul— where the eyes cannot open without receiving something that disturbs the mind, where the ear cannot hear anything except some poison that immediately attacks the heart. (*RMDMV*, 46–47)

The *tableau vivant* of the courtesan turned nun became a graphic indictment of a corrupt Versailles.

La Vallière's profession of vows on June 4, 1675, caused an even greater sensation. Queen Marie-Thérèse personally headed the delegation of lay witnesses. The court preacher, Bossuet, mounted the pulpit to preach a pointed sermon on the need of the mightiest to renounce sin and to seek the mercy of the Good Shepherd (see *RMDMV*, 82–124). Not without justification, Louis XIV privately condemned the spectacular mise-en-scène of La Vallière's vocation as a plot by his wife, his preacher, and the *parti dévot* to humiliate him publicly for his adultery and other immoralities.

During her thirty-six years as a Carmelite nun, La Vallière led a secluded life of prayer and mortification. Even by the austere standards of Carmel, La Vallière distinguished herself by the extremity of her fasts and vigils. She continued, however, to maintain contact with leading dignitaries of the Church and of the court. Bossuet, Rancé, Queen Marie-Thérèse, and even Mme de Montespan visited La Vallière in the convent.

Throughout her convent years, La Vallière continued her correspondence with Maréchal de Bellefonds, begun during her last years at Versailles. The letters to Bellefonds manifest the spiritual profile developed by La Vallière in Carmel. Like many members of the *école française* of ascetical and mystical theology, she emphasized abandonment to divine providence and complete abnegation of the will as the keystone of spiritual maturity:

> For a long time, through the grace of Jesus Christ, I've been persuaded and convinced of the nothingness of the things of this world. But it's not enough to be concerned about the things of heaven alone. Unfortunately, as long as the soul is united to the body, some spot always holds us firmly to earth. We always experience certain things that give us greater pain or pleasure in life, because we are not in that state of indifference where we should be in order to taste only the pure and intoxicating pleasure of loving God alone. (*L* 46: September 6, 1686; *RMDMV*, 219)

Complete indifference to the creatures of the world is the outward sign of a will truly abandoned to God's will. Much of the correspondence with Bellefonds details the practical and psychological obstacles in this path of spiritual surrender.

La Vallière's letters not only present her own struggles and interior lights; she also diagnoses the impiety that characterizes the aristocracy of the period. As her own sins had blinded her to God's existence, the disordered passions of her contemporaries lead to a practical atheism:

> Let us say to God's glory that His goodness extends over every living thing and that His mercy is limited neither by time nor by sin. We've experienced both in extraordinary ways. He enlightens us on our own misery in order to let us better understand His greatness and His omnipotence. Happy the soul who wants nothing more than to meditate the law of the Lord night and day! The more we grasp the nothingness of creatures, the more we admire the treasures of His wisdom. His yoke is so light to carry! But to whom exactly has God deigned to inspire all these thoughts? To you and to me! Let us tear down the veil that hides us from ourselves and dare to take a good look at ourselves just as we are. Forgive the comparison—I know that my crimes are much greater than yours. But isn't everything that offends God criminal? Let's take a good look at the life of society. What do we see there? A deplorable network of errors, of follies, of disorders, which all lead right up to the forgetting of God. (*L* 30; *RMDMV*, 185–186)

In this analysis of social corruption, La Vallière develops her theory of the sources of modern skepticism. The vices of the social elite not only oppose them to God and place them at risk of damnation; they succeed in suppressing any practical acknowledgment of God's very existence. A tacit atheism emerges. While the skeptics might express their irreligion in the form of intellectual argument, the roots of this contemporary "forgetting of God" lie hidden in the disordered regions of the passions and of the will.

After intense suffering from a strangulated hernia, Mlle de la Vallière died on June 6, 1710.

AN AUTHORSHIP CONTESTED

Louise de la Vallière's authorship of *Reflections on the Mercy of God* was never contested during her lifetime, nor is it contested today. The magisterial study of Jean-Christian Petitfils[15] has reconfirmed La Vallière's authorship of this work, even if a later editor probably introduced some stylistic changes to the original text. During the nineteenth and early twentieth centuries, however, several literary critics challenged La Vallière's claim to authorship. The false attribution of the work to male authors is a case study in how the works of women have been erased from the philosophical canon.

The work, *Les réflexions sur la miséricorde de Dieu,* first appeared anonymously in 1680, published by the Paris house of Antoine Dezallier, a publishing firm located near the Carmelite convent where La Vallière lived.[16] From the first, La Vallière was considered the book's author, a supposition she confirmed in her interviews with distinguished visitors to the convent parlor. Praised by the *Journal des Savants,* the book exhausted its first edition in a few months. By 1706, the book had undergone no less than ten editions. Simultaneous foreign editions (Frankfurt, 1683; Brussels, 1683) explicitly attributed the work to La Vallière.[17] The autobiographical references, the dominant image of the author as a "Magdalene," and the many parallels in form and content to La Vallière's correspondence confirmed the external attribution.

In the nineteenth century, several literary critics challenged this longstanding attribution. In 1852 M. Damas-Hinard published a work in which he discussed a 1688 edition of *Reflections* that had handwritten notes in the margins.[18] He argued that these notes had influenced the stylistic changes in the text of *Reflections* that appeared in an edition of 1716 and in subsequent editions of the work. More controversial was his claim that Bossuet himself was the author of these notes.

In 1855 Romain Cornut accepted this theory of Bossuet as the hidden editor in a new critical edition of *Reflections.*[19] Led by Sainte-Beuve, other literary critics dismissed the claims on the grounds that the handwriting did not match that of Bossuet and that the content of the notes did not correspond to Bossuet's preoccupations. While some minor stylistic changes to the text did occur in the 1716 edition, it was not even clear that the mysterious annotations of the 1688 version had any relationship to them.

A more sensational challenge to La Vallière's authorship emerged in the early twentieth century. In 1928 Abbé Marcel Langlois[20] announced that the real author of the work was not La Vallière at all, but a young courtier, Paul de Beauvillier, who formed part of the circle of devout laity at Versailles. The astonishing claim was dismissed by contemporary critics, such as J.-B. Eriau,[21] and subsequent critics, such as Petitfils,[22] as utterly without foundation. Nonetheless, Langlois's misogynist argument reveals one of the mechanisms by which women's authorship of philosophical works has been suppressed.

Put simply, Langlois argues that a woman could not possibly have written the text. First, women did not have such a philosophical and theological culture. Second, women could not speak as rationally and as authoritatively as the author of the work does:

> Let us return to the evidence left by the author in the text. Let us look at the style and the content. We notice that the author reads Holy Scripture in Latin, that he makes allusions to Aristotle and Descartes. A careful look at the text indicates that there is no trace of a feminine style and that we know that at this period Mlle de la Vallière was depressed and convalescent, and a very timid person all her life. On the contrary, on every page, one hears the voice of a man, of a director of conscience. This voice appeals to reason, refutes the objections of a woman, and firmly guides a vacillating will.[23]

The presuppositions here are clearly false. Many devout women of the period knew parts of the Latin Vulgate, through attendance at Mass, popular liturgical hymns, and use of the breviary, as well as through personal meditation with bilingual Bibles. La Vallière not only knew philosophical works; she had distinguished herself as a salon commentator precisely on the works of Aristotle and of Descartes.

The gendered analysis of the work ("feminine style" versus "masculine voice") unveils the gender biases of Langlois himself. If women cannot speak authoritatively on religious issues, then only a man could have written the work. If women use only emotion, not reason, in their arguments, then a woman could not have composed the book. Such a deductive gendered analysis simply ignores the empirical facts of La Vallière's longstanding philosophical interests and of her many efforts at spiritual direction in her letters to Bellefonds and in her parlor conversations at Carmel with perplexed aristocratic women.

Once Langlois has excluded all women as possible authors of a work of such philosophical and theological sophistication, he must find the male author. He lands improbably on an acquaintance of La Vallière, a young man in his twenties. Why a man would present himself as Mary Magdalene, why he would refer in the first person to his illnesses (clearly the illnesses of La Vallière during the composition of the book), and why an irreproachable layman would beg God's mercy for his sins of passion remain a mystery unclarified by the good *abbé*. While Langlois's thesis on Beauvillier's authorship immediately collapsed, it illustrates the misogynist bias by which the empirical facts of female authorship, let alone the quality of female philosophical reflection, can be dismissed.

A GENDERED VOICE

Reflections on the Mercy of God is a collection of twenty-four meditations on God's compassion. Written in the form of prayers, the meditations recount God's mercy to a sinner and describe the concomitant resolutions of the repentant soul. Composed primarily in the first and second person, *Reflections* is a passionate dialogue with God overheard by the reader. Often structured in the form of a litany, the work implores God's actions through a series of petitions.

Reflections is clearly an autobiographical work, written as a memorial of La Vallière's religious conversion in 1671. The original title of the book specifies the moment of its composition: *Reflections on the Mercy of God and on our Misery after a serious Illness.* The stated purpose of the work is to remind the author of resolutions made in the fervor of conversion: "A soul that God has made return to Him must thank Him every day for having opened its eyes to recognize its misery. We should write down the resolutions we took at the moment of conversion in order to see the obligations on which we will be judged in God's awesome judgment" (*RMD* 24; *RMDMV*, 305). In several passages, she underscores the necessity of a memorial of the conversion to avoid a return to the life of sin: "My God, what would become of all the promises that I made to you in fear and in danger, if Your mercy does not affix and support them in my soul when, to make me forget them, so many visible and invisible enemies come to tempt me by every seduction and flattery that nature has to offer?" (*RMD* 2; *RMDMV*, 231). Other allusions to her illness, to her psychological quirks (an over-enthusiastic temperament), and to her salon life mark the voice of the narrator as that of La Vallière herself.

Despite its autobiographical traces, *Reflections* is an oddly impersonal work. As the critic Romain Cornut argues,[24] the text lacks any allusion to specific personages, places, or events that shaped the dramatic court life of La Vallière. The passionate authorial voice seems to speak from a strangely atemporal and asocial landscape. Even the specific nature of her sin, adultery, is veiled. Political prudence explains in part this anonymous voice. Any pointed criticism of her own adultery would simultaneously condemn the immorality of the king. *Reflections'* narrative voice, however, is more complicated than that of a censored voice repressing politically damaging information. The persona of the work is not that of La Vallière alone. It is the elaborately gendered persona of the female saint.

The narrative voice of the work's repentant soul is not that of any redeemed sinner. It is the specific voice of biblical women: namely, the
Canaanite woman, the Samaritan woman, and St. Mary Magdalene. The
heading of "Reflection 3" states the purpose of the gendered voice: "On
the virtues necessary to approach Jesus Christ, according to the example
of the Canaanite woman, of the Samaritan woman, and of the Magdalene"
(*RMD* 3; *RMDMV,* 233). La Vallière's voice is assimilated to the paradigmatic experience of the women who personally encountered Christ's
mercy and the call to a penitential life.

La Vallière dwells at length upon each of the three figures of female sanctity. Each represents particular moral and religious sentiments essential for
the repentant soul. Each imposes herself as a canonical model for imitation by La Vallière and by other female penitents.

The Canaanite woman becomes the representative of humility. It is her
desire for divine mercy, expressed in exaggerated formulae of unworthi-
ness, that becomes the object of emulation:

> Give me this contrite and humbled heart whose weeping you never reject.
> Lord, let your holy grace inspire in me the same dispositions with which the
> Canaanite woman prostrated herself at your feet.
>
> Look at me approaching You as did this humble foreigner, as a miserable
> creature who considers herself all too happy to gather up the crumbs that fell
> from the table where You feed Your elect. (*RMD* 3; *RMDMV,* 234)

Strikingly, the first female saint invoked by La Vallière is not a biblical figure known for sexual sin. In fact, the scriptural account of the Canaanite
woman makes no mention of sin at all.[25] She is the petitioner in a healing
by Christ. Her healing manifests the divine power of Christ. Her status as
a Canaanite, the archetypal ethnic and religious antagonist of Israel, also
manifests Christ's outreach to the Gentiles and the future composition of
the Church as a reconciliation of Jew and Gentile.

La Vallière highlights the identity of the Canaanite woman as a foreigner.
She also adds stereotypically gendered gestures (weeping, prostration) to
the scriptural portrait of the Canaanite. The humility praised by La Vallière
is embodied in the palpably feminine figure of the tearful, prostrate outsider.

The second figure invoked by La Vallière is the Samaritan woman at the
well, featured in the Gospel according to St. John.[26] This woman, unmasked by Christ as an adulterer and as a bigamist, has traditionally served
as a biblical image of the sexual sinner. La Vallière parallels both her own
sin (sexual passion) and her own religious sentiments (the desire of forgiveness) with that of the Samaritan:

> Look with pity at this unhappy sinner who, still inflamed by the fire of her passions, asks You, as did the Samaritan woman, a drop of this living water with which You completely quelled the source of and the thirst for sin in her soul. (*RMD* 3; *RMDMV,* 234–235)

The passage underscores the similarity in the sinful tendencies of the two figures: in both cases, a longstanding sexual passion. It also manifests La Vallière's theory that grace must transform, rather than abolish or repress, the passions of the repentant sinner. In the analogy with the Samaritan woman, La Vallière evokes the passion to sin and to be redeemed as embodied in the figure of a woman with a pronounced history of sexual transgression.

The third and central woman saint cited in *Reflections* is St. Mary Magdalene. The Catholic cult of St. Mary Magdalene in the Counter-Reformation had in fact synthesized three distinct biblical women into a composite saint.[27]

The first strand in the synthetic portrait is that of Mary of Magdala, presented by the synoptic gospels as a disciple of Christ and as a prominent witness to the death, burial, and resurrection of Christ.[28] The Gospel according to St. John heightened her prominence by placing Mary of Magdala at the foot of the cross and by making her the first witness to the resurrection.[29] Christ's commission to her to announce to the apostles the gospel of His resurrection is the basis for St. Mary Magdalene's title, "Apostle to the Apostles," used in the Church's liturgical books.

The second strand is Mary of Bethany, the contemplative friend of Jesus in the Gospel according to St. John.[30] The third strand, presented by the Gospel according to St. Luke,[31] is the sinful woman who bathes the feet of Christ with her tears. Although the scriptural text makes no mention of the particular sin behind the gesture, patristic commentary and popular piety designated sexual sin, probably prostitution, as the hidden cause of the extravagant gesture. When this anonymous woman was fused with Mary of Magdala, the figure of St. Mary Magdalene as the archetype of the female public penitent with a history of sexual transgression was created.

The Counter-Reformational cult of St. Mary Magdalene emphasized both the peccatory and the apostolic traits of the saint. The medieval-modern emphasis upon St. Mary Magdalene as the repentant public sinner of sexual crime had become so pervasive that the term *Madeleine* became a common noun for all women repenting sexual sins, especially reformed prostitutes. Medieval tradition heightened the apostolic stature of St. Mary Magdalene by expanding her preaching role. According to French tradition, she finished her days preaching the gospel and creating a band of disciples in the Marseilles region.

Early in the seventeenth century, Marie de Gournay elaborated upon this feminist interpretation of the Magdalene:

> In the Church the Magdalene is called "Equal to the Apostles" by the apostles. Among other places, the Greek liturgical calendar published by Génebrard so names her. It is noteworthy that the Church and the apostles themselves permitted an exception to the rule of silence [the Pauline ban on women preaching] for her. She preached for thirty years in La-Baume-de-Marseilles, according to the tradition of all of Provence. And if someone reproaches this preaching of Mary Magdalene, let us ask him: Just what were the Sibyls doing when they prophesied by divine inspiration the advent of Jesus Christ to the entire universe? And afterward we must ask him if he denies the prophecies of St. Catherine of Siena, which the good and holy bishop of Geneva [St. Francis de Sales] has just taught us about?[32]

In this perspective, St. Mary Magdalene serves as the archetype of the woman commissioned by God to preach and to prophesy. The denial of the right of women to teach and to preach thus becomes an opposition to the will of God.

In *Reflections,* St. Mary Magdalene emerges as the model of repentance. It is the Lucan woman of remorse who is invoked by La Vallière:

> Most importantly, behold me without ceasing as the Magdalene and bring it about that, like this holy penitent, I may wash Your feet with my tears and that, in trying to love You much, I may try to wash away my many crimes. (*RMD* 3; *RMDMV,* 235)

The physical gesture of washing expresses the internal desire to erase the damage and the memory of sin. The religious sentiments of remorse, regret, and compunction embody themselves in the figure of the kneeling, weeping woman.

The three biblical woman saints not only provide a gendered voice for the narrator of *Reflections;* they act as intercessors for La Vallière. Authentic repentance and union with God is attained through the mediation of these three female figures:

> I implore You, by the intercession of these holy women, who are irreproachable witnesses to Your mercies, and who teach us what must be our hope in Your goodness, to grant me, before I approach Your sacred table and before I participate in Your divine mysteries, a lively and humble faith and a strong and constant charity. These two virtues contain both the accomplishment of Your law and the unshakable foundations of my salvation. (*RMD* 3; *RMDMV,* 235)

The traditional pedagogical role of the Magdalene is now extended to the Canaanite woman and to the Samaritan woman.

The female triptych not only witnesses to the effects of God's mercy; it teaches the suppliant about the nature of God's mercy and about the proper posture (hope) of the repentant soul. The intercessory saints manifest the sentiments of humility, repentance, and compunction in the irreducible voice and gestures of a woman. In so doing, they guide the repentant soul to the theological virtues of faith, hope, and charity. By assimilation of the sentiments of the women saints to the central virtues of the spiritual life, the entire act of salvation acquires a gendered contour.

TYPOLOGY OF VIRTUE

For La Vallière the theological virtues constitute the center of the moral as well as the spiritual life. La Vallière does not simply praise God for the gift of these virtues and beg God to deepen them within her; she develops a theory of the nature of these habits of the soul and a critique of the counterfeits of these virtues in the society of the period. Part of the interest of La Vallière's philosophy of the virtues resides in its examination of the skeptical and secularizing distortions of these virtues, distortions rooted in the characteristic vices of court and salon society.

FAITH AND SKEPTICISM

In "Reflection 4" La Vallière clarifies the nature of the faith she reveres as the central disposition of the penitent soul. Certain attributes of faith distinguish the virtue from false substitutes. Liveliness and firmness emerge as the first specifying attributes:

> O my God, give me therefore a living faith, that animates all my actions and that, despite my weakness, sustains Your love and Your grace in my heart; a firm faith that makes me believe in Your words and makes me remember, when the world wants me to follow it, that one cannot serve two masters. (*RMD* 4; *RMDMV*, 236)

The phrase "living faith" (*foi vive*) is not an anodyne appeal to an enthusiastic faith. One of the bitter polemics of the Reformation concerned the opposition between the Protestant conception of faith as *foi seule* (justification by faith alone, regardless of works) and the Catholic conception of faith as *foi vive* (living faith, justification by faith that manifests itself in works of justice and charity). La Vallière's immediate reference to the faith "that animates all my actions" confirms this distinctively Catholic approach to the nature of faith.

The firmness of faith (*foi ferme*) cited here also manifests a particular conception of the virtue of faith. On the one hand, faith indicates an assent of the intellect to the truths revealed by God ("makes us believe Your words"). On the other hand, faith guides the will in refusing the temptation to divided loyalties ("serve two masters"). The volitional dimension of faith balances the more intellectual component.

La Vallière adds two other attributes to clarify this concept of faith: humility and enlightenment:

> [Give me] a humble faith that teaches me to conform myself to Jesus Christ, that there is nothing I must avoid more than conformity to the world.
> Finally, [give me] an enlightened faith that, to prevent me from attachment to the world's grandeur, always places before my eyes the fact that this world passes away and that You, My God, are the only solid and eternal good. (*RMD* 4; *RMDMV,* 236–237)

Both of these attributes steel the soul for its combat with the world. Humility (*foi humble*) is not a matter of self-abasement. It is the stark refusal to surrender to the world's standards. Enlightenment (*foi éclairée*) is neither an illumination of the intellect nor a critical version of faith; it is the stout adherence of the will to God, an adherence that refuses the allure of all finite creatures.

In this perspective, the virtue of faith in itself empowers the soul to grasp and to combat the world's tendency to substitute itself for God. Rather than a simple habit of intellectual assent to revealed truth, faith is an inspired power of vision and will permitting the soul to wage a comprehensive combat against idolatry of the creature.

La Vallière decries the decline of the virtue of faith in contemporary society. She contextualizes the opposition to faith in the figure of the libertine, the skeptical habitué of salon society. Although at the moment of the composition of *Reflections* La Vallière believed that she still had a religious mission in the world, faith demands separation from its poisonous opponent: the seductive libertine.

> To bring to fruition the Christian sentiments You have given me, I will flee with horror all these evil people who parade their libertinism, who boast of their vices, and who, as Scripture says, never consider God in their ways of acting. Yes, Lord, no matter what interaction I may have with these militant libertines, who can only help to inspire irreligion, to destroy the purest reputation, to give us an exaggerated sense of self-worth that merits Your abandonment of us, to

honor evil and those who commit it—whatever attraction I may have for their mind or for their persons, I will faithfully, O my God, distance myself as far as is possible from business and friendship with them. Isn't hating the company of those who despise You the least I can do to thank You for having loved me so much? (*RMD* 15; *RMDMV,* 274–275)

Just as faith is not uniquely or primarily intellectual in La Vallière, unbelief is more of a flaw in the will than a blindness in the reason.

The self-proclaimed libertine (*libertins de profession*) defends a skeptical creed that masks and justifies immoral indulgence of the passions. The skepticism is the philosophical byproduct of the unbridled pursuit of pleasure. La Vallière's libertine is not any hedonist seeking excess. The libertine here is clearly a stock character of the court and salon. Malicious gossip ("destroy the reputation") and haughtiness ("exaggerated sense of self-worth") are the outward signs of the libertine dominating the floor of aristocratic receptions.

This contemporary form of unbelief also bears an unmistakable sexual stamp, since libertinism announces itself primarily through erotic conquest. La Vallière dramatizes the affective pull of this skepticism by admitting her own ambiguity toward libertine culture. She is opposed to the irreligious creed but attracted to the wit (*esprit*) and to the personality (*personnes*) of the libertines. Salon skepticism clearly remains a practical danger for La Vallière, as well as a corrosive intellectual and ethical enemy of faith.

Libertinism is not the only contemporary threat to the virtue of faith. In several meditations La Vallière diagnoses the counterfeit of faith presented by religious conventionalism. The conventional Christian adheres to the principles of the Catholic faith and engages in the required minimum of religious ritual. However, his or her moral life is anemic and his or her spiritual life is nonexistent. The ostentatiously affirmed "faith" of the conventional Christian only masks a practical denial of God, since all action is conducted as if God did not exist:

These are the people who, in the midst of the shadows that blind them, refuse to be enlightened by the light of these [religious] truths. We could say that a soul sunk in the world, without prayer, without reflection, and without consulting God on issues of conduct, is like a boat with neither captain nor rudder in the midst of a storm. It often mistakes a lie for the truth.

Moreover, we could say that it's a creature who believes that it knows God— even that it has faith, hope, and charity—but who doesn't really know any other God than its passions. It's a traveler in a strange land, without a guide, who only wanders further and further away from his or her native land. (*RMD* 22; *RMDMV,* 299–300)

The religious creed and practice of the conventional maintain appearances of the theological virtues. Since there is no contact with God through personal prayer, however, the apparent virtues are a sham.

The moral life declines, since personal access to God's grace, the guardian of moral fervor, has disappeared. The vocational and altruistic choices become chaotic, since divine inspiration, the proper guide for such choices, can no longer be detected by the insouciant soul. It is the lack of sustained personal prayer that is the key sign of this religious conventionalism. In fact, the final meditations for *Reflections* constitute an apology for the necessity of prayerful meditation by the Christian, if the virtue of faith is to thrive and to serve as an authentic compass of moral discernment. Otherwise, the public words and gestures of religion will deteriorate into a caricature of faith and will plunge the conventional Christian into a practical atheism.

La Vallière also suggests another contemporary threat to the virtue of faith: the challenge of rationalism. In her prelude to the critique of the conventionally religious, she sketches a portrait of the orthodox but tepid Catholic. The orthodoxy here is clearly a faith that has resisted the claims of rationalist criticism:

> I speak of those persons . . . who believe that there is a God, who are serenely convinced of this, and who are persuaded that there is no greater madness than to doubt it. Who are astonished to discover that there are people who believe the histories of Alexander and Caesar but who doubt the history of Jesus Christ.
>
> Who believe that the truth of the gospel preached by a dozen poor preachers and of the establishment of His Church founded upon an infinite number of miracles performed before the nations, cannot be truly doubted. . . .
>
> Who believe that so many mysteries incomprehensible to the human mind are pure effects of the omnipotence of Jesus Christ and of His infinite love toward His creatures. (*RMD* 22; *RMDMV*, 298–299)

Beneath the portrait of religious orthodoxy emerges a pronounced anxiety toward the contemporary inroads of rationalism. Authentic faith opposes the dismissal or diminution of Catholicism operated by a corrosive rationalism. It maintains the supernatural character of Christianity against the rationalist elimination of the miraculous. It defends the historicity of the gospel portrait of Jesus against the dissolution of scriptural claims by comparatist exegesis. It affirms the Catholic apologetic in favor of the Church's divine foundation against the rationalist preference for a purely interior religion. La Vallière's indirect critique of rationalism underscores the danger of an intellectual current that tends to diminish radically the content of faith, even if, unlike libertinism, it does not completely dismiss the value of Christianity.

Undoubtedly La Vallière's pointed brief against rationalism reflects the influence of her spiritual director, Bossuet. In the late 1670s Bossuet launched a crusade against the rationalistic theology of Richard Simon, an Oratorian priest.[33] An expert in biblical languages, Simon applied new historical-critical methods to the interpretation of the Bible itself. In his controversial 1678 work, *Histoire critique du Vieux Testament,* Simon argued that critical analysis of the Hebrew text of the Pentateuch, the opening books of the Bible, indicated that Moses could not possibly have been their sole author, as Jewish and Christian tradition had long maintained. Simon underlined the patent divergences in literary style among the various strands of the Pentateuch. More alarmingly, he noted the many contradictions in claims of fact in the book's disparate passages. He further argued that the standard Greek (Septuagint) and Latin (Vulgate) translations of the Hebrew original had seriously distorted numerous key Pentateuch passages.

Alarmed, Bossuet immediately denounced Simon's theories as an assault upon the divine inspiration of scripture and as a dangerous undermining of key Christian doctrines built upon scripture. He persuaded the French chancellor, Le Tellier, to condemn the book and to confiscate remaining copies. He pressured the Oratorian congregation to dismiss Simon. When Simon later published a critical edition of the New Testament, Bossuet renewed the assault against what he regarded as a denial of the truth of the biblical text. La Vallière's detailed defense of the literal truth of the New Testament's portrait of Jesus clearly echoes Bossuet's militant opposition to the historical-critical interpretation of scripture as the incursion of rationalism into the citadel of the Church.

In La Vallière the virtue of faith is neither a sentiment nor a simple intellectual assent. It is an inspired adherence to God, an adherence engaging both the intellect recognizing revealed truth and the will struggling against the world's idols. La Vallière's critique of libertinism, conventionalism, and rationalism as antagonists to the virtue of faith contextualizes the figure of unbelief. These challenges to faith not only represent the intellectual acids of modernity; they reflect specific demons in the culture of the court and of the salon.

HOPE AND PRESUMPTION

Like faith, the virtue of hope assumes specific contours in La Vallière. In "Reflection VII" La Vallière clarifies the nature of authentic hope and contrasts it with common distortions of the virtue. Again, the censured versions of hope reflect the particular social milieu La Vallière had encountered during her years at court.

Authentic hope manifests itself as a confident trust in God's mercy:

> I beg you, Lord, by the merit of this precious blood that flows from Your
> sacred wounds that You offer to the eternal Father as the price of my redemp-
> tion, a true confidence in Your mercies. (*RMD* 7; *RMDMV,* 246–247)

The hope is not earned by the penitent, although the hope is a personal
disposition of the penitent toward his or her salvation. The virtue is a gift
of Christ's redeeming sacrifice on the cross. Hope broadens the penitent's
witness to God's mercy from the experience of forgiveness of sin to a confidence in eternal life with God.

The virtue of hope can easily deteriorate into its caricature: presumption. The unscrupulous can manipulate God's mercy into an excuse for
continued sinful behavior:

> Do not permit me to abuse You in offending You even more. Do not let me
> enter that host of sinners who, without thinking to do penance, hope in Your
> goodness; who do not cease living in sin, without facing Your justice; who con-
> sider You more like the refuge and accomplice of their crimes than as the pro-
> tector of innocence and virtue. (*RMD* 7; *RMDMV,* 247)

Rather than conceiving hope as a deepening of the gratitude for sin for-
given, the presumptuous treat hope as a cheap title to avoid conviction of
sin and repentance. This abuse of God's goodness under the deceptive colors of hope flows from a divorce between God's mercy and human repentance engineered by those who seek to locate their eternal happiness
outside the logic of sin and redemption.

Avoidance of the collapse of hope into presumption requires more than
a penitential attitude on the part of the sinner. It demands a concept of
God that firmly balances the divine attribute of mercy with that of justice:

> Teach me, Lord, that if You are a God full of compassion for sinners who
> wholeheartedly return to You, hoping in Your mercies, You are a terrifying God
> toward those who trust in You only to multiply their offenses and who, having
> tasted the sweetness of Your graces, only mock and contemn them. Lord,
> weren't You speaking of these miserable people when You said that You would
> only treat mercifully those who sincerely beg Your mercy? (*RMD* 7; *RMDMV,*
> 279)

Ironically, the bitter presumption of the hardened sinner flows from a sentimental portrait of God. In this distorted theology, only the compassion,
the patience, and the tolerance of God are affirmed. The justice of God,
who will demand a strict accounting from every human being at the moment of death, is conveniently suppressed.

Presumption is not the only counterfeit of hope. La Vallière detects a particularly virulent distortion of hope in the venal aristocracy of the period. The virtue of hope has deteriorated into a passionate desire to possess ever greater wealth and honor:

> O my God, may this solid hope, showing me the nothingness and fragility of everything we call here below position, fortune, wealth, and greatness, make me no longer consider them as most people consider them. They act as if there is neither any other happiness nor any other life to hope for after this one. In knowing the true value of these things, may I only affix my heart's desires on these imperishable goods where truth itself assures us that we will find authentic joys. (*RMD* 16; *RMDMV*, 279)

Rather than aiming at a transcendent union with God, corrupted hope becomes an avarice for the next material conquest. The figure of the manipulative courtier, avid for ever greater possessions and titles, perfectly embodies the distorted hope that has degenerated into raw envy. God has simply disappeared under the veil of a hope that exhausts itself in the unending conquest of material goods and social acclaim.

CHARITY AND DETRACTION

The final theological virtue, charity enjoys a primacy among all the other virtues. Even when the other virtues exist in a weakened state, a moral life is possible if charity perdures. The absence of charity, however, signifies a complete ethical collapse since the proper motive for all action has disappeared:

> Faith, hope, and all the other virtues are nothing without charity. When I make mountains move and perform other miracles, but I do not love God, all my works are sterile and worthless in Your sight. Give me this charity that is the soul of all the other virtues and of all of our good actions. Give me a faithful and fervent love that uses every means to satisfy the ardent desire I have for conversion. (*RMD* 10; *RMDMV*, 259)

Charity here is neither the perfection of nor the auxiliary to the ensemble of the cardinal virtues: justice, temperance, fortitude, prudence. Charity is the necessary condition for the existence and flourishing of the moral virtues. Without charity's ecstatic love of God, the other virtues quickly deteriorate into calculating caricatures of themselves.

La Vallière clarifies this concept of charity. Radically theocentric, the virtue of charity focuses the penitent's affections upon God alone. "Reflection 11" provides a litany to God imploring a deeper imprint of charity. Each phrase of the litany focuses upon a greater attachment to God: to witness for God; to God's law; to fidelity to God; to sacrifice for God; to a preference for God over family (see *RMDMV,* 260–261).

Growth in charity requires a transformation of the center of the penitent's personality: the heart. Only God's gracious gift of a new heart can orient the person's affectivity toward authentic love of God:

> Create a new heart in me: a humble, firm, constant and courageous heart, free from the world and its creatures; a truly Christian heart, whereby I love You when I must sacrifice my life and fortune in witness to Your name and pay homage to the folly of the cross in the midst of a country and of a nation that considers it a scandal. (*RMD* 11; *RMDMV,* 260)

This passage links charity to other moral and theological virtues. The love inspired by charity is marked by a steely courage and constancy. All sentimentality is banished. Especially striking is the complex tie between charity and faith. Authentic charity expresses itself through courageous witness to Christ, a witness freely accepting the sacrifice of wealth and of life. It is the martyr, literally the confessor of the faith, who embodies the charity celebrated by La Vallière.

"Reflection 17" contextualizes the discussion of charity by locating the antagonist of the virtue in a typical salon practice: malicious gossip. The heading of the meditation sketches the opponent of charity in the figure of the backbiting courtier. "To conserve the charity we ought to have for our neighbors, it is not enough simply to abstain from destroying their lives, their honor, and their possessions. We must also avoid even the smallest mockeries and detractions" (*RMD* 17; *RMDMV,* 280). The meditation clearly aims at the refined gossip of salon society. Rather than outright lies, the hatred here expresses itself in the witty dissection of each other's actual faults and the sarcastic dismissal of all achievement. Veiled by humor, the salon detraction systematically assaults virtue by its destruction of all moral seriousness.

La Vallière admits that she personally sinned by her lively participation in the gossip of the salon. These "favorite sins" indicate how La Vallière typified her social milieu's distinctive vice, a systematic contempt for the human person masked by a brittle irony:

> Since we only value these gross sarcasms and personal attacks, unworthy even of a pagan, and we consider as of no consequence words which attack the very soul of our neighbors, which laughingly dissect their faults and which make them appear ridiculous—Since we dismiss as nothing the destruction of their

happiness and reputation as long as we do it with a laugh that entertains us—Lord, make me realize that those sins, which I can call my favorite sins, are even more disagreeable in Your eyes to the extent that they are pleasurable in human eyes and that they are only the unfortunate effects of my self-love. (*RMD* 17; *RMDMV,* 281–282)

The malicious gossip of La Vallière does not spring from her personal pride alone. The practice arises from an entire aristocratic milieu anxiously centered upon personal vanity and prestige. Perfected in the court at Versailles, the culture of gossip corrupts the traditional aristocratic virtue of honor by reducing it to a prickly pose of self-importance in the perpetual politics of the courtier's self-advancement.

PRAYER AND MIMESIS

Graciously bestowed by God, the theological virtues must be strengthened in the soul of the penitent. Serious prayer is the only method of deepening the imprint of faith, hope, and charity and nurturing other moral dispositions in their shadow. For La Vallière this summons to prayer cannot be fulfilled through participation in the church's liturgy and in popular devotions alone. Systematic meditation upon the life of Christ offers the only sure path for the affirmation of the moral habits proper to the soul of the redeemed:

O my God, at the same time that by Your grace you root out bit by bit all the bad habits from my soul, establish there all the virtues necessary to bring to fruition the work of my salvation. Bring it about that, in meditating with a lively faith on all the mysteries of Your life and of Your death, my heart is so inflamed that I have no other love or no other pleasure than that of pondering what You have graciously wanted to do and to suffer out of love for me. (*RMD* 6; *RMDMV,* 244)

Only in Christ, contemplated by the prayerful Christian, can the virtues emerge and mature.

La Vallière details how a particular mystery of the life of Christ can enrich and sustain a particular spiritual disposition. In "Reflection 6" she establishes a one-to-one correspondence between specific Christological mysteries and specific virtues. The birth of Christ in poverty encourages renunciation of material wealth (see *RMDMV,* 244). The hidden life at Nazareth favors renunciation of public esteem (245). The passion for the cross kindles horror for one's sin (245). The humiliation of Christ before Herod nurtures humility (246). The flagellation at the pillar and the crowning with thorns encourage an acceptance of humiliation (245). The cross focuses all desire on the unique hope of eternal salvation (246). This moral mimesis of Christ, nourished by rigorous scriptural meditation, is essential for the emergence of mature virtue within the Christian. Efforts to cultivate virtue in isolation from the economy of salvation end in failure.

NATURE AND ILLUSION

In this exaltation of the theological virtues, the "natural" virtues hold little place. In fact, La Vallière insists that the moral virtues have no value when divorced from the grace of Christ:

> Lord, help me to be strongly convinced that the life of the world is not the life of a Christian and that a God did not take flesh and die for us in order to grant our salvation through a comfortable life, according to the prudence of the senses and of the flesh. Help convince me that these moral virtues have no merit whatsoever before You, if they are not animated by the merits and by the virtues of Jesus Christ. (*RMD* 6; *RMDMV,* 243)

Tellingly, this dismissal of the natural virtues provides a particular censure of prudence, the most intellectual of the moral virtues. In La Vallière's spirituality, the cardinal moral virtues are neither a propadeutic to nor a guardian of the theological virtues. They constitute an obstacle to the life of grace, diverting the soul from the necessity of integral religious conversion and flattering the soul for an illusory self-sufficiency.

Reflecting the dismissal of the natural virtues, La Vallière's treatment of the virtue of wisdom starkly opposes the wisdom of the cross to the chimeric wisdom of the world. In the Aristotelian-Thomistic synthesis, wisdom functions as an intellectual virtue, the habit of grasping first causes. It frees the mind to recognize and to respect the hierarchy of truths. For La Vallière, however, the only authentic wisdom lies in the grace of the cross, which contradicts the shaky truths generated by pretentious human reason:

> Give me more simplicity and less confidence in my own reason, more works and less human and natural lights, out of fear that in following them rather than those of Your grace, I would lose myself. By following them, instead of becoming a humble Christian, my self-love would turn me into a socialite philosopher, more full of false maxims than of the science of the cross. O, the thoughts of people are in vain and erroneous when they are not ruled by the infallible wisdom of God! This is the wisdom that the world names folly and that it cannot recognize. This is the wisdom that God hides from the haughty and that

He reveals to the humble. This is the wisdom that overturns prudence and that follows the movements of grace from Jesus Christ. Finally, this is the wisdom wherein the fear of God has its beginning and its fullness. (*RMD* 5; *RMDMV*, 240–241)

This critique of natural wisdom proceeds by a series of antinomies: God/human, infallible/uncertain, cross/prudence, humility/pride, grace/reason. The cross imposes itself as the point of departure of authentic wisdom. The wisdom constructed by human reason independently of the cross only succeeds in generating metaphysical truths rooted in questionable virtue (prudence) and unquestionable vice (pride).

This analysis of wisdom is markedly gendered. La Vallière uses a feminine noun for "philosopher" (*une philosophe*) rather than the grammatically correct masculine noun (*un philosophe*). Further, this is a socialite woman philosopher (*une philosophe mondaine*), someone who prides herself upon her intellectual capacity and who, like the rest of her milieu, mocks the superior wisdom of the cross. The false wisdom condemned by La Vallière is not any pretension to comprehensive truth constructed by a vainly self-sufficient reason. It is specifically the wisdom of the *salonnière* exalted by her metaphysical culture and contemptuous of the religious wisdom of the humble.

In this dismissal of the wisdom of the salon, La Vallière engages in self-critique as a former salon Cartesian. Indeed, "Reflection 5" opens with an autobiographical contrast between divine wisdom and her erstwhile self-reliance:

Who am I? My Lord and my God! Who am I? A vain atom, a blind woman who wanders away as soon as Your light is no longer palpable, who merits to be thrown into the abyss of nothingness as soon as I pretend that I can elevate myself by my own virtue alone without waiting for the orders of Your wisdom. (*RMD* 5; *RMDMV*, 239–240)

La Vallière's embrace of the cross and rejection of the world's wisdom is not simply an avowal of her own sin of pride; it is a pointed critique of the philosophy of the salon, founded upon an aristocratic vainglory that can only oppose the cross as a disturbing folly.

PASSION AND CONVERSION

Despite its critique of natural virtue, *Reflections* offers a positive portrait of the passions, especially of the sentiments surrounding the moral life. Transformation of the passions, not their abolition or repression, reflects the work of grace. La Vallière uses the metaphor of friendship between God and the soul to illustrate the passions that should be transformed by the repentant soul's experience of conversion:

> Is it right that I should pride myself on being generous and full of probity, of tenderness, and of gratitude toward my friends, and yet that, toward God, I should present myself as a creature with neither faith nor friendship nor recognition? Is it right that my Creator, to whom I owe everything, only has the leftovers of His creature, only a weak acknowledgment, only weak desires, only the smallest part of myself?
>
> Is it right that, having forgotten nothing, and having always found everything possible to satisfy my passions, which only have idols for their objects, I find something difficult or impossible when I have to resurrect the passions and love You with all my heart? (*RMD* 12; *RMDMV,* 263)

The indwelling of charity in the soul does not abolish the passions that once served the idols of pleasure and of prestige. Authentic love of God requires a transformation of the passions into new sentiments of trust, confidence, and esteem for one's Creator. The repertoire of affections for one's closest friends is transferred and deepened as accompaniments of one's contrite, chastened love for God.

Contemplative prayer emerges as the privileged locus for this transformation of the passions. In dialogical prayer, the soul may present to God its destructive passions and invite the Holy Spirit to transmute the feelings of sadness and doubt into the sentiments of spiritual joy:

> Prepare my heart for the taste of the manna of prayer. This is the method to persevere at length in the pursuit of the good in the midst of the world. There You drive us away from the world and all its pleasures. There You make us find a holy and sovereign pleasure to love You above all things and to come often to speak with You, not only as our father and our God, but as the most tender friend that we could ever have. We come to lament before You about all of these passions that tyrannize us, about all these fears that shake us, and about all this sadness that exhausts us, so that, in the sweet exchange of prayer, we may show You the bottom of our hearts. (*RMD* 19; *RMDMV,* 290–291)

Contemplative prayer does not destroy the soul's pleasures. On the contrary, it transforms illicit pleasure, derived from attachment to the world, into the spiritual pleasures derived from redemptive attachment to God alone. Prayer is the ascetical arena where the penitent may offer at length his or her enervating passions to God, conceived as a patient friend, and slowly witness the transformation of these anxieties into the sentiments of serenity surrounding the new trust in God.

CRITICAL EVALUATION

Conceived as a testimonial to grace, *Reflections on the Mercy of God* permits La Vallière to elaborate an Augustinian position on the question of virtue and vice. She exalts the theological virtues of faith, hope, and charity as the necessary compass of moral endeavor. She denigrates the classical moral virtues, such as wisdom and prudence, as the debris of a vain neopaganism. Not only does she praise and blame the varieties of Christian and natural virtue; she elaborates a typology of virtue, carefully distinguishing authentic moral dispositions from their frequent caricatures.

The account of virtue embedded in La Vallière's theology manifests certain problems. The first concerns the autobiographical idiom in which she constructs her theory of virtue and vice. From the beginning to the end of her treatise, La Vallière addresses a merciful God known through her personal, idiosyncratic experience of repentance and conversion. She offers neither philosophical proof nor theological apology for the existence or the attributes of this deity. God's existence and salutary action, passionately affirmed rather than logically demonstrated, serve as a presupposition of La Vallière's arguments concerning the nature of authentic virtue. The ethical argument, often discursive in itself, rests upon a subjective spiritual experience that can only be evoked.

The second problem concerns the mystical rhetoric of the *Reflections*. Written in the second person, the treatise is a series of petitions addressed to God in impassioned prayer, often in the form of fiery imperatives. La Vallière's entreaties that God deepen her faith and hope often assert the primacy of these virtues rather than defining their precise nature. Her discussions of charity often describe the intensity of the virtue rather than explain the extent of the virtue's applications.

The passionate rhetoric of the text does not prevent La Vallière from developing a sophisticated argument on the necessity of the theological virtues and the illusion of ethical self-culture. On the contrary, it provides her with metaphors to etch the light of faith, the rock of hope, and the fire of charity. Nonetheless, the mystically emotive rhetoric of the work limits the more metaphysical argument on the nature of moral habits.

Despite these limitations, *Reflections on the Mercy of God* does develop a substantial moral philosophy, focused on issues of moral psychology. First, La Vallière sketches a consistently Augustinian account of virtue. The site for the emergence of virtue is not a generic human nature, abstracted from history. On the contrary, the site for the flourishing of virtue is always soteriological: that is, the actual history of sin and redemption by which humanity moves toward union with or opposition to God. Within the soteriological framework, the true face of virtue unveils itself as faith in God the redeemer, hope in eternal union with God, and ecstatic charity toward God and God's creation. The other moral dispositions essential for human interaction flow as subordinates to this trinity of graced habits.

Conversely, the effort to construct virtues and happiness upon human initiative alone inevitably fails, since it relies upon a concupiscent human nature bathed in ignorance and passion. The glittering neoclassical attempts to revive the virtues of antiquity lead only to the hubris of pagan pride.

Augustinian in its dismissal of the moral virtues and in its exaltation of the theological virtues, La Vallière's theory of virtue differs on several major points from the Augustinianism of Sablière studied in chapter 4. For Sablière, the passions as well as the natural virtues are dangerous, blocking the soul's ascent to God. For La Vallière, on the other hand, the passions are neutral, capable of being used for or against the ecstatic charity inspired by grace. God's redeeming activity alters rather than abolishes the passions.

La Vallière also differs from Sablière on the relationship between society and solitude. Although La Vallière ultimately abandoned the court for a strictly cloistered life in Carmel, *Reflections* defends the possibility of a virtuous life conducted in the world, even in the world of the court. Its insistence on the necessity of meditation to lead a virtuous life never becomes a categorical summons to the desert. In her positive evaluation of the sentiments and in her defense of a vocation within aristocratic society, La Vallière proposes a more temperate Augustinianism than that defended by Sablière.

Second, La Vallière's typology of the theological virtues offers a virtual sociology of moral temperament. Her study of faith addresses challenges to faith specific to the elite culture of the court: the skeptical courtier who contemns the Christian faith in order to pursue vicious passions; the conventional Christian who clings to a state cult without moral consequences; the rationalist scholar who destroys the credibility of Christianity by refusal of all evidence of the supernatural. Her analysis of hope detects the caricature of hope present in the *salonnière* whose life revolves around the fantasy of the greater title and the larger purse. In quasi-Pascalian terms she describes the aristocratic culture of diversion that suppresses questions of eternity in favor of gamelike conquest.

Her account of charity does not identify generic hatred as its enemy. Rather, she designates the network of salon gossip as the contemporary face of the passion to denigrate one's neighbor. Not content to provide a general table of virtue and vice, La Vallière contextualizes the theological virtues and their counterfeits in terms of the contemporary court and salon. This critical sociology of virtue constitutes one of the originalities of La Vallière's moral theory.

Finally, La Vallière constructs a gendered moral philosophy. The defining voice of the treatise is not that of the generic penitent. It is that of a woman penitent, witnessing to God's mercy toward a sexual transgression. It is the voice of the Magdalene. The entire discussion of virtue and vice arises within the framework of this gendered account of sin and redemption.

Moreover, the conversion of La Vallière, which constitutes the autobiographical pivot of the treatise, concerns not only the practical transition from the gender-specific role of royal mistress to that of cloistered nun; it also embraces an intellectual transition from the equally gendered role of salon philosopher to that of mystical theologian. It entails the abandonment of salon culture, epitomized by the novels of Mlle de Scudéry, in favor of an ascetical culture, codified by the works of St. Teresa of Avila. The canon of scripture supplants the earlier metaphysical canon of Aristotle and of Descartes. The theological virtues, rooted in the cross, replace the salon's virtue of prudence and its vice of pride. La Vallière's Augustinian account of the virtues does not arise out of simple scholarly conviction. It reflects an intellectual as well as vocational conversion embodied in a gendered experience of transgression and redemption.

CHAPTER VI

Madame de Maintenon: A Moral Pragmatism

True eminence consists in esteeming only virtue, in knowing how
to distance ourselves from fortune when it turns against us and
how to avoid being intoxicated by fortune when it goes our way.
— MME DE MAINTENON, *On Eminence*

Only a novelist could have invented Madame de Maintenon. The
impoverished daughter of a criminal, Françoise d'Aubigné, Marquise de
Maintenon (1635–1719), rose to become the spouse of Louis XIV and
arguably the most powerful woman in France. Founder of a celebrated
school for aristocratic girls, she revolutionized the education of women.

For her admirers, especially the faculty of her academy,[1] Maintenon was
a lay saint. Her nursing of her first husband, her governorship of the illegitimate children of Louis XIV, her reformation of her second husband,
Louis XIV, and her direction of the students at Saint-Cyr provided a model
of sanctity sensibly different from that of the cloister. To her detractors,
starting with the courtier Saint-Simon,[2] Maintenon was a consummate
schemer. Her piety only masked an insatiable ambition that coolly used the
suffering of a prestigious paralytic, the embarrassment of a royal mistress,
and the remorse of an aging king to insinuate herself into the pinnacle of
French society.

The preoccupation with Maintenon's moral character has never quite
obscured her pioneering role in the education of women. For more than
a century (1686–1793), the Royal Institute of Saint-Louis at Saint-Cyr imposed itself as the most prestigious academy for women in Europe. Founded
and personally directed by Maintenon, the school innovated by its original
lay inspiration, by the breadth of its curriculum, and by its emphasis on
artistic achievement.

Not only did Maintenon excel as an educational entrepreneur; in a flood

124

of works composed for the faculty and students of Saint-Cyr, she established herself as a philosopher of education. Numerous anthologies have provided extracts from Maintenon's works on education. However, the anthologies of Faguet,[3] Gréard,[4] and Prévot[5] drip an antireligious venom that eviscerates the theological heart of her educational philosophy. Moreover, Maintenon's writings on education remain largely unknown to the Anglophone public.

Within her educational theory, Maintenon elaborates a substantial moral philosophy, squarely based on the issue of virtue, the primary end of Maintenonian education. She develops an original interpretation of the cardinal virtues by the primacy she accords temperance. She examines the aristocratic spectrum of virtue with its distinctive emphasis upon politeness. If Maintenon's philosophy of virtue represents an apology for the era's aristocratic code of honor, it is a critical apology. The code's emphasis upon social rank is treated with suspicion by Maintenon, who is torn between an ethics of class and an ethics of merit.

AN EDUCATOR'S VOCATION

Born on November 27–28, 1635, Françoise d'Aubigné began her life in the prison of Niort.[6] Her father, Constant d'Aubigné, a career criminal, had been condemned for kidnapping (1613), for the murder of his first wife (1618), and most recently for treason and debt. Married in 1627 to Jeanne de Cardilhac, daughter of the prison warden, Constant was the disowned son of Agrippa d'Aubigné, the renowned Huguenot warrior and author. Baptized a Catholic by her mother, Françoise spent much of her early childhood with a beloved Protestant aunt, Mme de Villette, who converted her to Protestantism. A harrowing childhood included a failed political venture by her father in Martinique (1645–1647); a tempestuous visit with a Catholic aunt who used her as a domestic servant (1648); rebellious periods in the Ursuline convent schools at Niort and at Paris (1648–1649), where a nun converted her back to Catholicism; and a return to her impoverished mother (1649–1652), where she was periodically reduced to begging in the streets.

Her chaotic childhood included only sporadic formal instruction. However, under the tutelage of the Ursulines, she developed a limpid, vigorous writing style. At the insistence of her mother, she memorized passages from Plutarch's *Lives*. This exercise helped to cultivate her lifelong taste for morally edifying literature.

Without a dowry, the adolescent Françoise in 1652 accepted a marriage offer from an unlikely prospect: the burlesque poet Paul Scarron.[7] Paralyzed, impotent, sarcastic, and twenty-five years her senior, the writer skirted bankruptcy himself. Despite the mockery of salon circles, the improbable marriage proved a success. The tiny apartment of M. and Mme Scarron quickly became a fashionable literary salon, although the guests soon learned that food would not necessarily follow the witty conversation.

Mme Scarron developed her originally thin philosophical culture through contact with habitués of the salon: Vivonne,[8] Saint-Aignan,[9] Costar,[10] Ménage,[11] Benserade,[12] and Chapelain.[13] She read and approved the early writings of Descartes. The moralist Méré[14] particularly influenced her with his concept of the *honnête homme,* the temperate gentleman who would replace the warrior as the moral ideal of the aristocracy.

Renowned for her wit and for her literary judgment, Mme Scarron was hailed as a model *précieuse* by Mlle de Scudéry[15] and by Somaize.[16] The salon experience would influence her later conviction that dialogue, rather than reading and lecture, was the most effective means of education.

With the death of her husband in 1660, Mme Scarron faced a precarious future. During the following decade of obscurity, she deepened her friendship with prominent *salonnières,* such as the novelist Mme de Lafayette. Through her salon contacts, she befriended Mme de Montespan, then the mistress of Louis XIV.

In 1669, Mme Scarron began a delicate mission: the governorship of the children of Louis XIV and Montespan. First at a secluded chateau and later, after the king had legitimized the children in 1673, at court, the governess impressed the couple by her discretion and by her pedagogical skill. Her expert nursing of their sickly son, the Duc du Maine, brought about a miraculous improvement in his health. A grateful Louis XIV granted her an endowment in 1674, which permitted her to purchase the fief and the title of Maintenon. A financially secure Mme de Maintenon now took a prominent role in court society as a confidante of Louis XIV.

When the affair between Louis XIV and Montespan soured, Maintenon encouraged the king to reconcile with his estranged wife, Marie-Thérèse d'Autriche. The reasonably successful outcome of the reconciliation earned Maintenon the favor of the royal couple but the undying enmity of Montespan and her court allies. The sudden death of Queen Marie-Thérèse on July 30, 1683, drew Louis XIV and Maintenon even closer.

On October 9, 1683, they were married in a private religious ceremony conducted by Harlay de Champvallon, Archbishop of Paris. Morganatic, the marriage conferred neither the title nor the prerogatives of queen on Maintenon. Secret, the marriage was never publicly recognized either by Louis XIV or by Maintenon. Quickly, however, French society divined that a valid, sacramental marriage had occurred. In a celebrated portrait, Mignard depicted Maintenon in a cape lined with ermine decorated with fleurs-de-lys, clothing reserved for the French queen. Louis XIV's choice of a modestly born governess as his wife was simply too shocking to aristocratic propriety and to the longstanding policy of dynastic royal marriage.

During this decade, Mme de Maintenon's vocation as an educator matured. With two former Ursulines, Mme de Brinon and Mme de Saint-Pierre, she directed a school for impoverished servant girls, first at Montmorency (1680), then at Rueil (1681). She established a simple curriculum: religion, reading, writing, arithmetic, home economics. An entrepreneur, she negotiated with a textile firm to sell the pupils' products.

Flush with the acclaim garnered by the experiment at Rueil, Maintenon began to design her most cherished educational project: a royal boarding school for impoverished aristocratic girls. Opened temporarily at Noisy in 1684, the school gained a permanent home at Saint-Cyr, near Versailles, in 1686. Generously funded by Louis XIV, the Royal Institute of Saint-Louis was designed to receive 250 pupils, preferably drawn from the daughters of impoverished military officers. Maintenon carefully supervised every detail of the school, from the content of the curriculum to the color of the ribbons worn by each class.

Saint-Cyr divided its students into four classes: "reds" (7–11 years old); "greens" (11–14); "yellows" (14–17); and "blues" (17–20). The basic curriculum included courses in religion, reading, writing, arithmetic, music, and needlework. Older students received additional courses in history, Latin, painting, dancing, and home economics. The curriculum followed a strict gradation, the material taught increasing in difficulty at each successive level.

Each class had its internal hierarchical organization. A headmistress, assisted by several apprentice teachers, directed the class from the center of the classroom. Every class was divided into a series of "bands," each comprising approximately a dozen students, headed by a more advanced student. The head of each band conducted review sessions and discussions for her small group. She also assisted the headmistress in material chores.

Even more important than the innovative curriculum and class organization was the careful attention given to the formation of the teaching corps. Like Louis XIV, Maintenon disdained the then current convent education. She considered it completely ill-adapted to the vocational requirements of the typical laywoman. She founded the Dames of Saint-Louis as a lay community that would serve as the professorial corps of the schools. The Dames would live in community and pronounce a vow of celibacy, but they would belong to no religious order, would observe no cloister, and would practice only minimal communal prayer. Nothing would prevent the Dames from giving themselves completely to the educational needs of their students.

Professional competence was insufficient. In a torrent of conferences and letters, Maintenon instructed the Dames on the key virtues of a Saint-Cyr teacher: personal knowledge of each pupil's history and temperament and personal attention to each pupil's extracurricular life, whether spiritual or recreational.[17] In particular, the Dames were to be "reasonable." They would carefully explain to students the reasons behind a rule or a decision.

Maintenon also insisted that the Dames were to privilege a dialogical method of instruction. In every discipline, they were to encourage teacher-student discussion, and through the frequent use of the bands, they were to foster interstudent conversation. Numerous letters from Maintenon criticized teachers who use a vocabulary incomprehensible to young pupils or who prefer lecture to discussion in classroom conduct.[18]

In its first years (1686–1689), commonly called the "worldly years," Saint-Cyr glowed in its cultural achievements. Hardouin-Mansart designed its palatial buildings. Lulli composed its liturgical music. Fénelon and Bossuet preached in its chapel. Mlle de Scudéry wrote neoclassical skits for the students. The principal, Mme de Brinon, attempted to elevate the literary culture of the faculty. She baffled the Dames with readings from the Church Fathers and scandalized them with readings from Molière.

The artistic glory of Saint-Cyr reached its zenith on January 26, 1689, with the world premiere of Racine's *Esther,* specially commissioned for Saint-Cyr by Maintenon. With Louis XIV taking tickets at the door and Racine openly weeping at the beauty of the students' acting, the sumptuous production of *Esther* became a cultural sensation. The elite of Europe begged the king for a coveted ticket to subsequent performances.

The artistic triumph soon proved to be an educational disaster. The elaborate plays and concerts severely reduced the time for regular instruction. Maintenon quarreled with Mme de Brinon over the increasingly ostentatious religious offices. Star-struck by public adulation, surly students refused to do menial chores. Love affairs broke out, the most notorious being that between a sixty-year-old spectator, M. de Villette, and a student actress, Claire de Marrilly.

In 1691 a rueful Mme de Maintenon admitted the errors of the early years:

> I wanted the girls to have some wit. I wanted their heart to be elevated, their reason to be strengthened. I succeeded in this plan. They have wit and they use it against us. They have an elevated heart, and they are prouder and more arrogant than the most exalted princesses. We shaped their reason and ended up with the most presumptuous speech-makers. This is what happens when the desire to excel is your only principle.[19]

Maintenon firmly redressed the situation. She banned novels and neopagan works from the school. Out went the playlets of Scudéry. She simplified the uniforms and the decor. Out went the wigs and the ribbons. She revised the curriculum, excluding exercises that seemed to promote vanity. By a royal *lettre de cachet,* she removed Mme de Brinon from the premises. Her reforms gradually created a Saint-Cyr more committed to quiet moral improvement than to brilliant artistic achievement.

Having chased away the demon of coquetry, Maintenon now faced a new demon, that of spiritual illusion, during the second, "mystical" period of Saint-Cyr (1690–1697). Maintenon had invited Mme de Guyon to present spiritual conferences to the faculty and students. The leader of the Quietist movement, with its austere doctrine of abandonment to God through passive recollection, Guyon appeared the perfect antidote to the feverish worldliness of Saint-Cyr. Her pamphlet, *A short Method of Prayer,* circulated widely in aristocratic circles. Maintenon cherished her company and protected her against her ecclesiastical opponents. Guyon's lectures enraptured the school, especially a group of younger Dames.

Soon, however, the shadows of Quietism swept through the school. Students interpreted the doctrine of spiritual indifference as an invitation to neglect one's moral duties and one's work. The knitting needles stopped once again. Adolescents became intoxicated by discussions of their most recent mystical experiences.

In her memoirs, the Saint-Cyr teacher Mme Pérou recounts the exalted atmosphere of the early 1690s:

> The whole house became Quietist without knowing it. People talked about nothing but love, abandonment, holy indifference, simplicity. . . . You weren't supposed to worry about anything, even your own salvation. From that came the so-called resignation to God's will. They pushed it so far that you were supposed to accept serenely the possibility that you were damned rather than saved! . . . Their method of meditation consisted in placing yourself before God with neither preparation nor points of reflection nor desires. You were forbidden to use anything to raise the mind to God and excite the will to pursuit of the good. You just had to remain immobile and let God's Spirit act.[20]

Alarmed by the lethargy of the students, Maintenon turned against Guyon and her allies. An episcopal committee censured the doctrine of Guyon in 1694. In 1695 Guyon was arrested.

Personal visitations at Saint-Cyr from Bossuet (1696), from Godet des Marais, Bishop of Chartres (1697), and from Louis XIV himself (1698) attempted to stamp out the traces of Quietism. In 1697 royal *lettres de cachet* removed three recalcitrant Quietist teachers from the school. If Saint-Cyr continued to insist upon formation in piety as a principal objective, the Quietist episode stiffened Maintenon's resolve to promote a piety that was practical, a piety allergic to the first touch of mystical exaltation.

In the first decade of its existence, the teaching corps at Saint-Louis also underwent substantial transformation. Much to the regret of Louis XIV and of Maintenon, the Dames of Saint-Louis abandoned their lay status to become canonical religious following the rule of St. Augustine. Under Maintenon's personal patronage, however, the Dames maintained their distinctive identity as educators of aristocratic women. Maintenon frequently intervened to remind them that their first duty was to energetic service on behalf of their students and to challenge any deviation toward a more monastic lifestyle.

In the early years of the eighteenth century, Maintenon devoted even more personal attention to Saint-Cyr. Often on a daily basis, she appeared in the classrooms or in the chapel to give lectures or to field questions. She served as judge on the smallest issues: how to address servants, what hymns to sing, what punishment to give for a broken pot.

After the death of Louis XIV in 1715, Maintenon retired permanently to Saint-Cyr. Foreign dignitaries, such as Czar Peter I in 1717, went on pilgrimage to see the celebrated Saint-Cyr and its venerable founder. Even in her final years, Maintenon continued her daily round of lectures, correspondence, religious exercises, and weaving tapestries well into the night.

Madame de Maintenon died on April 15, 1719.

CONVERSATION AND CORPUS

Most of the works of Madame de Maintenon originally appeared in oral form. During the years at Saint-Cyr (1686–1719), Maintenon delivered hundreds of talks to the faculty and students. The Dames of Saint-Cyr made careful transcriptions of Maintenon's presentations. Maintenon reviewed and polished the transcripts to arrive at a final written text that would be copied and circulated by the Dames. In addition to these transcribed addresses, she composed a number of brief dialogues, morality plays to be performed by the students during recreation. Using these materials, the Dames produced a series of manuscript collections of Maintenon's works (1688, 1693, 1713, 1721, 1740). To the preceding materials, the Dames added other works by Maintenon: short stories, educational programs, brief essays. They also began to add material from Maintenon's voluminous correspondence of more than five thousand letters.[21]

The works of Maintenon fall into four major genres. The *Entretiens* (conferences) are talks given to the Dames of Saint-Cyr. Composed of questions and answers exchanged between Maintenon and the faculty, they treat primarily pedagogical issues. The *Instructions* (addresses) are talks given to the students themselves. Again primarily dialogical in form, they deal with the current problems in the school and with the virtues essential for the pupil. The *Conversations* (dialogues) are morality plays designed for informal performance by students. Often devoted to clarifying the nature of a specific virtue, the dialogues hold unusual philosophical as well as literary interest. The *Proverbes* (proverb plays) are brief skits acting out a popular French saying, often with a moral slant. Designed for the youngest pupils, these sketches celebrate simple schoolroom virtues: honesty, industry, cooperation.

The context of the composition of these works should influence the interpretation one gives to the moral philosophy proposed by Maintenon within them. First, the works are dialogical in form. Convinced that conversation rather than lecture was the most effective path to insight, Maintenon developed her moral theory through mutual interrogation. The theses on justice or civility are embedded either in an actual conversation between Maintenon and her interlocutors or in a fictional dialogue composed by Maintenon. Identifying the actual position of Maintenon in the chorus of conversational voices is not always an easy task.

Second, the works constitute practical responses to immediate problems. A prolific writer, Maintenon left no systematic treatise on virtue or education. It is in response to a particular quandary that Maintenon articulates her position on the questions of virtue and vice. Her theory of politeness or of temperance gradually emerges as she analyzes concrete questions of classroom behavior or of almsgiving on a tight budget.

Finally, Maintenon addresses herself to a particular social class: impoverished aristocratic women and their teachers. Maintenon's gendered arguments presuppose a fundamental difference between the social vocations of men and women. They focus on the cultivation of virtues deemed proper for women. Respectful of social hierarchy, they dwell on certain virtues, such as politeness, proper to the nobility. The tough, disabused tone of Maintenon's addresses reflects the economic and social precariousness of her students. Her repeated efforts to challenge their illusions concerning marriage or the cloister represent a sober appreciation of the grim prospects many of these impoverished women faced.

EDUCATIONAL PRAGMATISM

For Maintenon, the primary purpose of education is the cultivation of moral character. Religion, specifically Catholicism, provides the ultimate source and rule for this maturation in virtue. If the general end of education remains constant, the methods of instruction admit of legitimate variation. Curricular design and pedagogical technique are contingent, subject to continuous experimentation. Educational method must adapt itself to a particular end: the social rank and the social vocation of the student. This pragmatic adaptation of schooling to a specific social role governs Maintenon's philosophy of education. In a series of texts, Maintenon elaborates the details of education for different social orders: vowed religious, royalty, aristocracy, bourgeoisie, manual workers.

In a letter to a novice mistress (1686), Maintenon outlines the initial formation proper to a nun. The formation focuses on the cultivation of the will. Honesty, simplicity, and devotion are among the virtues to be fostered. Courage holds pride of place. "If they are courageous, they will be fervent and will progress with ease, despite any weakness of body or of mind."[22] Education of the nun should stress one particular means: a pervasive use of silence. "Accustom them to silence. . . . Scarcely any time at all should be left for any conversation among them."[23] Concomitantly, this ascetical formation should avoid any cultivation of elocution. "They should have no desire for eloquence. That could only arise from vanity."[24]

As in her other educational programs, Maintenon privileges the acquisition of moral virtue in the model education of the nun. However, the specific vocation of the nun, contemplative prayer, requires particular dispositions (perseverance) and specific means (silence) that differentiate this education from that designed for other classes.

Maintenon personally supervised the education of Marie-Adélaïde, Princesse de Savoie, Duchesse de Bourgogne, wife of Louis the grandson of Louis XIV and mother of Louis XV. In *Counsels for Mme la Princesse de Savoie* (1697), Maintenon argues that royal education must emphasize the virtues of discretion. Subject to unrelenting public scrutiny, the royal princess must master the rules of discretion in every public and private gesture:

> Speak, write, and perform all your actions as if you had a thousand witnesses. Recognize that sooner or later everything about you will be known. Writing especially is fraught with danger. . . . Confide nothing that could damage you if it were repeated. Recognize that well-kept secrets are well kept only for a time. Be wary of the taste you have for witty repartee. Most people will hate you because of it.[25]

Not only does royal education stress discreet conduct; it requires a distinctive curriculum. In a 1697 letter to Marquis de Dangeau, tutor of the princess, Maintenon approves his emphasis on historical instruction.[26] The royal personage must understand the past of the nation she symbolically represents. However, Maintenon insists on greater attention to mastering the art of conversation, essential for the hosting duties of the princess. Maintenon's theory of royal education contrasts with her model of aristocratic instruction, where history is minimized, and education for nuns, where silence suppresses conversation.

In a 1713 letter to two alumnae of Saint-Cyr, Mme de la Viefoille, Abbesse de Gomerfontaine, and Mme de la Mairie, Abbesse de Bizy, Maintenon discusses the education of the bourgeoisie. She insists that the educational program in these two convent schools, aimed at daughters of the local bourgeoisie, should differ clearly from the norm of schools for the aristocracy:

> You must educate your bourgeois pupils in a bourgeois way. They need neither poetry nor instruction in conversation. They don't need to embellish their wit. You should preach to them about family duties: obedience to their husband, child care, how to deal with servants, zeal in going to the parish church on Sundays and feasts. They should cultivate modesty with those who buy something from them and integrity in their business dealings.[27]

Since the bourgeoisie do not participate in political life, they should cultivate domestic virtues for the home and for the parish. Maintenon underscores key virtues in the economic sector: honesty in contracts, fair treatment of servants. The appropriate curriculum here involves extensive instruction in home economics and in family ethics. Pointedly, it excludes the more literary instruction reserved for royalty and aristocracy.

For working-class women, Maintenon underscores the centrality of manual labor in their curriculum. She also stresses the moral and religious virtues of resignation that must sustain a life of grueling physical work. Her *Maximes* (1682), composed for the impoverished working-class girls at her school at Rueil, typify Maintenon's concept of an education adapted to working-class concerns:

> God wanted you to serve. Make yourselves capable of doing so and adapt yourself to your fate.
>
> God wanted the rich to save themselves by giving of their wealth and the poor by not having any. . . .
>
> God wanted you to work hard. Don't hope for any other state in life. . . .
>
> If you don't submit to God's will for you, your misery will be as useless for the after-life as it is painful for you in this life.
>
> Your heart is happy when your body works. Most prominent people have a troubled heart, although they seem happy to us.[28]

Although Maintenon insists upon the necessity of basic literacy in the education of impoverished laborers (primarily to assure their salvation though catechesis), the primary emphasis is on training for and esteem of manual work.

Behind the surface virtues of industry and zeal emerge the cardinal virtue of resignation and the cardinal vice of envy. This fatalistic ethic expresses the anxiety of an ideology that blesses the current social hierarchy as an unalterable divine institution.

Incarnate in the school at Saint-Cyr, the education of aristocratic women constitutes the major pedagogical concern of Maintenon. Many of her works analyze the ends and methods proper to the education of the daughters of the impoverished nobility. In the pedagogy designed for the intermediate class of the aristocracy, Maintenon incorporates elements typical of instruction for the other classes. Like nuns, the Saint-Cyr gentlewoman must learn the values of silence, recollection, and meditation. Like royalty, she must master the code of politeness, not only in its exterior actions, but also in its interior sentiments of charity. Like the bourgeoisie, she must administer a household or a convent, often on a limited budget. Like the working class, she must esteem manual labor, even if her needlepoint represents a diversion rather than a livelihood. Nothing enrages Maintenon more than a Saint-Cyr pupil who refuses to grab a broom and sweep the hallway.

In this aristocratic education, Maintenon argues that reasonableness constitutes one of the fundamental virtues of the noblewoman. In her conferences with the teachers at Saint-Cyr, she insists that proper aristocratic instruction forms sound judgment rather than cultural sophistication:

> We should be less concerned to adorn their mind than to form their reason. This method, it's true, doesn't let the knowledge and the skill of the schoolmistress show through so clearly. A young girl who knows things by heart shines more in social gatherings and pleases her family more than does the girl whom we have formed to have good judgment, to know when to be quiet, who is modest and temperate, and who is never in a rush to give her opinion.[29]

It is the will, rather than the intellect or the memory, that is the object of this education.

The curriculum designed to foster this temperate reasonableness similarly favors solid instruction in morality rather than advanced study in the humanities:

> The external cultural accomplishments, the knowledge of foreign languages, and a thousand other talents that people desire for women of quality have se-

rious disadvantages. These concerns take up the time that we could put to better use. The pupils of the house of Saint-Louis should never be raised this way, when we can avoid it. Since they are without wealth, it is not proper to raise their mind and their heart in a way so foreign to their state in life and to their destiny.[30]

Too intellectual a formation not only damages the courteous prudence Maintenon considers essential in the well-bred aristocrat; it provides an alienating education for an impoverished gentlewoman who must face a stony future in a provincial manor or convent, where practical skill trumps a show of erudition.

Maintenon's pragmatic philosophy of differential education represents more than a technical adaptation of instruction to the demands of a particular workplace. It roots itself in a spirituality of states of life. A major theme of the Catholic Reform, especially in the Salesian tradition,[31] the theology of states of life argued that the discipleship of Christ could not confine itself to one generic set of acts, virtues, and sentiments. On the contrary, the way in which one followed Christ must vary according to one's basic vocation (cleric/lay; religious/secular), one's social rank (royal/aristocratic/bourgeois/laborer), and one's particular work.

As Maintenon argues in many addresses,[32] the discernment of one's vocation constitutes one of the key spiritual dramas of adolescence. The adherence to one's state of life, with its distinctive set of duties and of necessary virtues, is a central goal of education. Maintenon's pragmatic argument for differentiated models of education rests on a reverence for religious and political hierarchy. However, it also rests on a concept of salvation received and manifested through a series of contrasting vocational paths.

EMPIRE OF TEMPERANCE

In several texts, Maintenon provides a systematic treatment of the cardinal virtues. The dialogue *On the Cardinal Virtues* and the address *Of the Cardinal Virtues* analyze prudence, temperance, fortitude, and justice. They manifest the rationalist and pragmatic conception of virtue distinctive of Maintenon's philosophy. They also indicate the unusual primacy accorded temperance by Maintenon in the hierarchy of virtues proper to an aristocratic woman.

On the Cardinal Virtues presents four female characters who adopt respectively the personae of Fortitude, Justice, Prudence, and Temperance. The four virtues dispute which one of them is the most important. As the dialogue progresses, the traditional claim of justice as the central moral virtue is displaced by the claim of temperance, which imposes itself as the necessary moderator of the other virtues.

In claiming superiority over the other virtues, Justice defines itself in terms of its principal activities and relations:

> Nothing is as beautiful as Justice: it always has truth next to it; it judges without prejudice; it places everything in order; it knows how to condemn its friends and how to respect the right of its enemies; it can condemn even itself; it only esteems what is estimable.[33]

This concept of justice rests upon the traditional concept of judicial impartiality. It respects principles rather than persons.

Maintenon adds her own distinctive contours to this portrait of justice. Justice is the habit of imposing order on situations of confusion. The just respect hierarchy and rank. Justice also allies itself to honor by the exercise of esteem for those who merit it. Justice emerges as something other than giving each person his or her due. It represents a fundamental attitude of reverence before persons and events that command respect.

The claim of justice to primacy in the constellation of virtues is undercut by the counterarguments of Prudence and of Fortitude. Prudence claims to govern justice by forcing it to act in a more measured way: "I regulate its operations, prevent it from precipitation, make it take its time."[34] Fortitude disciplines justice by forcing it to act valiantly, when it must perform the repugnant act of punishing an ally. "You need me, because your sense of friendship makes you find it difficult to inflict any pain on a friend."[35]

In this perspective, prudence and fortitude emerge as more than complements to the virtue of justice. They are essential to the very operation of justice if it is to achieve its goal of impartial adjudication. Without prudence, justice deteriorates into a prosecutorial obsession that has lost all sense of proportion before the mixture of grave and minor evils that marks the human condition. Without fortitude, justice often finds itself incapable of applying its principles out of emotional attachment. As the dialogue argues, justice in itself can determine the proper dessert for each action and actor. Unperfected by prudence and fortitude, however, the exercise of justice inevitably misses its mark, due to implacability or impotence.

Maintenon's unusual treatment of prudence and fortitude reflects her broader theory of virtue. Prudence is no longer simply the capacity to discern the proper course of action. It emerges as the tutor of justice, prone to glacial severity. Fortitude is no longer the general habit of choosing the good against the appetite to avoid pain. It emerges as the particular habit of awarding dessert when emotional repugnance makes such award difficult. Vocationally both virtues modify the exercise of justice, which considered in isolation no longer represents the summit of moral conduct. This domesticated justice reflects Maintenon's moral ideal, wherein civility and politeness refine the traditional scale of virtue.

Trumping the three other virtues, temperance imposes itself as the central cardinal virtue. Its primacy derives from its role as the necessary moderator of the other virtues. Negatively, it prevents the other virtues from deteriorating into their negative stereotypes: fortitude into shrillness; justice into revenge; prudence into bashfulness. Positively, it frees the other virtues to accomplish their ends by providing the diplomatic edge necessary for successful action in society:

> In effect, I destroy gluttony and excess. I tolerate no outbursts. Not only am I
> opposed to all evil, I regulate the good. Without me, Justice would be insup-
> portable to human weakness, Fortitude would drive us to despair, Prudence
> would often prevent us from taking the actions we should and make us lose our
> time weighing every option. But with me, Justice becomes capable of circum-
> spection, Fortitude acquires suppleness, and Prudence continues to give ad-
> vice, but without undue hesitation, without too much or too little haste. In a
> word, I am the remedy to all extremism.[36]

The once principal role of temperance, the restraint of our tendency to choose sensory pleasure over the moral good, becomes secondary here. The primary work of temperance consists in the moderation of all virtues. It functions as the keystone of the moral life, inasmuch as its presence is necessary for the successful exercise of all other virtues, not only of justice.

Maintenon's apotheosis of temperance reveals the *salonnière*'s concern with the style, not only the content, of ethical conduct. The diplomatic action of the temperate frees the moral agent to attain certain goods inaccessible to the fanfare of fortitude and the whimpering of prudence. The encomium of temperance also reflects Maintenon's ascetical conception of the moral life. Sobriety, chastity, and abstemiousness are not minor chapters in moral endeavor. They constitute the center of an ethical life engendered by self-restraint. The primacy of temperance manifests Maintenon's aristocratic moral code, wherein discretion and delicacy characterize the soul of the gentlewoman.

Temperance not only governs the moral life in Maintenon, it also regulates the intellectual life. In response to Justice's exaltation of wisdom, Temperance replies: "You cannot ignore that wisdom requires sobriety. Don't search further. You can't do anything without me."[37]

Nowhere is the primacy of temperance clearer than in the dialogue's treatment of religion. Even salvation requires the moderating touch of temperance:

> I have to temper a religious zeal that is too busy, too excited, indiscreet. I have to encourage a conduct that avoids extremes. I moderate both the inclination to give alms and the inclination to hoard. I moderate the length of prayer, ascetical practices, recollection, silence, good works. I shorten a sermon, a spiritual dialogue, an examination of conscience. Finally, I even have to moderate religious fervor itself.[38]

Although the dialogue ends with a peremptory nod to the necessity of grace in the struggle against vice, temperance emerges as the principal architect of the moral agent's union with God as well as of the agent's union with other members of society. One of the originalities of Maintenon's moral philosophy is her transformation of temperance, an erstwhile secondary virtue, into the cornerstone of religious and intellectual, as well as ethical, maturity.

RATIONALIST VIRTUE

The address *Of the Cardinal Virtues* clarifies Maintenon's theory of virtue, especially her theory of justice. Like her other addresses to the students of Saint-Cyr, *Of the Cardinal Virtues* follows a dialogical structure. Four pupils pose and respond to questions that permit Maintenon to explain the purpose of the cardinal virtues and to detail the nature of each.

At the beginning of the address, Maintenon argues that the purpose of cultivating the cardinal virtues is to gain personal merit. Maintenon clarifies the content of this personal worth: "an assembly of virtues and of good qualities, especially of religion and of reason."[39] Maintenon establishes a framework in which the cardinal virtues are neither their own reward nor the means toward undifferentiated happiness. The cardinal virtues strengthen the rational and pious character of the moral agent. Reason here is not a Cartesian tool of certitude; it is reasonableness, a practical wisdom that maximizes the possibility of happiness in society. Religion here is neither mystical ecstasy nor a philosophical affirmation of God. It is temperate piety, which orders the agent's various duties by subordinating them to the supreme duty of the worship and service of God.

In elaborating the nature of the cardinal virtues, Maintenon provides a particularly detailed study of justice. The definition of justice is traditional: "rendering to each person his or her due and consenting that others render to us what we merit" (114). However, Maintenon modifies this concept of justice by linking it to the more intellectual notion of justness (*justesse*).

The just person knows how to form correct ideas and correct judgments, especially concerning persons and situations. The concept of equity (*équité*) includes this more intellectualist notion of justice:

> There is a judgment that is called equity, that makes us, without being preoccupied by our attractions or our repulsions, form just ideas about everything and distinguish good from evil. We can even see the faults of our friends, without being blinded by our friendship for them, and even happily recognize the good qualities that might be found in people we like less or who even actually oppose us. (115)

The virtue of justice here involves the capacity to think correctly, to find the *idée juste* that perfectly matches the actual state of a person or of an event. This reasonableness is practical, inasmuch as it involves a capacity to make a successful moral discernment of the situation confronted by the agent. Already tempered by prudence, this just or correct discernment presupposes a moral agent sufficiently freed from slavery to emotional attraction and repulsion. At its most mature, this justice expresses itself in the exercise of strictly impartial adjudication.

Maintenon concludes her study of justice by citing a type of justice even higher than that of equity: disinterestedness. This virtue transcends simple equity, a natural respect of just dessert, inasmuch as it involves the deliberate sacrifice of one's personal interests because of another's meritorious claim. "Disinterestedness makes us capable of deciding against ourselves in favor of those who have right on their side" (116). Under the guise of disinterestedness, justice emerges as a type of magnanimity.

In proving her thesis, Maintenon narrates an incident from the life of Louis XIV. The story concerns a lawsuit brought against the crown. A team of royal inspectors discovered that several homeowners had built their houses on land belonging to the king. The royal treasury demanded payment from the owners. The owners claimed ignorance of royal possession and asserted the property rights acquired by years of living on the land without previous legal challenge. The judges hearing the case split evenly, leaving the decision to the king himself. The king ruled on behalf of the owners and against himself, fearing even the appearance of personal interest in the administration of justice. Maintenon praises such disinterestedness as a supreme example of mature justice. This conception of justice as disinterestedness presents the virtue as the trait of a will so freed from prejudice that it sacrifices its own legitimate interests in order to accommodate the needs of another.

Prudence assumes a theological and aristocratic character in *Of the Cardinal Virtues:*

> Prudence is a virtue that rules all our words and our actions according to rea-
> son and to religion. It makes us discern what we must do and what we must
> avoid, whether we should speak or be silent, according to the occasion and the
> circumstances. It is opposed to indiscretion, which makes us speak in an inap-
> propriate way. (116)

This definition is traditional inasmuch as it conceives prudence as the
habit of knowing what to do in particular circumstances. But Maintenonian prudence bears its own distinctive colors. Although ruled by reason,
prudence is also regulated by religion. This religious tutelage of prudence
involves submission to the teaching authority of the Church in matters of
faith and morals, as Maintenon tirelessly reminds her pupils. It opposes the
appeal to private judgment by the Huguenot or the Jansenist. For Maintenon, the authentic exercise of prudence presupposes adherence to the
Church's moral law and to its principles for resolution of problems of conscience. Prudential deliberation operates within an ecclesiastical background.

The prudence here also reflects its aristocratic context. The regulated
activity is primarily one of speech. Knowing when to speak and when to be
silent, in sure knowledge of social conventions (*les occasions et les circonstances*), is major proof of possession of the virtue. Tellingly, the opposite
of the virtue is indiscretion. Often considered a minor flaw in nonaristo-
cratic milieux, indiscretion is a major one in aristocratic circles because it
can easily destroy reputation, the most important personal good according to Maintenon. Prudence emerges as a moral regulator of the central
activity of the salon and of the court: conversation.

Temperance acquires a strongly rationalist character:

> Temperance is a virtue that moderates us in all things and makes us hold a just
> middle between too much and too little. It is useful everywhere. It prevents all
> excess of passion, whether of joy or of sadness. If you laugh, it's with modera-
> tion and modesty. If you cry, it's without abandoning yourself completely to
> grief, by bearing your pain peacefully and patiently. If you eat, it's with mod-
> eration. Finally, temperance prevents all excess. (117)

This definition considerably expands temperance's empire. The virtue is
no longer limited to the rational control of the appetite for sensual pleasure. It restricts all human passions by barring emotional excess, whether
in reaction to pain or to the possibility of pleasure. Maintenonian temperance reflects its aristocratic provenance by the accent it places on the
rational control of grief and mourning, emotional states nobles must manifest in public.

Maintenon reinforces her thesis through the narrative of three sisters plunged into mourning by the death of their brother. She criticizes the sister who abandoned herself to excessive mourning, "banging her head against the wall, not wanting either to eat or to drink" (117). She praises the sisters who quietly mourned the brother, "not making a single gesture that suggested the least hint of being carried away" (117). Maintenon deepens the rationalist cast of temperance by posing the following question at the end of the narrative: "Which of these griefs do you find the more reasonable?" (117).

As prudence rationally frees the moral agent from prejudice, temperance rationally frees the agent from passion. As prudence governs conversation, temperance governs gesture. The salon ideals of deliberation, discretion, and self-mastery shape the temperance that characterizes all social interaction of the mature aristocrat.

In *Of the Cardinal Virtues,* fortitude closely allies itself to Maintenon's work ethic. Fortitude here is not generic courage; it is the particular courage to finish successfully those projects that provoke the hostility of others:

> Fortitude is a virtue that makes us pursue courageously our undertakings and overcome the obstacles that we find in others and in ourselves. We remain faithful to the good we are trying to achieve, without surrendering to difficulties, by accepting reversals with firmness and without dejection. (118)

The virtue strengthens the moral agent to conclude enterprises that draw the opprobrium of the world.

The suffering implicit in fortitude does not derive from simple fidelity to a moral ideal. It arises from the tenacity with which one undertakes and maintains a work in the face of the world's criticism. Such an interpretation of fortitude presupposes an extraordinary value placed upon work itself, especially controverted work of a creative nature. Maintenon reinforces this esteem of work in the conclusion of her study of fortitude: "Never forget, my children, that our merit depends on our work" (119).

This work-related framework for fortitude indicates the pragmatic cast of Maintenon's account of virtue. The purpose of fortitude is to free the agent to undertake a service consonant with his or her state of life. This service demands a labor marked by the sobriety of temperance but also by the courage to affront opposition.

This treatment of fortitude also manifests the more bourgeois accents of Maintenonian virtue. From the perspective of fortitude, neither family descent nor social rank determines personal worth. It is hard work pursued under duress that creates individual merit. The virtuous agent is in some measure the stubborn entrepreneur. As other addresses indicate, Maintenon leaves no doubt that her own tenacious tutelage of Saint-Cyr constitutes a recent chapter in the chronicle of this fortitude.

ARISTOCRATIC POLITENESS

Maintenon's theory of virtue does not limit itself to analysis of the cardinal virtues. In numerous works, she explores the nature of the virtues proper to the aristocracy, particularly to the noblewoman. Her presentation of aristocratic virtues focuses primarily on civility and politeness. She also treats several of the more controversial virtues cultivated by the nobility of the period: glory, eminence, wit. If Maintenon provides an elaborate justification for the ensemble of virtues the properly educated gentlewoman must acquire, the justification is nuanced. Arguments for reciprocity, individual merit, and social promotion through work undercut a code of virtue tied to rank.

In the address *On Politeness,* Maintenon studies the necessity, the nature, and the practical applications of politeness. Throughout the address Maintenon emphasizes that, unlike the cardinal virtues, politeness is a virtue proper to one particular class: the aristocracy. It is their birth and their rank that obliges the students at Saint-Cyr to master a series of practices associated with this virtue:

> Since God has made you ladies by birth, have a lady's manners. May those of you who have been well trained by your noble parents retain these manners and may the others acquire them. This is more important than you can imagine. Rudeness repulses everyone, even the most patient people.[40]

Politeness is not a secondary accomplishment for the aristocrat. Without its mastery, perfection in other virtues cannot compensate for the social opprobrium that the rude person will encounter:

> Since God has made you ladies by birth, take up the manners as well as the sentiments of a lady. Once and for all, be convinced that whatever virtue, whatever merit, whatever talent, and whatever good quality you might otherwise have, you will be insupportable to well-bred people if you don't know how to conduct yourselves properly. (182)

This passage expresses the hierarchical nature of Maintenon's theory of virtue. It is God who has summoned an elite, such as the pupils at Saint-Cyr, to belong to the nobility by birth. This social rank grounds a series of duties, such as the requirement to cultivate politeness, unknown to the peasant or to the day laborer.

In her concrete applications of politeness, Maintenon emphasizes linguistic behavior. The pupils must follow certain rules in speaking with each other. "Don't speak familiarly (*tutoyer*) to each other. Don't use nicknames. Rid yourselves of these grating vocal tones we are shocked to find in young ladies" (181). Even the briefest dialogue requires certain conventions in speech. "Never respond to anyone by simply saying 'yes' or 'no.' It is absolutely necessary for you to add 'Yes, Sir' or 'Yes, Madame' if you don't want to appear as rude as the most unlearned peasant" (182).

Politeness in speech covers more than the etiquette of address. It entails a mastery of French grammar and French style. Maintenon wages war against slang and neologisms. "Speak good French and do not invent thousands of words that mean nothing and do not correspond to proper usage" (182).

Maintenon's judgments on politeness in speech reflect the ethics of the salon. It is the style of conversation, more than its content, that reveals whether the speaker has in fact mastered politeness. Her judgments also constitute an apology for the literary culture of aristocratic women. The mastery of grammar, style, elocution, and composition are essential for the person who would cultivate politeness.

Politeness governs the least gesture, as well as the discourse, of the aristocrat. Maintenon details the etiquette of movement:

> Never throw open a door, a seat, or a book as if you were throwing a stone. Never pass in front of someone without bowing. Practice it with each other in order to be accustomed to it. Yield the entry to the door or at least make some sign of politeness before entering. Don't leave it up to someone else, as I've often seen you do. (181)

Not only does politeness govern the simple gesture of entering a doorway; it regulates the basic posture and countenance of the aristocrat:

> Your entire action should be full of composure. Stand up straight. Carry your head properly. Don't let your chin fall. Modesty is in the eyes, not in the chin. (182)

The complexity of politeness derives from its vocation to regulate the entire person. Posture, countenance, gaze, and gesture are the external grace of a refined soul.

The emphasis upon polite gesture reflects one of Maintenon's central theses on moral character: the necessity for diplomatic reason to overcome the immediate passions and interests of the person. The polite person will not betray herself easily, either through word or through gesture.

Politeness also modifies political behavior. Maintenon originally gave the address *On Politeness* to a select group of students from the "green" class (ages 11–14). In the educational system of Saint-Cyr, these pupils exercised a certain authority over other pupils through the supervision of study and work. Maintenon explains how the virtue of politeness must govern their exercise of power:

> Although you've been given a certain authority over your peers, that does not give you the right to speak to them in a domineering way, or with arrogance, or with rudeness. On the contrary, you must be committed more than anyone else to do your work with politeness, so as to serve as models for others. For example, say softly to one of them, 'Would you be willing to move back so that the light is not blocked for this pupil?' To another, 'Please make a little space for this pupil.' And to another, 'Would you be willing to help her finish her sewing, or help her review a subject on which the schoolmistress will test her today?'" (182)

The formulae of politeness proposed by Maintenon are more than decorative ornament. They initiate the student into the art of diplomacy. The polite student learns how to achieve the end of common work though suggestion and invitation rather than through stark command.

Politeness is not its own end. Nor is social advancement its primary purpose. Maintenon argues that the elaborate rules of etiquette serve one paramount moral purpose: the respect of others' persons:

> Whatever you say or do, be careful not to offend anyone or to embarrass anyone. This must be our principal preoccupation, if we don't want to displease the members of society. (183)

This is where politeness acquires its moral gravity. While the conventions of polite behavior may vary from one society to another, the motive for polite behavior is a moral constant. The polite aristocrat's care in speech and gesture expresses a respect for the human person as person.

CIVILITY AND RECIPROCITY

In the address *On Civility,* Maintenon refines her theory of politeness. Part of the interest of the address lies in its tension between an ethics of class and an ethics of reciprocity.

In Maintenon's framework, civility defines itself as a species of polite altruism. Attentive concern for the other emerges as the principal motive and sign of the virtue:

> Civility consists in freeing oneself in order to be busy about the needs of others, in paying attention to what can help or disturb them, in order to do the former and to avoid the latter. Civility means never talking about yourself, not making others listen to you too long, listening carefully to others, avoiding making conversation focus on you and your tastes, letting the conversation move naturally to accommodate the interests of others.[41]

More than a generic graciousness, civility involves a continuous decentering of one's self in order to hear the other and to respond to the other's needs. Behind the public works of service lies an attention to the other rooted in mature self-effacement.

Although in principle civility concerns all the public actions of the moral agent, Maintenon typically uses conversation as the paradigm of civil conduct. The external sign of the acquisition of civility is the speaker's willingness truly to engage the other by shifting the focus of conversation from the host's autobiography to the guest's narrative and to the needs of the guest that are transparent in the narrative.

Maintenon designates reciprocity as the cardinal moral principle underlying civil conduct. It is the golden rule of the Sermon on the Mount that provides the perfect guide for civil behavior:

> The Gospel strongly agrees with the duties of civic life. You know that Our Lord says that we should not do unto others what we don't want others to do unto us. This must be our great rule, which doesn't exclude certain customs traditional in our native countries.[42]

The final phrase poses an obvious challenge to the principle of reciprocity. How does one treat others as one wants to be treated when the customs of one's society demand a highly differentiated treatment of others according to social rank? The evangelical principle of equality stands in uneasy tension with a principle of deference and of hierarchy.

Deepening her appeal to an evangelical reciprocity as the fount of civility, Maintenon describes the cultivation of this virtue. Authentic civility, an interior sentiment rather than a collection of external practices, requires the maturation of other evangelical virtues, especially humility and charity, within the moral agent:

> I would like you to have these fine external manners, my children. Since you are so well trained, I would like you to add interior sentiments of charity and

of esteem for your neighbor with lowly sentiments concerning yourselves. This is what the Gospel orders you to do.[43]

Civil attention to the other can only flourish within the moral agent who has undergone a spiritual conversion. A charitable respect for the other, coupled with a sober assessment of one's faults, permits the virtue of civility to become a quality of moral perspective and not only of external action.

In Maintenon's account of it as "Christian politeness," civility transcends a strict reciprocity between the agent and the patient. Like the disinterestedness praised in the treatment of justice, Maintenonian civility involves a positive preference to serve the needs of the other rather than one's own needs, a preference quietly bearing the imprint of heroic charity.

The concluding section of *On Civility* qualifies, if it does not contradict, the appeal to universal reciprocity that dominates the opening. Four pupils ask questions regarding civil conduct in different social circumstances. Maintenon responds with a series of elaborate distinctions among persons drawn from different social ranks. Civility emerges as a calibrated differentiation of respect for persons according to the customs of social hierarchy. The capacity to recognize social difference, reflected in minute variations of word and gesture, now becomes the principal sign of civility's presence.

A careful casuist, Maintenon identifies the proper civil response for each occasion. One should thank a servant, but by a nod of the head, not by standing up. One should call a mechanic "Monsieur" if he seems sufficiently cultivated; otherwise, one should avoid the title. Minute nuances emerge in the treatments of whether one should accept holy water from an unknown man at the church door or whether one must accept tobacco from a social superior.

Maintenon's most delicious casuistry concerns etiquette in a carriage:

> We do not greet others when we are moving in a carriage unless it's a question of people we know well or persons of unusual social eminence. Then we stop the coach and we bow deeply, especially if it's the king or a prince or princess. All of this follows national custom. I've seen ambassadors stand up in their carriage and make a deep bow. In France, we don't stand, but we make a deep bow.[44]

In all of these occasions, the civil response expresses respect for the various persons. Indeed, in the treatment of servants and of workmen, Maintenon defends a comparatively liberal notion of civil conduct. Nonetheless, this portrait of civility as differentiated respect of persons according to social rank stands in tension with the earlier description of civility as evangelical reciprocity. The application of the golden rule here is problematic, inasmuch as the moral agent cannot treat the other as he or she desires to be treated. The civil agent must treat others differently, according to an etiquette consecrating the principle of social hierarchy over the principle of equality.

GLORY AND GENDER

If politeness constitutes the soul of an aristocratic ethic, it does not constitute the whole of the nobility's moral code. In numerous works Maintenon analyzes other qualities deemed essential to the aristocratic character. She devotes particular attention to three ancillary virtues: glory, eminence, and wit. In the treatment of each of these virtues, Maintenon once again evinces a tension between a theological conception of virtue and a conception more indebted to the metaphysics of social order. The analyses of these ancillary qualities permit Maintenon to specify the gendered nature of the virtue she is attempting to evoke before her students. In her study of these aristocratic virtues, Maintenon proposes a moral code for the gentlewoman that differs sensibly from that of the gentleman.

Descendant of the medieval code of chivalry and of the Renaissance cult of the hero, the virtue of glory (*la gloire*) divided French moralists in the seventeenth century. If all agreed that the cultivation of glory was central to the aristocratic character, the content of this glory proved elusive. The traditional site of glory, the bearing of arms, had faded as a preoccupation of the nobility. Barred from the military, women faced the perplexing question of whether people of their gender could even aspire to personal glory. In several works Maintenon defends a pacifistic concept of glory proper for all aristocrats, but especially for the noblewoman. Further, she argues for a version of glory that rejects any identification of the virtue with family, wealth, or social rank.

In the address *On True Glory*, Maintenon presents her theory of glory to students of the "blue" class (ages seventeen to twenty). She advances her thesis through sustained contrast between true glory (*la bonne gloire*) and false glory (*la mauvaise gloire*). The opening definition establishes the strictly ethical interpretation of this attribute. "I believe that true glory consists in loving one's honor and in never performing any base action."[45]

This definition places glory within a gendered framework. The emphasis upon honor reflects Maintenon's persistent argument that good reputation is the most important personal possession of a noblewoman. The reference to "base action" also contains a gendered reference. When the pupil Mlle des Bois offers robbery as an example of base actions, Maintenon counters with more subtle examples drawn from the experience of women: accepting gifts from men, receiving letters from unknown men, flirtation with men.[46] These approaches to the virtue not only link a woman's glory to sexual purity; they present sexual purity as strict abstention from any word or gesture smacking of impropriety.

Significantly, Maintenon rejects any attribution of baseness to the work or social status of a person. On the contrary, she praises hard work and thrift as quiet signs of glory:

> There is much more nobility in living from one's work and from one's saving than in being a burden to one's friends. . . . You must be accustomed early on to saving your money. I wouldn't tell rich people to sell their needlework, but I would tell those who aren't so rich to do so. There's nothing better for them to do.[47]

To illustrate her point, Maintenon presents an edifying tale drawn from the family of one of the Saint-Cyr students:

> I always loved the mother of a pupil of Saint-Cyr because of the life she led. She started to work early in the morning. She lived from her savings in order to avoid being a burden to her friends.[48]

This encomium of industriousness places a bourgeois figure upon the virtue of glory. It undercuts the aristocratic notion of glory on several levels.

First, it refuses to link authentic glory to social rank or familial origin. Second, it removes true glory from the traditional fora of arms, government, science, and art. Finally, in the narrative of the Saint-Cyr mother, it locates glory in a domain traditionally considered beneath the nobility: manual labor.

To clarify her concept of it, Maintenon defines true glory as a species of generosity. Greater than liberality, generosity distinguishes itself by its willingness to undertake the most demanding projects to help the other and by its courage in pursuing these projects despite every obstacle. Glory emerges in the desire for self-sacrifice, not in the external brio of the work undertaken. True glory consists essentially in a generous attitude of service:

> We ordinarily recognize glory by its honesty and even by its humility, by its concern to give pleasure to others, to relieve pain, to avoid giving offense, to render service.[49]

Maintenonian glory is the glow of a politeness transformed into ardent service of the suffering other.

Opposed to true glory, false glory is an assertion of honor based upon familial origin and social rank. Bereft of any moral virtue, this false glory scarcely masks a pride that fuels social hatred. Maintenon rebukes those who would distort glory into a class possession:

> False glory is the contrary of what I've called true glory. It's quite stupid always to be speaking about your parents, your nobility, and everything that concerns you in the nobility. People with this fault make themselves intolerable in society, as do people who act without concern and without consideration for others. . . . Remember and clearly understand that true nobles are not inclined to be haughty or to be contemptuous toward anyone. Proud, arrogant, and disdainful manners always indicate a small person.[50]

The vehemence of Maintenon's critique of pride-based glory expresses itself in the violence of her vocabulary: the stupidity (*fort sotte*) and the intolerable arrogance (*insupportable*) of those who flaunt a biological conception of glory. In her defense of true glory as an affair of laborious service, the voice of the humiliated, industrious child speaking to other impoverished adolescents emerges clearly.

So odd does Maintenon's theory of glory appear to the assembly that the student Mlle de Mornay complains that "we've wandered away from the subject of true glory that was supposed to be the subject of the conversation."[51] Maintenon disagrees, arguing that as pedestrian as the conclusions may seem, her topic is indeed the nature of authentic glory.

The novelty of Maintenon's theory is to remove glory from its traditional sites. She refuses to locate glory in warfare, in familial descent, in social position, in artistic achievement, in scientific accomplishment, in historical renown. She even refuses to locate it in heroic sanctity, with its danger of mystical exaltation. Maintenonian glory is decidedly inglorious. Its site is the patient, often hidden service of the vulnerable other.

EMINENCE AND THE STOA

The dialogue *On Eminence* studies one of the more elusive aristocratic virtues: eminence (*élévation*). The four characters in the dialogue concur on the importance of eminence in their social milieu. However, they confess their perplexity concerning its precise nature. Maintenon uses the dialogue to distinguish between authentic eminence, rooted in personal merit, and illusory eminence, based upon materialist ambition.

The initial definition establishes the traits of authentic eminence. "I think that eminence is having a heart greater than one's fortune and wanting to raise oneself above all by merit."[52] True eminence contains two distinct capacities. First, eminence permits the moral agent to maintain her integrity and serenity despite reversals in fortune. Clearly Stoical in inspiration,[53] this eminence enables the person to free herself from slavery to emotions or to material possessions. Second, eminence resides in the capacity of the moral agent to rise in social position through personal merit. Again, Maintenon praises the social status achieved by hard work. Justified claims of personal merit rightly alter the social hierarchy of rank.

The dialogue clarifies both poles of authentic eminence. Maintenon adds a Christian gloss to the Stoical conception of eminence as the capacity to maintain one's equilibrium in the midst of reversal of fortune. This self-mastery, once an avenue to isolation from society, becomes for Maintenon the path to a more intense social solidarity:

> True eminence consists in esteeming only virtue, in knowing how to distance ourselves from fortune when it turns against us and how to avoid being intoxicated by fortune when it goes our way. It consists in sharing the fate of the unfortunate and in never holding them in contempt.[54]

Eminence here entails the capacity to face suffering with equanimity. It is the wisdom of those who lucidly accept the quirky turns of the wheel of fortune. However, this indifference to the peripeties of fate does not issue in a steely indifference to the fortune of others. On the contrary, a truly elevated acceptance of fate opens the moral agent to a greater compassion toward others. In times of good fortune, the agent recognizes the duty to share her bounty with the destitute. In moments of bad fortune, the agent intensifies her respect for the poor, knowing from personal experience how much misery proceeds from the inscrutable decrees of fate rather than from individual responsibility.

Maintenon defends the personal ambition that also constitutes authentic eminence. She praises those who desire to raise their social status, on condition that this social ascension arises from personal merit composed of outstanding service and moral character. Admittedly, this concept of meritorious elevation challenges a social order based on biological descent:

> There are different degrees of nobility. We have to see ourselves as we are. We should only raise ourselves through our merit. That is where we find authentic eminence.[55]

Contested by several dialogue characters as a species of insolence, this social ascension is illustrated by Maintenon through an edifying tale. It concerns a commoner who rises to the rank of general by dint of courageous military service. When criticized by a prominent noble because of his low birth, the general tartly responds: "It's true that I'm nothing. And frankly I'm convinced that if you had been born as I was, you would never have reached the rank that I hold."[56]

This military example is not neutral. Aristocratic opinion of the period considered the officer corps, like the episcopal corps, an exclusive club for the younger sons of the nobility. Maintenon's approval of ascension through merit in the military reflects her own provocative actions in the political order. Her morganatic marriage to Louis XIV, her efforts to legitimize his illegitimate children, and her attempts to secure their rights of succession stunned the aristocracy, with its strict canons of social propriety and familial privilege. While not directly challenging the social order of the *ancien régime,* Maintenon's theory of social eminence by merit celebrates an aristocracy of personal achievement that uneasily coexists with the traditional aristocracy of descent.

TRUE WIT

By the time Mme de Maintenon composed her works, no one disputed the value of wit in an aristocratic woman. The ornament of the salon had become the necessary quality of the gentlewoman, expected to master the art of conversation. A quarrel simmered, however, over the nature of the wit proper to the cultivated woman. In this debate, Maintenon defends an anti-intellectualist position, opposing the acquisition of an extensive literary and scientific culture by women. Maintenonian wit carries a decidedly moralistic stamp. Maintenon's position on the proper role of wit in women reflects her theories in the more fundamental dispute over the education appropriate to women.

The dialogue *On True Wit* contrasts two theories concerning the wit proper for the aristocratic woman. The first exalts the figure of the *salonnière,* distinguished by a broad literary culture and by libertine friendships. The second vaunts the figure of the housewife, typified by hard manual labor and by religious devotion. Maintenon clearly endorses the latter and dismisses the former as a species of pride.

The opening definition of wit (*esprit*) echoes the salon provenance of the virtue:

> I believe that wit is a more or less extended light, which gives a certain taste for everything that has a certain brilliance. It inflames the imagination. It makes conversation more pleasant. It increases the delight of oneself and of others.[57]

The definition breathes the spirit of the *précieuse.* Wit here is a decorative auxiliary of intelligence. It embellishes, it intensifies, it colors. It ornaments the key activity of the salon: conversation. Devoted uniquely to the expansion of pleasure, it resides more in the faculty of imagination than in that of reason.

When the dialogue turns to a definition of true wit (*le bon esprit*), the salon accouterments suddenly disappear. True wit emerges as a species of Maintenonian politeness:

> I believe that true wit is to have a well-disciplined mind, to adapt oneself to everything, to make one's pleasure the pleasure of others, to love solid things, to proportion one's tastes to one's state in life, to enjoy pleasures with those who have them, to know how to give up pleasures with those who do not. We should not vaunt the advantages that our wit gives us over those who are less agile than we are.[58]

This definition of authentic wit sternly moralizes the virtue. The love of the brilliant becomes esteem of the solid. Imagination yields to an intelligence well proportioned to one's social duties. Pleasure remains a key preoccupation, but the intensification of pleasure is supplanted by strict moral duty: serving the pleasure of others. True wit retains its mental agility, but the agility now manifests itself as a readiness to spot the needs of the other and sympathetically to accommodate them. Rather than singularizing herself, the witty moral agent now effaces herself out of respect for the mental limits of the other.

This domesticated concept of wit provokes a dispute between two of the dialogue characters, Augustine and Célestine. Clearly gendered, the dispute involves a fundamental difference on the proper social role for women. Augustine endorses this concept of authentic wit as especially appropriate for women:

> We are of a sex with a greater obligation to have a well-disciplined mind than to have a mind with extensive knowledge. Moreover, we can see far enough, if we understand that there is nothing more solid than to work at our salvation and to choose the state that will make our salvation more certain and much easier.[59]

This position on female wit reflects Maintenon's broader theory of gender differentiation. Unlike men, called to speculation and to public service, women are called to master practical judgment in the moral and religious conduct of the family. Solid judgment, not speculative brilliance, is the noetic ideal for women. Not only is extensive literary and scientific culture unnecessary for women; it is dangerous, since it easily thwarts the cultivation of the religious devotion and the discreet service that typifies their particular domain.

Appalled by the suffocation of women's talents, Célestine opposes this moralizing concept of wit. She defends the right and the duty of women to develop a broad intellectual culture and to refuse enclosure within the household:

> You [Augustine], therefore, agree with the position of those who want to take away from our sex the benefits of being scholars (*savantes*). I just don't understand what pleasure you can take in being with people who know neither history nor current events nor literature. What value is there in women who are so absorbed by housekeeping that they don't even know the differences among an elegy, an ode, and a lyric poem?[60]

Célestine's speech constitutes a pointed apology for the access of women to literary culture and to informed participation in public affairs. It is an acerbic critique of those who would confine women to household chores in the name of a gendered duty that only rationalizes the subjection of women. The social ideal here is clearly the *salonnière*, whose scholarship permits her to make subtle distinctions among literary genres.

As the dialogue progresses, the conflict between the two visions of women's social role hardens. The moral value of domestic service contests the intellectual value of conversation with "rhetoricians, poets, and philosophers."[61] The religious value of disinterested work battles the aesthetic value of sparkling conversation. The debate is unequal. Maintenon progressively tips the conflict in favor of Augustine's ideal of the virtuous housewife.

Célestine's feminist apology falters on two scores. First, her motive reveals itself as social snobbery rather than sincere concern for the development of women's talents:

> I would never be able to live in the way that farm women do! What! Get up early in the morning as country women do! They've scarcely gotten out of bed before they send the family out to work and start the endless routine of housework![62]

Second, the intellectual culture vaunted by Célestine turns out to be bogus. She sheepishly admits her passion for astrology:

> Célestine—I'm presently diverting myself with astrologers.
> Augustine—Do you think that good judgment has anything to do with astrology? Whoever believes that she knows the secrets of the stars and can map them out for us does not know how to conduct herself.[63]

Célestine's superficial culture contrasts unfavorably with Augustine's prudent work on behalf of others. True wit imposes itself as solid judgment rather than as erudition or as ironic humor.

CRITICAL EVALUATION

Madame de Maintenon's educational practice and theory rest upon a series of paradoxes. An opponent of convent education, she perfected the model of the convent boarding school, right down to the etiquette lessons and the embroidery. A distinguished *salonnière,* she stripped women's education of literary and scientific ambition. An enigmatic social outsider, she defended a moral code drenched in the aristocratic ethos of rank. Patron of the Catholic Reform, she defended a deistic piety of good works, hostile to the speculative brio and the mystical passion of the Reform. Apologist of the monarchy, she celebrated a remarkably bourgeois moral ideal of thrift, sobriety, and hard work.

As an educational theory, the limits of Maintenon's philosophy are obvious. Based on the conviction that gender difference entails decisive differences in social vocation, Maintenon's model of education bars women from serious access to the liberal arts and sciences. If the Saint-Cyr curriculum is comparatively broad, its focus is the cultivation of practical virtues: those moral habits central to the good Catholic and those everyday skills essential to the gentlewoman who governs a provincial household or a modest convent. The study of history or of literature is meant to provide a minimum of culture for polite conversation. The pursuit of mathematics only helps the students to live on a balanced budget. The humanistic appeal to the intrinsic value of these disciplines or to the innate beauty of the cultivated mind finds no echo in this pragmatic account of education.

The Maintenonian account of virtue betrays a similar weakness. In this schema, the intellectual and religious virtues enjoy little autonomy. They are firmly subordinated to the moral virtues. Maintenonian wit and wisdom emerge as variations of prudence. Maintenonian piety establishes itself as moral earnestness, with grace and prayer in secondary roles. Even the spectrum of moral virtue constricts. The dominant ethos of politeness reduces justice to thoughtfulness, fortitude to integrity, prudence to restraint. This account of the moral virtues manifests a clear consistency in its celebration of temperance and in its systematic softening of more acerbic qualities, such as wit and glory. Nonetheless, the repeated reduction of virtues to a polite desire to serve provides a thin, monochromatic theory of moral character.

Another limitation of Maintenon's moral philosophy resides in its uncritical embrace of social hierarchy. The overriding concern to form po-

lite women tends to canonize the elaborate hierarchy of rank and deference of monarchial France. Although Maintenon bluntly describes the
moral tares of the authorities a Saint-Cyr alumna must face, the disabused
commentary emerges within a fundamental deference to the figures of the
father, the husband, the king, and the bishop. Maintenon's theory of personal merit qualifies this respect for social rank. Nonetheless, it offers little challenge to the alleged divine origin or to the basic benignity of the
stratified social order of the period. A moral philosophy so focused on reverence and restraint offers scant space for critical distance or prophetic
censure.

Despite its narrowness, Maintenon's moral philosophy makes several important contributions. In the area of educational theory and practice,
Maintenon defends a dialogical model of learning. Maintenon not only believes that the polite woman must master the art of conversation; she argues that the very formation of the virtuous woman must be dialogical in
nature. Her interactive addresses, her moral dialogues for performance,
and her conferences with her faculty underscore her conviction that moral
insight emerges only within a conversational setting.

Her attack on the cult of the book and the magisterial lecture is more
than an expression of anti-intellectualism. It reflects the conviction that
the knowledge proper to a gentlewoman can only surface through participation in classroom conversation, guided by skilled teachers, and in the
performance and imitation of dialogues designed to inculcate virtue. Not
only is this stress on dialogue a matter of pedagogical method; it involves
a moral principle, inasmuch as the most important forum for the expression of virtue resides in the practice of conversation. By her insistence on
a pedagogy of dialogue and by her construction of a philosophical corpus
composed of dialogues, Maintenon places the central activity of the salon,
polite conversation, at the heart of the moral enterprise.

Another key contribution of Maintenon's moral philosophy is its recon-
struction of virtue along the lines of class and gender. Unlike the Augustinian critics Sablière and La Vallière, Maintenon never dismisses the
classical edifice of moral virtue itself. Nonetheless, she transforms the traditional account of the virtues by recasting them in light of certain class
concerns. A major part of Maintenon's polemic attempts to demonstrate
that the twin virtues of the aristocracy, politeness and civility, concern more
than etiquette. They are class-specific variations on charity that touch the
keystone of moral conduct: the respect of the human person. Maintenon
tends to subordinate the ensemble of cardinal virtues to this overarching
class ethics of politeness. Justice emerges as magnanimity, prudence as delicacy, fortitude as honor. Temperance imposes itself as the paramount
virtue. This is an unusual primacy in the history of philosophy, but an in-

evitable one in an ethics that privileges the civil word and the polite gesture.

Maintenon also recasts the virtues through a focus on gender. Qualities traditionally associated more with women, such as temperance and piety, acquire a new primacy. Attributes traditionally associated more with the male domain of public affairs, such as fortitude and justice, recede. By a gendered reinterpretation of virtue, Maintenon manages to transform traits once associated primarily with men into clear characteristics of women. Glory, once the unique possession of the warrior, becomes the virtue of the zealous mother. Wit, the accessory of the *honnête homme*, becomes the province of the industrious housewife. Rather than insisting that women cultivate virtues traditionally ascribed to men, Maintenon argues that greater prominence must be accorded the virtues traditionally pursued by women and that many virtues must be redefined to reflect the gender-specific experiences of women.

Finally, Maintenon relativizes virtue by the pragmatic framework into which she casts it. Since different people play contrasting social roles, they must cultivate different habits and dispositions. Not all are called to master resignation, industriousness, wit, discretion, and magnanimity—at least, not to the same degree. This insistence on the variability of the virtues reflects Maintenon's theology of states of life and her metaphysics of social order. It also indicates her pedagogical conviction that no uniform ideal exists for the education of the human person taken in abstraction. If education must adapt itself to a variety of social classes, virtue must present itself as a plurality of moral habits specific to gender, work, rank, and religious vocation. The humanistic ideal of the universal cultivated gentleman recedes in favor of irreducible difference.

CHAPTER VII

Conclusion: Unmasking Virtue

Suppressed for centuries, the moral philosophy developed by the *salonnières* of neoclassical France indicates certain directions for current efforts to expand the canon of philosophy. It underscores the need to attend to the distinctive sites and genres wherein women pursued philosophical reflection. It suggests the importance of retrieving a fuller range of women's voices, including those indifferent or hostile to egalitarian doctrine. The significance of the philosophy of virtue sketched by Mme de Sablé and her colleagues is not merely historical. Their works explore certain gendered virtues, such as politeness, widely ignored by recent philosophers. Their skeptical unmasking of the hidden vice animating virtue also raises pointed questions about our current philosophical enthusiasm for an ethics of virtue and character.

EXPANDING THE CANON

Since histories of philosophy are written predominantly by academics, they tend to focus upon a unique site for philosophy: the university. Even if a philosopher does not personally enjoy an academic post, he or she should be a clear object of interest and commentary by professors in a collegiate philosophy department. Thus, if anyone is a philosopher in neoclassical France, it is Descartes, contested but never ignored by the Sorbonne.

As the philosophical canon expands to include the voices of women, unsurprisingly it privileges those women with the greatest proximity to the male professorate. Elisabeth of Bohemia (1618–1680) and Christina of Sweden (1626–1689), epistolary students of Descartes, naturally rise to prominence. The recent interest in Anna Maria van Schurman (1607–1678)[1] reflects in part a fascination with the first woman admitted to uni-

157

versity lectures in northern Europe, even if she was segregated and hidden from the male students, seated alone in a darkened balcony.

Such an academic expansion of the canon has retrieved the philosophical voices of women long ignored by the history of modern philosophy. The three aforecited women are incontestably authors of serious philosophical and theological culture. But such an approach tends to turn women into satellites of the main philosophical event, still firmly anchored in the exclusively male bastion of the early modern university. No longer absent from the history of philosophy, the woman philosopher emerges as an intellectual helpmate: the disciple, the secretary, the correspondent. It is her reaction to the dominant male authors and theories of the period, rather than her own original philosophical construction, that remains the focus of the expanded chronicle of early modern philosophy.

This book presents the different history of early modern philosophy that can emerge when philosophical sites more central to women are explored. A focus on the salon not only retrieves a number of silenced women authors; it also indicates how the philosophical reflection by women represented an alternative to the university model. The venue of the salon fostered a mode of philosophical argument characterized more by debate and by epigrammatic commentary than by the lecture and the treatise. Thematically, it privileged the moral issues tied to love. If it discussed at length the perennial philosophical topic of the virtues, it transposed this debate into a gendered key. Sablé's defense of the authentic virtues of friendship and La Vallière's account of divine attributes and theological virtues exemplify the salon's translation of the philosophical debate over virtue into an irreducibly feminine voice.

In form as well as content, the salon empowered women to experiment with alternative methods of philosophical analysis. The salon's patronage of novel genres of moral argument constitutes one of its signal contributions to ethical inquiry. Sablé used the maxim to generate a series of theses on the ways in which vice camouflages itself as virtue. Sablière employed the same genre to sketch an Augustinian account of virtue, where the theological virtues displace any claims of the natural virtues to moral primacy. Deshoulières transformed the idyll into an instrument of critical analysis that systematically reduces claims of virtue to evidence of instinct. Retrieving the most ancient genre of philosophical reflection, Maintenon used the dialogue to propagate a figure of virtue adapted to an exclusively female audience. Shaped by the salon's conventions of polite conversation, these genres grounded a detailed argument on moral psychology in the works of each of these women. Nonetheless, the formal distance of these works from the dominant genre of the academic treatise has long isolated them from sustained philosophical scrutiny.

As this study of the moral philosophy generated by seventeenth-century *salonnières* has indicated, the expansion of the philosophical canon requires strategies other than the simple hunt for hidden women philosophers and their texts. It demands attention to the venues in which women pursued their own philosophical inquiry. Structurally different from the university and the academy, the world of the salon, like the worlds of the convent and of certain correspondence networks, fostered a philosophical culture that privileged moral preoccupations and methods of moral analysis tied to the specific experience of aristocratic women. The weight of canonical sites and genres poses as serious an obstacle to the very perception, let alone the appreciation, of the alternative moral philosophies developed by women as does the authority of canonical texts.

PROBLEMATIC RETRIEVAL

The fate of the salon *corpus* indicates the broader problems involved in the retrieval of women's philosophical voices. One problem concerns the tacit frontier between literature and philosophy. When not simply ignored, the works of the *salonnières* have been routinely classified as a specimen of light literature. Literary scholars noted the wit and the charm of these works, but the substantive philosophical arguments on the illusions of virtue or the link between power and knowledge faded into obscurity. Deshoulières's shepherdesses, not her critique of reason, survived in the anthologies. While the categorization of the salon works in moral psychology as a secondary branch of *belles-lettres* ensured their literary survival, it has routinely marginalized them as decorative rather than substantive enterprises. The philosophical pedigree of these works and their vigorous moral arguments lie dormant.

If the retrieval of women's philosophical voices from early modernity requires a new map of philosophy sites and genres, it also invites a critical assessment of the feminist perspectives guiding the current expansion of the canon. Unquestionably, the second wave of feminism in the 1970s fueled the current retrieval and analysis of hitherto forgotten women authors in the early modern period. A torrent of new editions, new translations, and new encyclopedias has altered the history of philosophy by the inclusion of women's voices. Like any recreation of the canon, however, the current enterprise carries its own partial interests. While these biases have resurrected certain women writers, they have obscured others.

Illustrative of this bias in the expansion of the early modern French canon is the case of Marie le Jars de Gournay (1565–1645).[2] At the moment Marie de Gournay is probably the best-known woman philosopher from seventeenth-century France. Numerous commentaries praise her philosophical vigor. She is acclaimed, and rightly, as a pioneer of feminist thought. She argues for the fundamental equality between the sexes and explicitly decries the denial to women of access to public office and to humanistic education.

Her lifestyle has furthered her appeal. Neither a nun nor a married woman, Gournay attempted to live from her writing and editorial work as a professional single woman in Paris. Gournay's works are certainly of a high literary and philosophical caliber. However, part of the contemporary passion for her work lies in the almost perfect correspondence between her substantive positions and the dominant creed of contemporary academic feminism. Tellingly, the one area where Gournay departs from secular feminism, her lengthy theological appeals to the Bible and patristic authors, receives scant contemporary attention.

The exaltation of egalitarian-feminist heroes like Gournay tends to obscure the contribution of women writers who appear to oppose current academic orthodoxy on sexual equality. The current estate of Madame de Maintenon is a case in point. Her pioneering work in the education of women is undisputed. Her massive collection of writings constitutes a literary landmark. Her skillful dialogues, often focused on virtue, would seem an obvious candidate for inclusion in an expanded philosophical canon. However, even sympathetic contemporary editors of her work are clearly uneasy with her. This derives largely from the simple fact that Maintenon does not tell us what we want to hear on education and on morals. A reformer of education for women, Maintenon refuses to condone the thesis that women should receive the same education as men. Classical languages and the sciences will remain a closed book for the students at Saint-Cyr. In her transposition of virtues, she prizes politeness over justice, piety over courage. Although she defends the vocational freedom of her pupils, their freedom is finally limited to two conventional choices: the convent or marriage.

While recognizing her literary and philosophical acumen, commentators routinely criticize Maintenon for missing the golden opportunity to turn Saint-Cyr into a model humanistic-scientific *collège* for women. Since her educational project does not conform to contemporary notions of gender equality, her alternative philosophy of education and the theory of differentiated virtue embedded in that philosophy remain suspect.

The marginalization of Maintenon also indicates the current fate of early women philosophers perceived as too religious, especially those considered too sectarian in outlook. Like the line between philosophy and literature, the tacit frontier between philosophy and theology must also be challenged to retrieve the full spectrum of women's philosophical voices in an expanded canon. The dismissal of authors who appeal to theological

authorities or to personal mystical experience as nonphilosophical effectively suppresses the works of a number of early modern women authors
who have developed a substantial philosophical argument on the nature
of virtue. La Vallière's philippic against rationalism and Sablière's apology
for charity have as great a claim to philosophical attention as does the mor-
dant skepticism of a Deshoulières. The autobiographical framework of personal conversion in the *Reflections on the Mercy of God* does not diminish the
sophistication of La Vallière's critical sociology of virtue and vice. The overarching Augustinian theology of *Maximes Chrétiennes* does not invalidate
Sablière's trenchant critique of the humanistic account of virtue.

QUESTIONING CHARACTER

The moral philosophy developed by the women studied in this volume does not have only historical value. This *corpus* raises a pointed set of
questions about the "revival of virtue ethics" that has become so prominent
a feature of recent ethical and political theory.

First, a number of these authors question the standard list of virtues that
commands our philosophical and political interest. Despite recent work on
the relativity of virtues—on how, for example, virtues may vary according
to one's work—the nomenclature of virtues has varied little from the
Athens of Aristotle. Justice, fortitude, temperance, and prudence retain
pride of place. Philosophical treatises still try to clarify the preeminent
virtue of justice. Educational reformers insist that the formation of character must still pivot around the student's acquisition of temperance, the
capacity to forsake pleasure for the sake of the good, and of fortitude, the
capacity to accept pain for the sake of the good.

This concept of virtue, however, clearly privileges the life of the affluent
male as normative for all human nature. The impoverished have few pleasures to renounce and thus little opportunity to practice temperance. The
fortitude here quickly manifests itself as military and athletic courage. Justice, wherein one gives each person his or her due, presupposes a certain
social and economic capacity to execute one's duties in this area.

The philosophers presented in this volume attack the classical litany of
virtues from several angles. Sablé insists on the habits associated with
friendship as the core of virtue. This primacy of friendship is all the sharper
given Sablé's dismissal of such political virtues as justice and courage as the
outcroppings of courtier ambition. Such an insistence on the authenticity
of friendship privileges one of the central relationships women enjoyed
among themselves and one of the few relationships based on freedom,
equality, and reciprocity. The private sphere, in which most women passed
their existence, now trumped the public sphere as the authentic *locus* of

virtue. The capacity to be faithful to a freely chosen friend displaced the virtue of chastity, which for an aristocratic woman was often tied to an arranged marriage. In her dismissal of the traditional ensemble of virtues and in her concomitant exaltation of the sole virtue of friendship, Sablé firmly attacks the gender bias dominating the older conception of virtue.

Maintenon also challenges the traditional edifice of virtue. Her method is more irenic than that of Sablé's acerbic circle. She never dismisses the standard virtues of antiquity and of modern Christian humanism. But she systematically changes their content to incorporate the experience of women. Glory is demilitarized and emerges as the endurance of the housewife. Eminence involves personal constancy, not political preeminence. Maintenon gently demolishes the gender prejudice that confined certain virtues to the experience of politically powerful men by redefining them as perfectly attuned to the typical tasks and achievements of women of her era.

Maintenon makes an especially important contribution to the philosophy of virtue in her insistence on politeness and civility as cardinal habits to be acquired by her students. In Maintenon's perspective, politeness becomes the fulcrum of the other virtues. This primacy of politeness contrasts with the cavalier dismissal of the virtue in contemporary moral philosophy.

Standard ethics textbooks often open with a distinction between manners and morals. "Manners" concerns issues of etiquette, such as where to place the fork. These are of no concern to the philosopher. "Morals" concerns questions of serious universal import, such as whether one can kill the burglar who just broke into the apartment. These issues are precisely what the philosopher studies. Popular opinion, however, has never accepted such a demarcation. Millions of people avidly read Ann Landers, Abigail Van Buren, and Judith Martin ("Miss Manners") for advice on everyday issues of politeness: expressing gratitude for a gift, dealing with a garrulous relative, tactfully resolving a family dispute. There is more than the fork at stake here. The everyday ethical questions grouped under the rubric of "politeness" remain largely ignored by philosophers, although they remain serious moral dilemmas for millions of moral agents.

Maintenon's insistence on the primacy of politeness in moral habits is more than an echo of the class-based concerns of an aristocratic boarding school; it emphasizes that many of the key dispositions necessary for the moral life, such as discreet concern for the happiness of others, are wrongly ignored by academic philosophy, with its taste for dramatic moral dilemmas. People *are* bothered by the cousin who never thanked them for the Christmas gift and by the faculty member who always interrupts his colleagues at department meetings. Maintenon addresses this chagrin at length, but professional philosophers rarely explore it.

The emphasis of Maintenon and a host of salon authors on the primacy of politeness not only challenges a recurrent omission in the traditional account of virtue; it forcefully allies virtue theory with the distinctive experience of women. While both genders were expected to acquire the virtue of politeness, women were expected to excel at it. Women were to model the quiet respect for the dignity of others that manifests itself through a repertoire of gracious words and gestures. The very mission of the salon was literally to "polish" the temperament, language, and ritual of society. By making politeness the keystone of authentic virtue, Maintenon privileges the home, rather than the battlefield or the court, as the central testing ground for moral character.

Several of the philosophers studied in this book provide another contribution to virtue theory. They place the question of vice and virtue, indeed the entire project of moral conduct, into a broader metaphysical framework. Deshoulières and Sablière offer the most systematic efforts in this area. Deshoulières's critique of virtue rests on her metaphysical conviction that reality is nothing other than matter, atomically arranged, and that material causation can explain the most "spiritual" of human actions. Philosophical confusion over the nature of virtue reflects a more fundamental philosophical confusion over the nature of reality and action. Sablière provides a more theological framework for her analysis of virtue. It is the economy of redemption, the fundamental drama of sin and redemption in Christ, that controls her dismissal of the "natural" moral virtues and her apotheosis of the theological virtues of faith, hope, and charity. The critique and praise of specific virtues arises from an overarching theology of grace.

Acutely sensitive to the minute social stratifications of their own culture, the philosophers analyzed in this book also lend substantial attention to the social context of the practice of virtue. Sablé focuses on the feigned virtues of the aristocracy of the salon and court. It is the subtle manipulation of noble titles, royal offices, and polite conversation that attracts her attention more than does the general issue of justice. La Vallière's analysis of the theological virtues elaborates upon class-specific distortions of these virtues: how, for example, the hope in eternal life can mutate into the courtier's hope of promotion. Even Maintenon, utterly conventional in her political creed, systematically undercuts the dominant social conception of virtue when she transforms the glory of the warrior and the wit of the intellectual into the sturdy perseverance of the rural housewife. More than an implicit reflection of their aristocratic background, the moral theory developed by these women philosophers explicitly recognizes and critiques the distorted figures of virtue that were dominant in their social milieu.

Finally, the *salonnières* studied in this book make their most pointed contribution to virtue theory by their very skepticism about the entire project. Many contemporary theories of virtue limit themselves to describing the virtues and to discussing their interrelationships. The neoclassical women presented in this volume question the motives behind the practice of the virtues and the very demarcation between virtue and vice.

Sablé uses the maxim to explore how vice, particularly pride, motivates apparent displays of virtue. Ambition often fuels the love of neighbor. Hate can easily drive truth-telling. The desire for esteem can cause ostentatious respect for another's property. Sablé does not criticize the standard definitions of virtue. But she suspects the motives behind the exercise of virtue. Rather than opposing virtue, vice emerges as the covert motor of virtue itself.

Sablé deepens her critique of virtue by her political analysis. The vice motivating displays of virtue is not generic pride. It is specifically the pride of the ambitious seeking to gain leverage over subordinates and superiors. It is the power struggle of the court that clearly fuels the rapacious pride driving a thousand apparent acts of justice and charity. In establishing the link between power and defective virtue, Sablé transcends the limits of the simple unmasking of virtue that occupied all the members of her salon.

From a more theological perspective, Sablière and La Vallière also undercut the traditional claims of virtue. Faithful to the Augustinian tradition, they insist on the primacy of the theological virtues of faith, hope, and charity. Not only do the classical moral virtues mask serious vice; they enclose sinners in self-sufficiency. For Sablière and La Vallière, talk of human justice is illusory if not rooted in justification by Christ. Efforts at temperance and fortitude are in vain when divorced from the grace of the cross. Prudence becomes an obstacle to the heroic charity that must be the mark of the redeemed.

Both authors insist on a distinctively Christian ethic and account of virtue. The matrix of the moral life is the theological virtues, a gift of God's grace, not a creation of human freedom. The humanistic insistence on the value of the cardinal and other allied moral virtues rests upon a false estimate of the power of humanity to save itself through its own freedom and ascetical struggle.

The Augustinian account of virtue defended by Sablière and La Vallière responds to a perennial question in theological ethics: the specificity of Christian ethics. Both authors insist that Christian ethics cannot be understood as an expansion or deepening of a generic moral project. Whereas other ethical systems originate in human pride and in that pride's efforts at self-salvation, Christian ethics must begin in Christ's act of redemption. It is the experience of that redemption through the habits of faith, hope, and charity that grounds the Christian moral life. Rather than adding to a corrupt human nature and to the vain virtues fabricated by that nature, the theological virtues represent an economy of salvation authored by God alone.

From a decidedly more skeptical perspective, Deshoulières provides the most pointed critique of the entire edifice of virtue. She transcends the dismissal of virtue as a mask of vice. She challenges the very possibility of virtue and vice, since she questions the reality of reason and free will themselves. In her critique, will is simply disguised instinct. The prudent person does not dash into the middle of the street. Neither does a healthy dog. The courageous person faces enemies. So does a tigress when her offspring are attacked. For Deshoulières, our illusions about virtue go beyond our omnipresent pride, the target of so many salon *moralistes*. The "pride" itself is illusory, since this alleged vice only designates the instinct of self-preservation that guides the human person as surely as it does the lamb and the nightingale.

Deshoulières's critique of virtue is an anthropological critique. Errors concerning the virtues and the vices spring from a misunderstanding of human nature. Philosophers' imperious claims to rationality, freedom, and immortality blind them to their all too material constitution. In Deshoulières's ecological perspective, the most intractable human pride lies in the refusal to recognize that humanity is part of, not master of, nature itself.

MIRROR AND WARNING

The moral philosophy developed by the *salonnières* echoes the creeds and forms of a vanished culture. It is only with difficulty that we can grasp the moral import of the disputes so central to their reflection. Obscure quarrels on grace and elaborate discussions of court etiquette seem as remote as their parlor games featuring Cupid. If they developed a gendered ethics, they also developed a class ethics, an ethics perfectly mirroring the conventions, aspirations, and anxieties of an aristocracy that has long since disappeared. But in their suspicion of virtue, the *salonnières* continue to deliver a warning. Sablé, Deshoulières, Sablière, La Vallière, and Maintenon question whether our own list of virtues reflects the experience of women, especially the experience of women in friendship, in child rearing, and in religious ecstasy. Their suspicion of virtue raises an even more troubling issue. They question the very substance of our grandiloquent discourse on virtue. With a witty smile they ask whether our vaunted justice and our earnest courage might have more to do with God and matter than we would wish.

Maximes *de Madame de Sablé*

1. Comme rien n'est plus faible et moins raisonnable que de soumettre son jugement à celui d'autrui, sans nulle application du sien, rien n'est plus grand et plus sensé que de le soumettre aveuglément à Dieu, en croyant sur sa parole tout ce qu'il dit.

2. Le vrai mérite ne dépend point du temps, ni de la mode. Ceux qui n'ont point d'autre avantage que l'air de la Cour le perdent quand ils s'en éloignent; mais le bon sens, le savoir et la sagesse rendent habile et aimable en tout temps et en tous lieux.

3. Au lieu d'être attentifs à connaître les autres, nous ne pensons qu'à nous faire connaître nous-mêmes. Il vaudrait mieux écouter pour acquérir de nouvelles lumières que de parler trop pour montrer celles que l'on a acquises.

4. Il est quelquefois bien utile de feindre que l'on est trompé. Car lorsque l'on fait voir à un homme artificieux qu'on reconnaît ses artifices, on lui donne sujet de les augmenter.

5. On juge si superficiellement des choses que l'agrément des actions et des paroles communes, dites et faites d'un bon air, avec quelque connaissance des choses qui se passent dans le monde, réussissent souvent mieux que la plus grande habilité.

6. Être trop mécontent de soi est une faiblesse. Être trop content de soi est une sottise.

7. Les esprits médiocres, mais mal faits, surtout les demi-savants, sont plus sujets à l'opiniâtreté. Il n'y a que les âmes fortes qui sachent se dédire et abandonner un mauvais parti.

8. La plus grande sagesse de l'homme consiste à connaître ses folies.

9. L'honnêteté et la sincérité dans les actions égarent les méchants et leur font perdre la voie par laquelle ils pensent à arriver à leurs fins, parce que les méchants croient d'ordinaire qu'on ne fait rien sans artifice.

10. C'est une occupation pénible aux fourbes d'avoir toujours à couvrir le défaut de leur sincérité et à réparer le manquement de leur parole.

11. Ceux qui usent toujours d'artifice devraient au moins se servir de leur jugement, pour connaître qu'on ne peut guère cacher longtemps une conduite artificieuse parmi des hommes habiles, et toujours appliqués à la découvrir, quoiqu'ils feignent d'être trompés pour dissimuler la connaissance qu'ils en ont.

12. Souvent les bienfaits nous font des ennemis et l'ingrat ne l'est presque jamais à demi. Car il ne se contente pas de n'avoir point la reconnaissance qu'il doit, il voudrait même n'avoir pas son bienfaiteur pour témoin de son ingratitude.

13. Rien ne nous peut tant instruire du dérèglement général de l'homme que la parfaite connaissance de nos dérèglements particuliers. Si nous voulons faire réflexion sur nos sentiments, nous reconnaîtrons dans notre âme le principe de tous les vices que nous reprochons aux autres; si ce n'est par nos actions, ce sera au moins par nos mouvements. Car il n'y a point de malice que l'amour-propre ne présente à l'esprit pour s'en servir aux occasions, et il y a peu de gens assez vertueux pour n'être pas tentés.

14. Les richesses n'apprennent pas à ne se point passioner pour les richesses. La possession de beaucoup de biens ne donne pas le repos qu'il y a de n'en point désirer.

15. Il n'y a que les petits esprits qui ne peuvent souffrir qu'on leur reproche leur ignorance parce que, comme ils sont ordinairement fort aveugles en toutes choses, fort sots, et fort ignorants, ils ne doutent jamais de rien et sont persuadés qu'ils voient clairement ce qu'ils ne voient qu'au travers de l'obscurité de leur esprit.

16. Il n'y a pas plus de raison de trop s'accuser de ses défauts, que de s'en trop excuser. Ceux qui s'accusent par excès le font souvent pour ne pouvoir souffrir qu'on les accuse ou par vanité de faire croire qu'ils savent confesser leurs défauts.

17. C'est une force d'esprit d'avouer sincèrement nos défauts et nos perfections, et c'est une faiblesses de ne pas demeurer d'accord du bien et du mal qui est en nous.

18. On aime tellement toutes les choses nouvelles et les choses extraordinaires qu'on a même quelque plaisir secret par la vue des plus tristes et des plus terribles événements, à cause de leur nouveauté et de la malignité naturelle qui est en nous.

19. On peut bien se connaître soi-même mais on ne s'examine point assez pour cela, et l'on se soucie d'avantage de paraître tel qu'on doit être que d'être en effet ce qu'on doit.

20. Si l'on avait autant de soin d'être ce qu'on doit être que de tromper

les autres en déguisant ce qu l'on est, on pourrait se montrer tel qu'on est, sans avoir la peine de se déguiser.

21. Il n'y a personne qui ne puisse recevoir de grands secours et de grands avantages des sciences, mais il y a aussi peu de personnes qui ne reçoivent un grand préjudice des lumières et des connaissances qu'ils ont acquises par les sciences, s'ils ne s'en servent comme si elles leur étaient propres et naturelles.

22. Il y a une certaine médiocrité difficile à trouver avec ceux qui sont au-dessus de nous, pour prendre la liberté qui sert à leurs plaisirs et à leurs divertissements, sans blesser l'honneur et le respect qu'on leur doit.

23. On a souvent plus d'envie de passer pour officieux que de réussir dans les offices, et souvent on aime mieux pouvoir dire à ses amis qu'on a bien fait pour eux que de bien faire en effet.

24. Les bons succès dépendent quelquefois du défaut du jugement parce que le jugement empêche souvent d'entreprendre plusieurs choses que l'inconsidération fait réussir.

25. On loue quelquefois les choses passées pour blâmer les présentes, et pour mépriser ce qui est, on estime ce qui n'est plus.

26. Il y a un certain empire dans la manière de parler et dans les actions, qui se fait faire place partout et qui gagne par avance la considération et le respect. Il sert en toutes choses et même pour obtenir ce qu'on demande.

27. Cet empire qui sert en toutes choses n'est qu'une autorité bienséante qui vient de la supériorité de l'esprit.

28. L'amour-propre se trompe même par l'amour-propre, en faisant voir dans ses intérêts une si grande indifférence pour ceux d'autrui qu'il perd l'avantage qui se trouve dans le commerce de la rétribution.

29. Tout le monde est si occupé de ses passions et de ses intérêts que l'on en veut toujours parler sans jamais entrer dans la passion et dans l'intérêt de ceux à qui on en parle, encore qu'ils aient le même besoin qu'on les écoute et qu'on les assiste.

30. Les liens de la vertu doivent être plus étroits que ceux du sang, l'homme de bien étant plus proche de l'homme de bien par la ressemblance des moeurs que le fils ne l'est de son père par la ressemblance du visage.

31. Une des choses qui fait que l'on trouve si peu de gens agréables et qui paraissent raisonnables dans la conversation, c'est qu'il n'y en a quasi point qui ne pensent plutôt à ce qu'ils veulent dire qu'à répondre précisément à ce qu'on leur dit. Les plus complaisants se contentent de montrer une mine attentive, au même temps qu'on voit dans leurs yeux et dans leur esprit un égarement et une précipitation de retourner à ce qu'ils veulent dire, au lieu qu'on devrait juger que c'est un mauvais moyen de plaire que de chercher à se satisfaire si fort, et que bien écouter et bien

répondre est une plus grande perfection que de parler bien et beaucoup, sans écouter et sans répondre aux choses qu'on nous dit.

32. La bonne fortune fait quasi toujours quelque changement dans le procédé, dans l'air et dans la manière de converser et d'agir. C'est une grande faiblesse de vouloir se parer de ce qui n'est point à soi. Si l'on estimait la vertu plus que toute autre chose, aucune faveur ni aucun emploi ne changerait jamais le coeur ni le visage des hommes.

33. Il faut s'accoutumer aux folies d'autrui et ne se point choquer des niaiseries qui se disent en notre présence.

34. La grandeur de l'entendement embrasse tout. Il y a autant d'esprit à souffrir les défauts des autres qu'à connaître leurs bonnes qualités.

35. Savoir bien découvrir l'intérieur d'autrui et cacher le sien est une grande marque de superiorité d'esprit.

36. Le trop parler est un si grand défaut qu'en matière d'affaires et de conversation, si ce qui est bon est court, il est doublement bon, et l'on gagne par brièveté ce qu'on perd souvent par l'excès des paroles.

37. On se rend quasi toujours maître de ceux que l'on connaît bien, parce que celui qui est parfaitement connu est en quelque façon soumis à celui qui le connaît.

38. L'étude et la recherche de la vérité ne sert souvent qu'à nous faire voir par expérience l'ignorance qui nous est naturelle.

39. On fait plus de cas des hommes quand on ne connaît point jusqu'où peut aller leur suffisance, car l'on présume toujours davantage des choses que l'on ne voit qu'à demi.

40. Souvent le désir de paraître capable empêche de le devenir, parce que l'on a plus d'envie de faire voir ce que l'on sait que l'on n'a de désir d'apprendre ce qu'on ne sait pas.

41. La petitesse de l'esprit, l'ignorance et la présomption font l'opiniâtreté, parce que les opiniâtres ne veulent croire que ce qu'ils conçoivent et qu'ils ne conçoivent que fort peu de choses.

42. C'est augmenter ses défauts que de les désavouer quand on nous les reproche.

43. Il ne faut pas regarder quel bien nous fait un ami mais seulement le désir qu'il a de nous en faire.

44. Encore que nous ne devions pas aimer nos amis pour le bien qu'ils nous font, c'est une marque qu'ils ne nous aiment guère s'ils ne nous en font point quand ils en ont le pouvoir.

45. Ce n'est ni une grande louange, ni un grand blâme quand on dit qu'un esprit est ou n'est plus à la mode. S'il est une fois tel qu'il doit être, il est toujours comme il doit être.

46. L'amour qu'on a pour soi-même est quasi toujours la règle de toutes nos amitiés. Il nous fait passer par-dessus tous les devoirs dans les rencon-

tres où il y va de quelque intérêt, et même oublier les plus grand sujets de ressentiment contre nos ennemis quand ils deviennent assez puissants pour servir à notre fortune ou à notre gloire.

47. C'est une chose bien vaine et bien inutile de faire l'examen de tout ce qui se passe dans le monde si cela ne sert à se redresser soi-même.

48. Les dehors et les circonstances donnent souvent plus d'estime que le fond et la réalité. Une méchante manière gâte tout, même la justice et la raison. Le "comment" fait la meilleure partie des choses, et l'air qu'on leur donne dore, accommode et adoucit les plus fâcheuses. Cela vient de la faiblesse de la prévention de l'esprit humain.

49. Les sottises d'autrui nous doivent être plutôt une instruction qu'un sujet de nous moquer de ceux qui les font.

50. La conversation des gens qui aiment à régenter est bien fâcheuse. Il faut toujours être prêt de se rendre à la vérité et à la recevoir de quelque part qu'elle nous vienne.

51. On s'instruit aussi bien par le défaut des autres que par leur instruction. L'exemple de l'imperfection sert quasi autant à se rendre parfait que celui de l'habileté et de la perfection.

52. On aime beaucoup mieux ceux qui tendent à nous imiter que ceux qui tâchent à nous égaler. Car l'imitation est une marque d'estime et le désir d'être égal aux autres est une marque d'envie.

53. C'est une louable adresse de faire recevoir doucement un refus par des paroles civiles, qui réparent le défaut du bien qu'on ne peut accorder.

54. Il y a beaucoup de gens qui sont tellement nés à dire "non" que le "non" va toujours au-devant de tout ce qu'on leur dit. Il les rend si désagréables, encore bien qu'ils accordent enfin ce qu'on leur demande ou qu'ils consentent à ce qu'on leur dit, qu'ils perdent toujours l'agrément qu'ils pourraient recevoir s'ils n'avaient point si mal commencé.

55. On ne doit pas toujours accorder toutes choses, ni à tous. Il est aussi louable de refuser avec raison que de donner à propos. C'est en ceci que le "non" de quelques-uns plaît davantage que le "oui" des autres. Le refus accompagné de douceur et de civilité satisfait davantage un bon coeur qu'une grâce qu'on accorde sèchement.

56. Il y a de l'esprit à savoir choisir un bon conseil, aussi bien qu'à agir de soi-même. Les plus judicieux ont moins de peine à consulter les sentiments des autres, et c'est une sorte d'habilité de savoir se mettre sous la bonne conduite d'autrui.

57. Les maximes de la vie chrétienne, qui se doivent seulement puiser dans les vérités de l'Évangile, nous sont toujours quasi enseignées selon l'esprit et l'humeur naturelle de ceux qui nous les enseignent. Les uns par la douceur de leur naturel, les autres par l'âpreté de leur temperament tournent et emploient selon leur sens la justice et la miséricorde de Dieu.

58. Dans la connaissance des choses humaines, notre esprit ne doit jamais se rendre esclave, en s'assujettissant aux fantaisies d'autrui. Il faut étendre la liberté de son jugement et ne rien mettre dans sa tête par aucune autorité purement humaine. Quand on nous propose la diversité des opinions, il faut choisir, s'il y a lieu; sinon, il faut demeurer dans le doute.

59. La contradiction doit éveiller l'attention, et non pas la colère. Il faut écouter, et non fuir celui qui contredit. Notre cause doit toujours être celle de la vérité, de quelque façon qu'elle nous soit montrée.

60. On est bien plus choqué de l'ostentation que l'on fait de la dignité que de celle de la personne. C'est une marque qu'on ne mérite pas les emplois, quand on se fait de fête; si l'on se fait valoir, ce ne doit être que par l'éminence de la vertu. Les Grands sont plus en vénération par les qualités de leur âme que par celles de leur fortune.

61. Il n'y a rien qui n'ait quelque perfection. C'est le bonheur du bon goût de la trouver en chaque chose. Mais la malignité naturelle fait souvent découvrir un vice entre plusieurs vertus pour le révéler et le publier, ce qui est plutôt une marque du mauvais naturel qu'un avantage du discernement, et c'est bien mal passer sa vie que de se nourrir toujours des imperfections d'autrui.

62. Il y a une certaine manière de s'écouter en parlant qui rend toujours désagréable. Car c'est une aussi grande folie de s'écouter soi-même quand on s'entretient avec les autres que de parler tout seul.

63. Il y a peu d'avantage de se plaire à soi-même quand on ne plaît à personne. Car souvent le trop grand amour que l'on a pour soi est châtié par le mépris d'autrui.

64. Il se cache toujours assez d'amour-propre sous la plus grande dévotion pour mettre des bornes à la charité.

65. Il y a des gens tellement aveuglés, et qui se flattent tellement en toutes choses, qu'ils croient toujours comme ils désirent et pensent aussi faire croire aux autres tout ce qu'ils veulent; quelque méchante raison qu'ils emploient pour persuader, ils en sont si préoccupés qu'ils leur semble qu'ils n'ont qu'à le dire d'un ton fort haut et affirmatif pour en convaincre tout le monde.

66. L'ignorance donne de la faiblesse et de la crainte; les connaissances donnent de la hardiesse et de la confiance; rien n'étonne une âme qui connaît toutes choses avec distinction.

67. C'est un défaut bien commun de n'être jamais content de sa fortune, ni mécontent de son esprit.

68. Il y a de la bassesse à tirer avantage de sa qualité et de sa grandeur pour se moquer de ceux qui nous sont soumis.

69. Quand un opiniâtre a commencé à contester quelque chose, son es-

prit se ferme à tout ce qui le peut éclaircir. La contestation l'irrite, quelque juste qu'elle soit, et il semble qu'il ait peur de trouver la vérité.

70. La honte qu'on a de se voir louer sans fondement donne souvent sujet de faire des choses qu'on n'aurait jamais faites sans cela.

71. Il vaut presque mieux que les Grands recherchent la gloire, et même la vanité dans les bonnes actions, que s'ils n'en étaient point du tout touchés. Car encore que ce ne soit pas les faire par les principes de la vertu, l'on en tire au moins cet avantage que la vanité leur fait faire ce qu'ils ne feraient point sans elle.

72. Ceux qui sont assez sots pour s'estimer seulement par leur noblesse méprisent en quelque façon ce qui les a rendus nobles, puisque ce n'est que la vertu de leurs ancêtres qui a fait la noblesse de leur sang.

73. L'amour-propre fait que nous nous trompons presque en toutes choses, que nous entendons blâmer et que nous blâmons les mêmes défauts dont nous ne nous corrigeons point, ou parce que nous ne connaissons pas le mal qui est en nous, ou parce que nous l'envisageons toujours sous l'apparence de quelque bien.

74. La vertu n'est pas toujours où l'on voit des actions qui paraissent vertueuses. On ne reconnaît quelquefois un bienfait que pour établir sa réputation et pour être plus hardiment ingrat aux bienfaits qu'on ne veut pas reconnaître.

75. Quand les Grands espèrent de faire croire qu'ils ont quelque bonne qualité qu'ils n'ont pas, il est dangereux de montrer qu'on en doute. Car en leur ôtant l'espérance de pouvoir tromper les yeux du monde, on leur ôte aussi le désir de faire les bonnes actions qui sont conformes à ce qu'ils affectent.

76. La meilleure nature, étant sans instruction, est toujours incertaine et aveugle. Il faut chercher soigneusement à s'instruire, pour n'être ni trop timide ni trop hardi par ignorance.

77. La société, et même l'amitié de la plupart des hommes, n'est qu'un commerce qui ne dure qu'autant que le besoin.

78. Quoique la plupart des amitiés qui se trouvent dans le monde ne méritent point le nom d'amitié, on peut pourtant en user selon les besoins comme d'un commerce qui n'a point de fonds certain, et sur lequel on est ordinairement trompé.

79. L'amour, partout où il est, est toujours le maître. Il forme l'âme, le coeur et l'esprit, selon ce qu'il est. Il n'est ni petit ni grand selon le coeur et l'esprit qu'il occupe, mais selon ce qu'il est en lui-même. Et il semble véritablement que l'amour est à l'âme de celui qui aime ce que l'âme est au corps de celui qu'elle anime.

80. L'amour a un caractère si particulier qu'on ne peut le cacher où il est, ni le feindre où il n'est pas.

81. Tous les grands divertissements sont dangereux pour la vie chrétienne, mais entre tous ceux que le monde a inventés, il n'y en a point qui
soit plus à craindre que la comédie. C'est une peinture si naturelle et si
délicate des passions qu'elle les anime et les fait naître dans notre coeur,
et surtout celle de l'amour, principalement lorsqu'on se représente qu'il
est chaste et fort honnête. Car plus il paraît innocent aux âmes innocentes,
et plus elles sont capables d'en être touchées. On se fait en même temps
une conscience fondée sur l'honnêteté de ces sentiments, et on s'imagine
que ce n'est pas blesser la pureté que d'aimer d'un amour si sage. Ainsi on
sort de la comédie le coeur si rempli de toutes les douceurs de l'amour, et
l'esprit si persuadé de son innocence qu'on est tout préparé à recevoir ses
premières impressions, ou plutôt à chercher l'occasion de les faire naître
dans le coeur de quelqu'un, pour recevoir les mêmes plaisirs et les mêmes
sacrifices que l'on a vus si bien représentés sur le théâtre.

Note: This text is based on Madame de Sablé, *Maximes de Mme de Sablé,* ed. Damase Jouaust
(Paris: Librairie des bibliophiles, 1870).

Réflexions diverses *de Madame Deshoulières*

I.

Que l'homme connaît peu la mort qu'il appréhende,
　　Quand il dit qu'elle le surprend!
Elle naît avec lui, sans cesse lui demande
Un tribut dont en vain son orgueil se défend.
Il commence à mourir longtemps avant qu'il meure;
Il périt en détail imperceptiblement.
Le nom de mort qu'on donne à notre dernière heure
　　N'est que l'accomplissement.

II.

Êtres inanimés, rebut de la nature,
　　Ah! que vous faites d'envieux!
　　Le temps, loin de vous faire injure,
　　Ne vous rend que plus précieux.
On cherche avec ardeur une médaille antique;
D'un buste, d'un tableau, le temps hausse le prix,
Le voyageur s'arrête à voir l'affreux débris
D'un cirque, d'un tombeau, d'un temple magnifique;
Et pour notre vieillesse on n'a que du mépris.

III.

　　De ce sublime esprit dont ton orgueil se pique,
　　Homme, quel usage fais-tu?
　　Des plantes, des métaux tu connais la vertu;
　　Des différents pays les moeurs, la politique;
　　La cause des frimas, de la foudre, du vent;
　　　　Des astres le pouvoir suprême:

175

Et, sur tant de choses savant,
Tu ne te connais pas toi-même!

IV.

La pauvreté fait peur; mais elle a ses plaisirs.
Je sais bien qu'elle éloigne, aussitôt qu'elle arrive,
La volupté, l'éclat, et cette foule oisive
Dont les jeux, les festins, remplissent les désirs;
Cependant, quoi qu'elle ait de honteux et de rude
Pour ceux qu'à des revers la fortune a soumis,
Au moins, dans leurs malheurs, ont-ils la certitude
De n'avoir que de vrais amis.

V.

Pourquoi s'applaudir d'être belle?
Quelle erreur fait compter la beauté pour un bien?
À l'examiner, il n'est rien
Qui cause tant de chagrin qu'elle.
Je sais que sur les coeurs ses droits sont absolus;
Que tant qu'on est belle on fait naître
Des désirs, des transports, et des soins assidus:
Mais on a peu de temps à l'être,
Et longtemps à ne l'être plus.

VI.

Misérable jouet de l'aveugle fortune,
Victime des maux et des lois,
Homme, toi qui, par mille endroits,
Dois trouver la vie importune,
D'où vient que de la mort tu crains tant le pouvoir?
Lâche, regarde-la sans changer de visage;
Songe que, si c'est un outrage,
C'est le dernier à recevoir.

VII.

Que chacun parle bien de la reconnaisance!
Et que peu de gens en font voir!
D'un service attendu la flatteuse espérance
Fait porter dans l'excès les soins, la complaisance:

À peine est-il rendu, qu'on cesse d'en avoir.
De qui nous a servis la vue est importune:
    On trouve honteux de devoir
    Les secours que dans l'infortune
On n'avait point trouvé honteux de recevoir.

VIII.

Quel poison pour l'esprit sont les fausses louanges!
Heureux qui ne croit point à de flatteurs discours!
Penser trop bien de soi fait tomber tous les jours
    En des égaréments étranges.
L'amour-propre est, hélas! le plus sot des amours;
Cependant des erreurs il est la plus commune.
Quelque puissant qu'on soit en richesse, en crédit,
Quelque mauvais succès qu'ait tout ce qu'on écrit,
    Nul n'est content de sa fortune,
    Ni mécontent de son esprit.

IX.

    On croit être devenu sage,
Quand, après avoir vu plus de cinquante fois
    Tomber le renaissant feuillage,
On quitte des plaisirs le dangereux usage.
    On s'abuse. D'un libre choix
    Un tel retour n'est point l'ouvrage;
Et ce n'est que l'orgueil dont l'homme est revêtu
    Qui, tirant de tout avantage,
    Donne au secours de la vertu
    Ce qu'on doit au secours de l'âge.

X.

En grandeur de courage on ne se connaît guère
Quand on élève au rang des hommes généreux
Ces Grecs et ces Romains dont la mort volontaire
    A rendu le nom si fameux.
Qu'ont-ils fait de si grand? Ils sortaient de la vie
    Lorsque, de disgrâces suivie,
Elle n'avait plus rien d'agréable pour eux;
Par une seule mort ils s'en épargnaient mille.
Quelle est douce à des coeurs lassés de soupirer!

Il est plus grand, plus difficile
De souffrir le malheur que de s'en délivrer.

XI.

L'encens qu'on donne à la prudence
Met mon esprit au désespoir.
À quoi donc nous sert-elle? À faire voir d'avance
Les maux que nous devons avoir.
Est-ce un bonheur de les prévoir?
Si la cruelle avait quelque règle certaine
Qui pût les écarter de nous,
Je trouverais les soins qu'elle donne assez doux;
Mais rien n'est si trompeur que la prudence humaine.
Hélas! presque toujours le détour qu'elle prend
Pour nous faire éviter un malheur qu'elle attend
Est le chemin qui nous y mène.

XII.

Palais, nous durons moins que vous,
Quoique des éléments vous souteniez la guerre,
Et quoique du sein de la terre
Nous soyons tirés comme vous.
Frêles machines que nous sommes,
À peine passons-nous d'un siècle le milieu.
Un rien peut nous détruire; et l'ouvrage d'un Dieu
Dure moins que celui des hommes.

XIII.

Homme, vante moins ta raison;
Vois l'inutilité de ce présent céleste
Pour qui tu dois, dit-on, mépriser tout le reste.
Aussi faible que toi dans ta jeune saison,
Elle est chancelante, imbécile;
Dans l'âge où tout t'appelle à des plaisirs divers,
Vile esclave des sens, elle t'est inutile;
Quand le sort t'a laissé compter cinquante hivers,
Elle n'est qu'en chagrin fertile;
Et quand tu vieillis, tu la perds.

XIV.

Les plaisirs sont amers d'abord qu'on en abuse.
          Il est bon de jouer un peu;
Mais il faut seulement que le jeu nous amuse.
          Un joueur, d'un commun aveu,
          N'a rien d'humain que l'apparence;
Et d'ailleurs il n'est pas si facile qu'on pense
D'être fort honnête homme et de jouer gros jeu.
Le désir de gagner qui nuit et jour occupe
          Est un dangereux aiguillon;
Souvent, quoique l'esprit, quoique le coeur soit bon,
          On commence par être dupe,
          On finit par être fripon.

XV.

Souvent c'est moins bon goût que pure vanité
Qui fait qu'on ne veut voir que de gens de mérite:
          On croirait faire tort à sa capacité,
Si du monde vulgaire on recevait visite.
Cependant un esprit solide, éclairé, droit,
Du commerce des sots sait faire un bon usage;
          Il les examine, il les voit,
          Comme on fait un mauvais ouvrage.
Des défauts qu'il y trouve il cherche à profiter:
          Il n'est guère moins nécessaire
          De voir ce qu'il faut éviter,
          Que de savoir ce qu'il faut faire.

XVI.

Qui dans son cabinet a passé ses beaux jours
À pâlir sur Pindare, Homère, Horace, Plaute,
          Devrait y demeurer toujours.
S'il entre dans le monde avec un tel secours,
          Il y fera faute sur faute;
          Il portera partout l'ennui.
          Un ignorant, qui n'a pour lui
Qu'un certain savoir-vivre, un esprit agréable,
À la honte du grec et du latin, fait voir
          Combien doit être préférable
          L'usage du monde au savoir.

XVII.

Que l'esprit de l'homme est borné!
Quelque temps qu'il donne à l'étude,
Quelque pénétrant qu'il soit né,
Il ne sait rien à fond, rien avec certitude:
De ténèbres pour lui tout est environné.
La lumière qui vient du savoir le plus rare
N'est qu'un fatal éclair, qu'une ardeur qui l'égare;
Bien plus que l'ignorance elle est à redouter.
Longues erreurs qu'elle fait naître,
Tous ne prouvez que trop que chercher à connaître
N'est souvent qu'apprendre à douter.

Note: This text is based on Madame Deshoulières, *Réflexions diverses*, in Madame et Mademoiselle Deshoulières, *Oeuvres* (Paris: Stéréotype d'Hernan, 1803), 1.199–205.

Maximes Chrétiennes *de Madame de la Sablière*

1. Baptême: La naissance que nous recevons dans le baptême et qui nous fait chrétiens, nous élève bien au-dessus de tout ce que nous sommes, et par la nature et par la fortune.

2. La Loi: La prière a pour fin l'accomplissement de la Loi; ainsi, qui s'acquitte de quelque devoir prescrit par la Loi, fait quelque chose de plus agréable à Dieu, que de prier.

3. Hypocrites: Le culte sans morale fait des hypocrites, ou des superstitieux. La morale sans culte fait des philosophes et des sages mondains. Pour être chrétien, il faut joindre ensemble ces deux choses.

4. Grands: Les grands vivent presque toujours sans réflexion; cependant, ils sont plus obligés que les autres, de rentrer souvent en eux-mêmes, pour se dire de certaines vérités qu'ils ne doivent pas espérer apprendre d'ailleurs.

5. Orgueil: Il y a une singularité vicieuse qu'inspire l'orgueil, et c'est ce que le Fils de Dieu condamne si souvent dans les pharisiens; mais il y a une singularité évangélique qui s'oppose au torrent du siècle, qui en condamne l'usage, et c'est le véritable caractère qui distingue des justes des mondains et des pécheurs.

6. Grands: Quand les Grands, en donnant lieu de croire qu'ils veulent être flattés, empêchent qu'on leur découvre les vérités qui pourraient les instruire, l'ignorance dans laquelle ils vivent est en quelque façon volontaire, et ne les exempte point de péché.

7. Conseil: Rien n'est plus capable de rendre un bon conseil, non seulement inutile, mais même préjudiciable, que de l'accompagner d'un mauvais exemple.

8. Incertitude: Il n'y aurait aucune incertitude dans la morale chrétienne, si les hommes, qui conviennent presque toujours des règles générales et des principes, en tiraient les conséquences sans consulter leurs passions.

9. Charité: La charité sanctifie les actions les plus communes, et l'orgueil corrompt les plus sublimes vertus.

10. Défauts: Les gens de bien par leurs bons exemples, corrigent souvent les défauts des autres sans les reprendre; et ceux qui ne le sont pas, reprennent souvent les défauts des autres sans les corriger.

11. Foi: La Foi nous fait regarder comme des biens ce que le monde regarde comme des maux; et comme des maux, ce que le monde appelle des biens; et c'est de la différence de ces idées que naît la différente conduite des justes et des pécheurs.

12. Occupés: Nous sommes sans cesse occupés d'un avenir incertain, qui souvent ne nous regarde pas; et nous ne pensons point à celui qui ne peut manquer d'arriver, et d'où dépend notre bonheur, ou notre malheur éternel.

13. Salut: Quand nous négligeons notre salut, ce n'est pas la charité qui nous fait travailler à celui des autres.

14. Désirs: Ce qui nous empêche d'exécuter nos bons desseins, c'est que nous ne pensons qu'à notre faiblesse, et que nous ne faisons pas réflexion qu'il est aussi aisé à Dieu de nous faire faire de saintes actions, que de nous inspirer de saints désirs.

15. Bonheur éternel: Il n y a point de moment où nous ne puissions mériter un bonheur éternel; le temps est donc une chose si précieuse, que le monde n'a rien d'un assez grand prix pour nous payer celui que nous lui donnons.

16. Supplice du coeur: Il n'y a point de créature qui ne devienne le supplice du coeur qui cherche son repose en elle.

17. Amusements frivoles: Les amusements frivoles du siècle ne nous ôtent pas moins le goût et le discernement des vrais biens, que les passions les plus criminelles.

18. Usage: L'usage ne peut jamais servir d'excuse et de prétexte pour pécher; comme c'est le monde qui l'établit, il doit toujours être suspect aux chrétiens, qui ont fait serment dans leur baptême de renoncer au monde et à ses maximes.

19. Incrédulité de l'esprit: L'incrédulité de l'esprit vient presque toujours de la corruption du coeur. On ne peut se résoudre à croire ce qui fait violence à la nature.

20. Défiance: Nous avons une défiance timide de la Providence de Dieu dans les affaires temporelles; et pour l'affaire du salut, nous avons une confiance téméraire en sa miséricorde.

21. Habitudes: Les habitudes dans la vieillesse ne sont pas de moindres obstacles pour le salut que les passions dans la jeunesse.

22. Défauts: On corrige plutôt les défauts des autres en les souffrant avec patience, qu'en les reprenant avec orgueil.

23. Superbe: On établit souvent des maximes sévères par superbe; on aime à se parer de cette apparence de vertu, et il ne coûte rien de rendre insupportable pour les autres un joug que l'on ne veut pas s'imposer à soi-même.

24. Humilité: Les sentiments d'humilité que nous faisons paraître par nos paroles, ne sont pas sincères, si nous sommes fâchés de persuader les autres de ce que nous disons de nous-mêmes.

25. Fuir: Nous ne pourrions souffrir que les autres prissent autant de soin de nous fuir, que nous en prenons de nous fuir nous-mêmes en nous répandant au dehors.

26. Corriger: On prend aisément en général la résolution de se corriger; on jouit avec plaisir de l'idée de la vertu; mais sitôt qu'il se présente quelque passion à combattre, cette résolution s'affaiblit et l'on ne se sent plus capable d'exécuter un dessein que l'on avait formé sans peine, mais que l'on ne peut exécuter sans se faire violence.

27. Confesser: S'il suffisait pour être sauvé de se confesser à l'heure de la mort, il ne serait pas vrai que la voie du salut fut si étroite, et qu'il y eut si peu d'élus.

28. Vice: Le torrent du siècle ne manquera pas de nous entraîner du côté du vice, si nous ne faisons de continuels efforts pour nous avancer dans le chemin de la vertu.

29. Chrétiens: Si l'on se faisait une idée de l'Évangile sur la vie de la plupart des chrétiens, on le croirait plein de maximes directement contraires à celles que Jésus-Christ a établies.

30. Passions: Nous prenons souvent le repentir qui naît de notre inconstance, ou du malheureux succès de nos passions, pour le remords d'une véritable pénitence.

31. Dégoût: Quand le dégoût que nous avons pour le monde n'est pas un effet de la grâce, mais de l'orgueil et de l'amour-propre, il nous ramène bien à nous-mêmes, mais il ne nous conduit point à Dieu.

32. De l'âme: Il est autant impossible à l'âme de se soutenir dans la grâce sans la prière, qu'il l'est au corps de subsister sans nourriture.

33. De l'âme: Tout ce qui se passe avec le temps est court, et ne mérite point d'attirer l'attention d'une âme, qui marche sans cesse vers l'Éternel.

34. Pécheur: Il n y a point d'état plus déplorable que celui d'un pécheur qui ne trouve point d'obstacle à ses désirs, et que Dieu abandonne à la merci de ses passions.

35. Salut: Les chaînes qui nous liaient aux créatures sont souvent rompues, que nous demeurons encore attachés à la terre par notre propre poids. Cet obstacle qui s'oppose à notre salut, et qui subsiste dans les différentes âges de la vie, n'est pas moins difficile à vaincre que les autres.

36. Passions: Il est difficile de vaincre ses passions, mais il est impossible de les satisfaire.

37. Vengeance: La vengeance procède toujours de la faiblesse de l'âme, qui n'est pas capable de supporter les injures.

38. Péchés: Les hommes se plaignent de leur peines, et ne se repentent point des péchés qui les attirent.

39. Devoirs du chrétien: Les omissions des devoirs du chrétien, et de ceux de la condition où l'on se trouve, sont des péchés souvent imperceptibles aux personnes mêmes qui les commettent; cependant l'Évangile condamne le serviteur inutile aux mêmes peines que le rebelle.

40. Péchés: Nous ne haïssons pas assez fortement le péché, si cette haine ne nous fait éviter avec soin les occasions qui nous ont été des pièges.

41. Volonté de Dieu: On ne résiste point à la volonté de Dieu, elle s'accomplit toujours en nous, ou par notre obéissance, si nous nous y conformons, ou par notre châtiment, si nous révoltons contre elle.

42. Projets: Les projets que nous faisons de nous convertir un jour, ne servent le plus souvent qu'à étouffer les remords présents. On se repose sur des desseins chimériques que l'on exécute jamais, et par là on se dérobe la vue de ses crimes, ou l'on croit en quelque façon les réparer.

43. Fausses et trompeuses: Toutes les différences que l'opinion met entre les hommes sont fausses et trompeuses; il n'y a que la grâce qui les distingue, on n'est véritablement que ce qu'on est aux yeux de Dieu.

44. Persécution: Il faut respecter ceux qui nous persécutent, et les regarder comme des exécuteurs de la justice de Dieu qui nous châtie.

45. Fidèles: Si les fidèles qui s'assemblent dans les Églises pour prier, se regardaient comme des coupables qui viennent implorer la miséricorde de leur juge, leurs prières seraient plus humbles et plus ferventes.

46. Amour de Dieu: L'amour que Dieu demande de nous n'est pas un amour sensible, mais un amour de préférence qui nous engage à sacrifier toutes choses plutôt que de lui déplaire.

47. Desseins: Si dans tous nos desseins nous ne pensions qu'à plaire à Dieu et à faire sa volonté, quelque succès qu'ils puissent avoir, nous serions toujours contents.

48. Vertu des païens: La vertu des païens les a portés quelquefois à mépriser le monde, mais il n'y a que la vertu chrétienne qui puisse faire désirer d'en être méprisé.

49. Vertu: Toutes les vertus éclatantes nous doivent toujours être suspectes, il n'y a que l'amour de l'humiliation dont le démon ne peut jamais nous faire un piège.

50. Coeur élevé: Un coeur élevé par la grâce ne trouve rien dans le monde qui ne soit au-dessous de lui.

51. Vertu: Si nous considérons que les vertus qui s'acquièrent avec tant de peines, se perdent quelquefois en un moment dans le commerce du

monde; bien loin de nous y plaire, nous les fuirions comme un ennemi qui ne pense qu'à nous enlever nos plus précieux trésors.

52. Conversation: Il se mêle ordinairement dans les conversations les plus saintes, un certain levain d'orgueil et de vanité qui en empêche tout le fruit.

53. Salut: Les bons desseins que nous formons et que nous n'exécutons pas, ne servent qu'à nous rendre plus coupables, et qu'à mettre de nouveaux obstacles à notre salut.

54. Tristesse: Il n'y que la tristesse de la pénitence qui soit une tristesse raisonnable; toutes les autres sont des marques de la faiblesse, ou de la corruption de la nature.

55. Désirs: Le désir est la prière du coeur; Dieu qui connaît nos désirs, entend toujours, et exauce souvent cette prière.

56. Chute: Il est juste que celui qui ne fuit point les occasions de pécher, et qui s'expose témérairement au péril, soit puni de sa présomption par sa chute.

57. Séparer du monde: Il est plus aisé de se séparer du commerce du monde, que de vivre dans le monde avec aussi peu d'attachement que si l'on en était séparé. Cependant l'un ou l'autre est nécessaire pour se sauver.

58. Prospérité: Dieu qui nous promet de ne nous pas abandonner dans la tribulation, ne nous fait pas espérer la même grâce dans la prospérité.

59. Chrétiens: La véritable gloire d'un chrétien ne consiste pas à s'élever au-dessus des autres, mais à s'abaisser pour se rendre plus conforme à Jésus-Christ.

60. Tranquillité du pécheur: La tranquillité du pécheur au milieu de ses crimes, est une léthargie spirituelle.

61. Mérite: Le mérite de nos souffrances est bien d'un prix plus grand devant Dieu, que celui de nos actions.

62. Punition: La pénitence ne punit pas assez sévèrement le pécheur, si elle n'imite la colère de Dieu, ne prend pas la place de sa justice.

63. Plaisir assuré: Un plaisir dont on est assuré de se repentir ne peut jamais être tranquille.

64. Recueillement: Le recueillement est une espèce de solitude, où il faut souvent se retirer au milieu des conversations profanes du siècle, pour n'être pas infecté de l'air contagieux que l'on y respire.

65. Grandes choses: C'est moins en faisant de grandes choses, qu'en s'acquittant facilement des plus petites, que l'on devient saint.

66. Inquiétude: Pour juger du trouble et de l'inquiétude des pécheurs, il ne faut que les consulter eux-mêmes au milieu de tous leurs plaisirs. Ils ont la bonne foi d'avouer qu'ils ne peuvent parvenir à se rendre heureux.

67. Prières: Nous voulons que Dieu nous écoute dans nos prières, et nous ne nous écoutons pas nous-mêmes.

68. Dieu punit: Dieu punit souvent les désirs déréglés du coeur par les ténèbres de l'esprit.

69. Hypocrisie: L'hypocrisie est une espèce de sacrilège, qui fait servir au crime les apparances de la vertu.

70. Sexe: Dans le commerce le plus innocent entre des personnes de différent sexe, il y a toujours une espèce de sensualité spirituelle qui affaiblit la vertu, si elle ne la détruit pas entièrement.

71. Caractère du chrétien: Être sévère pour soi, et indulgent envers les autres, est le véritable caractère du chrétien.

72. Prudence: La prudence est lâche et timide, si elle n'est animée par le zèle de la charité, et le zèle est indiscret, s'il n'est reglé et conduit par la prudence.

73. De l'âme: Une âme, qui par la prière entre souvent en commerce avec Dieu, se dégoûte aisément du commerce du monde.

74. Iniquité: Le juste s'aime véritablement, pusiqu'il se procure le plus grand de tous les biens. Celui qui aime iniquité perd son âme, et se hait soi-même.

75. Orgueil: L'orgueil est la source de toutes nos agitations et de tous nos troubles, il n'y a que l'humilité qui puisse procurer à l'âme une véritable et solide paix.

76. Séparer du monde: Il faut nous séparer du monde, et en quelque façon de nous-mêmes, pour écouter Dieu dans la retraite. Le tumulte du siècle et celui des passions, nous empêchent souvent de l'entendre.

77. Négligence: La négligence dans les petites choses, est toujours une espèce d'infidélité, qui est souvent punie par de grandes chutes.

78. Affliction: Quand nous nous affligeons de nos fautes sans nous en corriger, c'est une marque que cette tristesse ne procède point de la grâce, mais de l'orgueil et de l'amour propre.

79. Trouver Dieu: Comment peut-on espérer de trouver Dieu au moment de sa mort, si on ne l'a jamais cherché pendant sa vie?

80. Espérances: Si les espérances que nous formons pour notre salut, ne sont pas fondées sur la parole de Dieu, elles sont fausses et trompeuses, en vain nous nous promettons à nous-mêmes ce que Dieu ne nous promet pas.

81. Amour de Dieu: L'amour de Dieu n'exclut point la crainte de ses judgments, plus on l'aime et plus on craint d'être à jamais séparé de lui.

82. Libertins: Si les libertins, qui ne veulent croire que ce qu'ils peuvent comprendre, ne conviennent point de leur extravagance et de leur folie, qu'ils sentent au moins leur présomption et leur témérité.

83. Mort: Dieu nous a caché le moment de notre mort pour nous obliger d'avoir attention à tous les moments de notre vie.

84. Passions: Les désirs qu'inspirent les passions, sont des envies de malade, que l'on ne peut satisfaire sans se nuire et sans se rendre malheureux.

85. Vertu: À mesure que l'on avance dans la vertu, on perd le goût des plaisirs du monde; comme à mesure que l'on avance en âge, on méprise les amusements de l'enfance.

86. Paresseux: L'âme du parasseux ressemble à une terre qu'on ne cultive pas, elle ne produit que des ronces et des chardons.

87. Humilité: Dieu humilie souvent par le péché ceux qui ne se sont pas humiliés par la grâce.

88. Immutabilité: Quand on ne veut que ce que Dieu veut, on participe en quelque façon à son immutabilité.

89. Piété: Il y a des actions de piété qui paraissent méprisables aux yeux des hommes, et qui sont d'un grand prix devant Dieu.

90. Demande à Dieu: Nous demandons souvent à Dieu des choses que nous devons craindre d'obtenir.

91. Paix avec soi-même: Comment peut-on avoir la paix avec soi-même, quand l'on est en guerre avec Dieu?

92. Voie: Puisqu'il y a une voie qui paraît droite à l'homme, et qui conduit à la mort, quelle doit être notre attention pour ne pas marcher dans cette voie, où l'on s'égare infailliblement sans le savoir?

93. Cache de Vérité: Que l'on cache de vérités par crainte de déplaire. Le silence de la flatterie n'est pas moins criminel que son langage.

94. Devoirs: Il ne suffit pas de s'acquitter des devoirs communs à tous les chrétiens, il faut encore remplir ceux de sa profession et de son état.

95. Préceptes: Il est difficile d'accomplir tous les préceptes, si notre zèle ne nous porte quelquefois jusqu'à la pratique des conseils.

96. Souffre: Tout ce que l'on souffre, on le souffre justement; ainsi l'on ne peut jamais se plaindre sans injustice.

97. Chute des Justes: Il faut profiter de la chute des justes, aussi bien que de leurs bons exemples.

98. Fond du coeur: Il n'y a que ceux à qui Dieu parle dans le fond du coeur, qui puissent connaître toute l'étendue de leurs obligations.

99. Espérer de Dieu: Il faut tout espérer de Dieu, quand on a sincèrement recours à lui, quelqu'indigne que l'on soit de ses grâces.

100. Justes: Il y a des Justes que Dieu retient dans le commerce du monde, pour éclairer et pour condamner les pécheurs.

Note: This text is based on Madame de la Sablière, *Maximes Chrétiennes,* in *Réflexions ou Sentences et maximes morales de Monsieur de la Rochefoucauld, Maximes de Madame la marquise de Sablé, Pensées diverses de M.L.D. et les Maximes Chrétiennes de M***** (Amsterdam: Pierre Mortier, 1705), 277–310.

Sur les vertus cardinales *de Madame de Maintenon*

Victoire: Pour entrer dans le dessein que l'on a de nous rendre capables de conversations raisonnables, j'ai pensé que nous devions prendre aujourd'hui les vertus cardinales pour sujet de la nôtre, et dire sur chacune ce qui nous viendra dans l'esprit.

Pauline: Voilà qui est fait, je prends la Justice.

Victoire: Et moi la Force.

Euphrasie: Et moi la Prudence.

Augustine: Vous ne me laissez pas à choisir, mais je suis contente de mon partage et ravie d'être la Tempérance.

La Justice: Je ne crois pas qu'aucune de vous prétende s'égaler à moi. Rien n'est si beau que la Justice. Elle a toujours la Vérité auprès d'elle, elle juge sans prévention, elle met tout dans son rang, elle sait condamner son ami et donner le droit à son ennemi, elle se condamne elle-même, elle n'estime que ce qui est estimable.

La Force: Tout cela est vrai, mais vous avez besoin de moi et vous vous lasseriez si je ne vous soutenais.

La Justice: Pourquoi me lasserais-je?

La Force: Parce que votre personnage est triste, que vous déplaisez souvent et qu'on ne vous aime guère, qu'on vous craint, et qu'il faut un grand mérite pour s'accommoder de vous.

La Prudence: C'est à moi à régler ses démarches, à l'empêcher de se précipiter, à lui faire prendre son temps, et vous gâteriez tout l'une et l'autre sans moi.

La Justice: Est-ce qu'il ne faut pas être toujours juste?

La Prudence: Oui, mais il ne faut pas toujours être sur son tribunal à rendre justice. Il faut mettre tout à sa place.

La Force: Vous pouvez en effet rendre quelques services à la Justice, mais les miens vous sont nécessaires. Vous êtes plus propre à la retenir qu'à la faire agir, si je ne vous donne à toutes deux mon secours.

La Justice: Je ne vous comprends point. Quoi! J'ai besoin de votre secours pour voir que mon ami a tort et mon ennemi raison!

La Force: Non, vous le voyez par vous-même, mais vous avez besoin de moi pour oser le dire, car votre amitié vous fait trouver de la peine à fâcher votre ami.

La Justice: Il me suffit qu'une chose soit juste pour la soutenir.

La Force: Oui, je suis avec vous, mais c'est que vous ne me voulez pas voir, vous donnez à la Justice ce qui est à la Force, et vous voilà injuste.

La Tempérance: Je vous admire, Mesdemoiselles, de croire que vous pouvez vous passer de moi, et que je vous suis nuisible parce que je n'empresse pas de parler.

La Prudence: Voudriez-vous aussi faire la nécessaire?

La Tempérance: Je le suis si fort que je vous défie toutes trois de vous passer de moi.

La Force: Et que ferez-vous avec votre froideur?

La Tempérance: Je vous empêcherai de pousser tout le monde à bout.

La Justice: Quel service me rendrez-vous?

La Tempérance: Je modérerai votre justice souvent amère et désagréable.

La Prudence: Je ne pense pas que vous prétendiez rien sur moi.

La Tempérance: Je m'opposerai à vos incertitudes, à votre timidité qui va souvent trop loin.

La Force: À vous entendre, vous l'emporteriez donc sur nous toutes?

La Tempérance: Sans doute, vous penchez toutes aux extrémités si je ne vous modère. C'est moi qui mets des bornes à tout, qui prends ce milieu si nécessaire et si difficile à trouver, et qui m'oppose à tous les excès.

La Prudence: Je vous avais toujours regardée comme opposés à la gourmandise, et rien de plus.

La Tempérance: C'est que vous ne me conaissez pas. Je détruis en effet la gourmandise et le luxe, je ne souffre aucun emportement. Non seulement je m'oppose à tout mal, mais il faut que je règle le bien. Sans moi la Justice serait insupportable à la faiblesse des hommes, la Force les mettrait au désespoir, la Prudence empêcherait souvent de prendre des partis qu'il faut prendre, et perdrait son temps à tout peser. Mais avec moi la Justice devient capable de ménagement, la Force s'adoucit, la Prudence donne des conseils, sans trop affaiblir; elle ne va ni trop vite ni trop lentement, et en un mot je suis la remède à toutes les extrémités.

La Justice: Je suis surprise de ce que j'entends. Ne conviendrez-vous que la sagesse se peut passer de vous?

LA TEMPÉRANCE: Vous répondriez vous-même à cette question, car vous n'ignorez pas qu'il faut être sobre dans la sagesse. Ne cherchez pas davantage, Mademoiselle, on ne peut rien faire de bon sans moi.

LA PRUDENCE: Au moins ferons-nous notre salut sans vous?

LA TEMPÉRANCE: Difficilement. J'ai à tempérer le zèle trop actif, amer et indiscret. Il faut que je fasse prendre une conduite qui évite les extrémités, que je modère l'inclination à donner et l'inclination à garder, que je règle le temps de la prière, les austérités, le recueillement, le silence, les bonnes oeuvres, que j'abrège une exhortation, que je raccourcisse une consultation, un examen, enfin j'ai à modérer jusqu'aux désirs de la ferveur.

LA JUSTICE: Vous avez bien des affaires.

LA TEMPÉRANCE: Mon caractère ne me permet pas d'en être fatiguée. J'agis doucement et paisiblement.

LA FORCE: Tout cela conclut que nous avons besoin de vous, mais n'avez-vous besoin de personne?

LA TEMPÉRANCE: Non, je me suffis à moi-même.

LA FORCE: Ne peut-on pas être trop modéré?

LA TEMPÉRANCE: Ce ne serait plus modération, car elle ne souffre ni le trop ni le trop peu.

LA PRUDENCE: Vous me dégoûtez de mon état, et j'envie le vôtre.

LA TEMPÉRANCE: C'est que vous aviez trop bonne opinion de vous; cependant vous êtes toutes très estimables. Y a-t-il rien de plus beau que la Justice, toujours fondée sur la vérité, incapable de prévention, incorruptible, désintéressée, se jugeant elle-même malgré son amour-propre?

LA JUSTICE: Avec tout cela vous dites que je suis haïe.

LA TEMPÉRANCE: C'est que vous ne flattez pas, et on veut être flatté.

LA FORCE: Et pour moi je gâterai tout sans vous?

LA TEMPÉRANCE: Oui, mais vous faites merveille avec moi, vous animez toutes les vertus, vous poursuivez vos entreprises jusqu'à la fin, et vous ne vous lassez jamais.

LA PRUDENCE: Et je ne fais qu'hésiter.

LA TEMPÉRANCE: Vous savez choisir les temps, vous êtes accommodante, vous prévoyez les inconvénients, vous prenez des mesures, et vous êtes absolument nécessaire, pourvu que je vous garantisse de l'extrémité.

LA FORCE: Vous voulez nous consoler, mais enfin notre personnage est inférieur au vôtre.

LA TEMPÉRANCE: Que serai-je sans vous? Employée seulement et souvent inutilement à m'opposer aux excès et aux passions des hommes. Mon bel endroit est d'être nécessaire pour modérer les vertus.

LA FORCE: Sommes-nous des vertus si nous avons besoin de vous pour éviter quelque extrémité? La vertu tient le milieu.

LA TEMPÉRANCE: C'est moi qui fais connaître ce milieu. Je ne dis pas que vous fissiez de grands maux, mais vous pourriez aller trop loin.

LA JUSTICE: Je pourrais être trop juste?

LA TEMPÉRANCE: Non, mais juger trop souvent, être par là à la charge de tout le monde. La Force jointe à la sécheresse de la Justice la rendrait encore plus fâcheuse.

LA PRUDENCE: Je pourrais y rémedier.

LA TEMPÉRANCE: Vous les embarrasseriez souvent. Nous avons besoin les unes des autres. Vivons bien ensemble et sans jalousie. Unissons-nous contre la corruption du monde, plus forte que toutes les vertus, si la grâce ne venait à leur secours.

Note: This text is based on Madame de Maintenon, *Sur les vertus cardinales,* in Madame de Maintenon, *Conseils et instructions aux demoiselles pour leur conduite dans le monde,* ed. Théophile Lavallée (Paris: Charpentier, 1857), 1.258–261.

Notes

Chapter I. Introduction: Salon Philosophy

1. The term "Augustinianism" is widely but loosely used to designate a certain current of piety, theology, and philosophy in French Catholicism during the seventeenth century. Literally the term designates a renewed enthusiasm for the works and theories of St. Augustine. New critical editions of Augustine, starting with the six-volume Louvain edition (1576–1577), and fresh French translations, especially by the Jansenists Antoine Arnauld and Robert Arnauld d'Andilly, assured wide diffusion of the Augustinian canon. So pervasive was Augustine's influence on the literature of the period that literary critic Philippe Sellier simply calls the era "the century of Saint Augustine." The century's Augustinianism, however, involved more than reference to a patristic text; it indicated a particular outlook on the controversies of the age. In the longstanding quarrel concerning grace, the Augustinians stressed divine initiative in salvation and minimized the role of human freedom and cooperation. In moral matters they insisted on a rigorous interpretation of the law and denounced apparent compromises with the world, such as attendance at theatrical performances. In philosophy they disdained the Aristotelianism of the Sorbonne as an arid exercise in logic, tainted by biological materialism. Suspicious of his methodic doubt, they still welcomed Descartes's *cogito* argument and ontological proofs for God's existence as a salutary retrieval of earlier Augustinian theories. In politics the Augustinians allied themselves with the *parti dévot*, the political faction that insisted that French foreign policy should promote a coalition of the European Catholic powers to fight Protestantism and Islam. Throughout the century they bitterly criticized the nationalist policies of the French throne, which systematically waged war on Spain and sought alliances with Protestant and Moslem powers to enhance French territory and prestige.

2. The following works study the intellectual development of women in seventeenth-century France: Gustave Reynier, *La femme au XVIIe siècle* (Paris: Plon, 1933); Wendy Gibson, *Women in Seventeenth-Century France* (New York: St. Martin's Press, 1989); Linda Timmermans, *L'accès des femmes à la culture* (Paris: Champion, 1993).

3. For a study of the role of nuns and laywomen in the schools of the French Counter-Reformation, see Elizabeth Rapley, *The Dévotes: Women and Church in Seventeenth-Century France* (Kingston, Ont.: McGill-Queen's University Press, 1989).

4. See St. François de Sales, *Introduction to the Devout Life,* trans. John K. Ryan (Garden City, N.Y.: Doubleday, 1972).

5. See Madeleine Daniélou, *Madame de Maintenon éducatrice* (Paris: Bloud et Gay, 1946), 156.

6. See Jacqueline Pascal, *Règlement pour les enfants*, in *Lettres, opuscules et mémoires de Madame Périer et de Jacqueline, soeurs de Pascal, et Marguerite Périer, sa nièce, publiés sur les manuscrits originaux par M. P. Faugère,* ed. M. P. Faugère (Paris: A. Vaton, 1845), 252.

7. See Marcel Langlois, *Madame de Maintenon* (Paris: Plon, 1932), 9.

8. Anne Le Ferre Dacier (1651–1720), classicist and translator; renowned for her translation of Homer into French.

9. Marie-Madeleine-Gabrielle de Rochechouart de Mortemart, Abbesse de Fontevrault (1645–1704), translator of Plato and author of treatises on politeness and monastic rule.

10. Antoinette du Ligier de la Garde, Mme Deshoulières (1630–1694), leading poet, translator of Lucretius, and disciple of Epicurus and of Gassendi. See chapter 3.

11. François Poullain de la Barre, *De l'égalité des deux sexes, discours psychique et moral, où l'on voit l'importance de se défaire des préjugés* (Paris: Jean du Puis, 1656).

12. René Descartes, "Lettre au Père Vatier" (22 février 1638), in *Oeuvres de Descartes,* vol. I, ed. Charles Adam and Paul Tannery (Paris: Cerf, 1899), 560.

13. See Blaise Pascal, *Provinciales,* in *Oeuvres complètes,* ed. Jacques Chevalier (Paris: Gallimard-Pléiade, 1954), 684.

14. Nicolas Malebranche, *De la recherche de la vérité,* in *Oeuvres complètes,* vol. 1, ed. Geneviève Rodis-Lewis (Paris: Gallimard-Pléiade, 1979), 200.

15. Jacques Rouhault (1620–1675), Cartesian philosopher, physicist, and mathematician. His major work was *Oeuvres posthumes* (Paris: Desprez, 1682), a collection of scientific treatises.

16. See Jacques Rouhault, *Traité de physique* (Paris: Desprez, 1676).

17. Claude Clerselier (1614–1684), early editor of the works of Descartes. He popularized Cartesian philosophy and physics.

18. Louis de Lesclache (1620–1671), philosopher and teacher; author of works on logic (1648), spelling (1649), moral philosophy (1655), the passions (1660), and the history of philosophy (1665).

19. See Louis de Lesclache, *Abrégé de la philosophie en tables* (Paris: s.n., 1652).

20. For a discussion of the intersection between philosophical and scientific formation of women during this period, see Reynier, *La femme au XVIIe siècle,* 51–55.

21. See Bernard le Bovier, M. de Fontenelle, *Éloge des savants* (Paris: Vrin, 1981); based on the edition of 1767.

22. François de Grenaille, sieur de Chatounières, *L'honneste fille,* vol. 1 (Paris: Paslé, 1639), vols. 2–3 (Paris: Sommaville et Quinet, 1640).

23. See Poullain de la Barre, *De l'égalité des deux sexes.*

24. See Marie-Éléonore de Rohan, Abbesse de Malnoue, *La morale du sage* (Paris: Claude Barbin, 1667), 3–10.

25. The following works provide detailed studies of the salons of the period: Roger Picard, *Les salons littéraires et la société française 1610–1789* (New York: Brentano's, 1943); Elizabeth C. Goldsmith, *"Exclusive Conversations": The Art of Interaction in Seventeenth-Century France* (Philadelphia: University of Pennsylvania Press, 1988); Carolyn C. Lougée, *Le Paradis des Femmes: Women, Salons, and Social Stratification in Seventeenth-Century France* (Princeton, N.J.: Princeton University Press, 1976); Jolanta K. Pekacz, *Conservative Tradition in Pre-Revolutionary France: Parisian Salon Women* (New York: Peter Lang, 1999).

26. Marguerite de Valois (1553–1615), French queen. She hosted a circle of artists and poets; was the patron of Ronsard; and authored poetry, memoirs, and letters.

27. See Timmermans, *L'accès des femmes,* 177ff.

28. For a discussion of the link between letter-writing and conversation, see Goldsmith, *"Exclusive Conversations,"* 28–39.

29. Marie de Rabutin-Chantal, marquise de Sévigné (1626–1696), salon hostess, letter-writer, and partisan of Descartes along with her daughter, Mme de Grignan.

30. Anne-Marie Louise d'Orléans, duchesse de Montpensier (1627–1693), salon hostess and partisan of the Fronde, celebrated for her literary portraits. Her memoirs were published posthumously in 1724.

31. See Antoine de Baudeau, sieur de Somaize, *Le grand dictionnaire des prétieuses, historique, poétique, géographique, cosmographique et armorique,* 2 vols. (Paris: s.n., 1661).

32. See Jean de la Forge, *Cercle des femmes savantes* (Paris: Loyson, 1663).

33. See Marguerite Buffet, *Éloges des illustres scavantes tant anciennes que modernes* (Paris: Jean Cusson fils, 1668).

34. See Gilles Ménage, *Historia mulierum philosopharum* (Lugduni: Apud Anissonios, Joan, Poseul, et Claudium Rigaud, 1690).

35. For a description of the history and structure of Rambouillet, see Barbara Krajewska, *Mythes et découvertes: Le salon littéraire de Madame de Rambouillet dans les lettres des contemporains* (Paris and Seattle: Papers on French Seventeenth-Century Literature, 1990).

36. See Picard, *Les salons littéraires,* 109.

37. For a discussion of the "literature of the desert," in which both La Vallière and Sablière figure prominently, see Bernard Beugnot, *Le discours de la retraite au XVIIe siècle* (Paris: Presses Universitaires de France, 1996).

38. The argument in this subchapter is indebted to the earlier work of Eileen O'Neill on the causes of the "loss" of women philosophers in the early modern period: see Eileen O'Neill, "Disappearing Ink: Early Modern Women Philosophers and Their Fate in History," in *Philosophy in a Feminist Voice: Critiques and Reconstructions,* ed. Janet Kourany (Princeton, N.J.: Princeton University Press, 1998), 17–62.

39. A typical example of this rationalistic tendency is Erica Harth's critique of the philosophical work of the salon as too tied to religious orthodoxy. "Excluded from the more powerful dissent of the academy and harboring possibly more subversive ideals of their own, women had little opportunity for contributing to the larger historical movement of the seventeenth and eighteenth centuries by which a discourse of dissent rose to dominance" (Erica Harth, *Cartesian Women: Versions and Subversions of Rational Discourse in the Old Regime* [Ithaca, N.Y.: Cornell University Press, 1992], 63). The presupposition here is that philosophical vigor, at least in this period, is tied to religious skepticism.

40. A recent example occurs in Simone Bertière, *Les femmes du Roi-Soleil* (Paris: Éditions de Fallois, 1998), which provides an excellent study of the relationship of Louis XIV to Louise de la Vallière and to Madame de Maintenon, as respectively mistress and wife. Bertière, however, dismisses their theoretical contributions. On La Vallière's book on God's mercy: "Nothing very original in this text with its verbose phrases. It's entirely conventional" (202). On Maintenon's writings: "For years she worked to construct, to sculpt her posthumous image through her letters, lectures, and educational chats. She carefully mixed moral teaching with properly slanted revelations about her life" (546).

41. See Gibson, *Women in Seventeenth-Century France,* 38ff.; and Harth, *Cartesian Women,* 64–122.

42. See Nicolas Boileau-Despréaux, *Satire X,* in *Oeuvres complètes,* ed. Françoise Escal (Paris: Gallimard-Pléiade, 1966), 62–80.

Chapter II. Madame de Sablé: A Jansenist Code of Moderation

1. Sainte-Beuve, *Port-Royal,* ed. Maxime Le Roy (Paris: Gallimard, 1953–1955), 3.70–71.

2. This subchapter uses biographical information concerning Mme de Sablé contained in the following sources: Victor Cousin, *Madame de Sablé* (Paris: Didier, 1854); Vincenza Guidarelli, "The Salon of Mme de Sablé: Foyer of Literary Jansenism" (Ph.D. dissertation,

Fordham University, 1979), 7–151; Nicolas Ivanoff, *La Marquise de Sablé et son salon* (Paris: Les Presses Modernes, 1927).

Also central for biographical information on Sablé are the *Portefeuilles de Dr. Valant* conserved at the Bibliothèque Nationale de France (Richelieu) in the *Fonds français* under nos. 17044–17058. These manuscripts, collected by Sablé's personal physician, Valant, contain much of Sablé's correspondence and many of the papers relative to her salon.

Hereafter the *Portefeuilles de Dr. Valant* will be cited as BNF(R) Ffr., followed by the folder number(s).

3. The descendant of the sixteenth-century Catholic *Ligue,* the *parti dévot* was a loose coalition of militant Catholics attempting to make religious principles the centerpiece of French politics. In domestic policy they supported programs of moral reform for the clergy and the court. In foreign policy they supported a great coalition of Catholic powers (France, Spain, Austria) to oppose Protestantism. They bitterly contested the nationalist foreign policy of the French monarchy (Louis XIII/Richelieu; Louis XIV/Mazarin), which opposed Spain and which formed alliances with non-Catholic powers (Sweden, the Netherlands, the Ottoman Empire) to aggrandize French territory.

4. See Baltasar Gracián (1601–1658), *Oráculo manual y arte de prudencia; the Spanish text and a new English translation,* ed. L. B. Walton (New York: Salloch, 1953).

5. Mme de Motteville, *Mémoires* (Amsterdam: Chauguion, 1750), 1.13.

6. See Tallement des Réaux, *Les historiettes,* ed. Louis-Jean-Nicolas Monmerqué (Paris: Garnier frères, 1932), 3.75ff.

7. Catherine de Vivonne, Marquise de Rambouillet (1588–1665), conducted her salon in the celebrated *chambre bleue.* Devoted primarily to literature and to drama, her salon also grouped many partisans of the Fronde.

8. Vincent Voiture (1597–1648) was a poet and essayist who dominated the literary discussions of the Hôtel de Rambouillet.

9. See Jean Chapelain, *Lettres de Jean Chapelain,* ed. Philippe Tamizey de Larroque (Paris: Imprimerie Nationale, 1880), 1.639–640.

10. Madeleine de Scudéry (1607–1701), as an author primarily known for *Artamène ou le Grand Cyrus* (1649–1653), a novelistic treatment of members of the Fronde. Her final works elaborate her moral theories: *Conversations morales* (1686); *Nouvelles considérations morales* (1688); *Entretiens sur la morale* (1692).

11. Valentin Conrart (1603–1675) was an author and a co-founder of the Académie française. His principal work, *Mémoires sur l'histoire de son temps* (Paris: Monmergué, 1825), is useful for its account of the Parisian salons of the period.

12. Madeleine de Scudéry, *Artamène ou le Grand Cyrus* (Paris: Courbé, 1650), 6.116.

13. Anne-Marie-Louise d'Orléans, Duchesse de Montpensier, Fronde leader, disgraced in 1652, author and head of a literary salon. Her principal works include *Rélations de l'Île invisible* (1659), *Divers portraits* (1659), and *Mémoires* (1724).

14. See Mlle de Montpensier, *L'histoire de la Princess de Paphlagonie,* in Jean Segrais, *Oeuvres* (Geneva: Slatkine, 1968), 218.

15. Ibid.

16. See Guidarelli, "Salon of Mme de Sablé," 9–96.

17. See Antoine Arnauld, *De la fréquente communion,* 9th edition (Lyon: Plaignaud, 1683).

18. See Guidarelli, "Salon of Mme de Sablé," 105–115.

19. For a survey of the "crisis of the signature," see Louis Cognet, *Le Jansénisme* (Paris: Presses universitaires de France, 1961), 48–84.

20. Mme de Sablé, "Lettre à Choiseul," BNF(R) Ffr. 10584, f.75.

21. Mme de Sablé, "Lettre au Cardinal de Rospigliosi," BNF(R) Ffr. 10583, f.6.

22. Marie de Rabutin-Chantal, Marquise de Sévigné (1626–1696), author of letters,

which were successively shaped into collections: *Mémoires de Bussy* (1696), *Lettres* (1697), *Nouvelles lettres* (1709).

23. Marie-Madeleine Pioche de la Vergne, comtesse de la Fayette (1634–1692), novelist and epistoler. Her principal works included *La Princess de Clèves* (1678) and *Histoire de Mme Henriette d'Angleterre* (1700).

24. Marie-Madeleine-Gabrielle de Rochechouart de Mortemart, Abbesse de Fontevrault (1645–1704) was an essayist and a classicist reputed to have translated Plato's *Symposium*. Her major work was *Question sur la politesse*, available in *Recueil de divers écrits sur l'amour et l'amitié* (Paris: s.n., 1736).

25. Marie-Éléonore de Rohan, Abbesse de Caen et de Malnoue (1628–1681) was a reformer, classicist, and author. Her major work was *Morale du sage et paraphrase des psaumes de la pénitence* (Paris: Barbin, 1667).

26. Gilberte Pascal Périer (1620–1687) was an epistoler and the biographer of brother Blaise and sister Jacqueline Pascal. See her *La vie de Monsieur Pascal suvivi de la vie de Jacqueline Pascal* (Paris: La Table Ronde, 1994).

27. Antoine Arnauld (1612–1695), priest, Jansenist leader and philosopher. His principal works include *La logique de Port-Royal* (1662), dedicated to Mme de Sablé, and *Réflexions sur la nature et la grâce* (1685).

28. Pierre Nicole (1625–1695), moralist and professor at the schools of Port-Royal, was coauthor (with Arnauld) of *Logique de Port-Royal*. In 1671 he published the first of thirteen volumes of *Essais morales*.

29. Jean Domat (1625–1696), legal scholar, editor of Pascal. His major works include *Les lois civiles* (1689–1694) and *Le droit public* (1697).

30. Jacques Esprit (1611–1678), Oratorian priest and essayist. His principal works include *La fausseté des vertus humaines* (1678) and *Maximes politiques mises en vers* (1669), both composed in Sablé's salon.

31. Blaise Pascal (1623–1663), philosopher, mathematician, and participant in Sablé's salon, entered the Port-Royal circle in 1654. Pascal's *Provinciales* (1656–1657) and the posthumous *Pensées* reflect the epigrammatic genres and Jansenist anthropology of the salon.

32. François, Duc de la Rochefoucauld (1613–1680) achieved literary fame through the publication of his *Maximes* and his *Mémoires*. His early career was spent in political intrigue. Appointed governor of the province of Poitou in 1646, he quickly become a partisan of the aristocratic leaders of the Fronde (1648–1653). Wounded in three battles, he permanently lost his health. For his part in the rebellion he suffered imprisonment, exile, and the destruction of his ancestral castle. A close friend and protegé of Madame de Sablé, La Rochefoucauld frequented her salon and mastered the genre of the *maxime*. The publication of his *Réflexions ou sentences et maximes morales* in 1665 established his literary reputation. Although his uncompromising dissection of the corruption hidden behind apparent virtue was widely praised by the Jansenist members of Sablé's salon, La Rochefoucauld himself remained aloof from the Jansenist movement.

33. A Jesuit theologian, Molina published *De concordia liberii arbitrii cum divinae gratiae donis* in Lisbon in 1588. In the simmering dispute over the relationship between divine grace and human freedom, Molina stressed the role of human freedom and moral responsibility. The "Augustinians" (including the Jansenists) condemned the work as denying the necessity of grace in salvation.

34. Dominique Bouhours, S.J. (1628–1702), literary critic and spiritual author. His major work is *Manière de bien penser dans les ouvrages d'esprit* (Paris: Mabre-Cramoisy, 1687).

35. René Rapin, S.J. (1621–1687), classicist, literary critic, and opponent of Jansenism. His major work is *Réflexions sur la poétique d'Aristote* (Paris: Chez F. Muguet, 1674).

36. See Cousin, *Madame de Sablé,* 72.

37. See Marquis de Sourdis, "Pourqoui l'eau monte dans un tuyau," BNF(R) Ffr. 17050, f.20.

38. Charlotte Saumaize de Chazon, comtesse de Brégy (1619–1696), poet and letter-writer. Her principal works include *Lettres et poésies* (Leyden: Antoine du Val, 1666).

39. See "Pensées sur l'esprit," BNF(R) Ffr. 17050, f.22.

40. See "Conférence sur le Calvinisme," BNF(R) Ffr. 17056, ff.17–19.

41. See Antoine Arnauld and Pierre Nicole, *De la perpétuité de la foi de l'église catholique* (Paris: Chez l'Abbé M., 1841).

42. See "Pensées sur la guerre," BNF(R) Ffr. 17056, f.26.

43. See Arnauld d'Andilly, "Pourquoi nous devons préférer nos amis à notre pays," BNF(R) Ffr. 10587, f.123.

44. Marquis de Sourdis, "Questions sur l'amour," BNF(R) Ffr. 17056, f.196.

45. Marquis de Sourdis, "De l'amour," BNF(R) Ffr. 17056, ff.197–198.

46. For a study of the genesis of the *Maximes,* see Susan Read Baker, *Collaboration et originalité chez La Rochefoucauld* (Gainesville: University of Florida Press, 1980).

47. See Cousin, *Madame de Sablé,* 132–143.

48. La Rochefoucauld, "Lettre à Sablé," in La Rochefoucauld, *Oeuvres complètes,* ed. Louis Martin-Chauffier (Paris: Gallimard-Pléiade, 1950), 481.

49. La Rochefoucauld, "Lettre à Sablé," BNF(R) Ffr. 17045, f.153.

50. Mme de Sablé, "Lettre à La Rochefoucauld," BNF(R) Ffr. 17045, f.155.

51. See Cousin, *Madame de Sablé,* 161–162.

52. Mme de Rohan, "Lettre à La Rochefoucauld," BNF(R) Ffr. 17045, ff.164–165.

53. Mme de Sablé, "Lettre à La Rochefoucauld," BNF(R) Ffr. 17048, f.369.

54. For a comparative presentation of the original Sablé draft with the *Journal des Savants* article, see Cousin, *Madame de Sablé,* 140–146.

55. Blaise Pascal, "Lettre à Mme de Sablé," BNF(R) Ffr. 17045, f.243.

56. Marquis de Sourdis, "Lettre à Mme de Sablé," BNF(R) Ffr. 17050, f.22.

57. Nicolas, Abbé d'Ailly (1640–1712), priest and author. He edited Sablé's *Maximes* (1678), to which he adds his own maxims under the pseudonymn "M.L.D." His principal work is *Sentiments et maximes sur ce qui se passe dans la société civile* (Paris: s.n., 1697).

58. See Mme de Sablé, *Maximes de Madame la Marquise de Sablé; suivies de Pensées de M.L.D.,* ed. Nicolas, Abbé d'Ailly (Paris: Mabre-Cramoisy, 1678). A reedition, *Maximes de Mme de Sablé,* ed. Damase Jouaust (Paris: Librairie des bibliophiles, 1870), was published in 322 copies. Unless otherwise noted, this chapter's citations of Sablé's *maximes* refer to the Jouaust edition. The translations from the French text are my own.

59. See Mme de Sablé, *Maximes.*

60. For a discussion of these misattributions, see Jean Lafond, *La Rochefoucauld: Maximes et refléxions* (Paris: Gallimard, 1978), 305.

61. For an inexpensive but scholarly edition of Sablé's *maximes,* see "Maximes de Madame de Sablé," in Jean Lafond, *La Rochefoucauld,* 227–247. For an accessible bilingual presentation, see Arthur Chandler, "Maxims of Madame de Sablé" (http://charon.sfsu.edu/sable).

62. Victor Cousin, *Madame de Sablé,* 84–85.

63. Jean Lafond, *La Rochefoucauld,* 303–304.

64. Mme de Sablé, *Maximes,* 14. For the rest of this chapter, citation of the *Maximes* will be by page number in the text.

65. See Pierre Nicole, *Traité de la Comédie,* ed. Georges Couton (Paris: Les Belles Lettres, 1961). The leading moral theologian of the Jansenist circle, Nicole (1625–1695) insisted that attendance at theatrical performances contradicted Christian morals, because of the

vanity nurtured in both the actors and the audience, even when the plays were not particularly licentious. The quarrel over the theatre was part of the larger polemic between Jansenists and Jesuits over morality. The Jesuits provided a qualified defense of theatrical performances, deeming them worthwhile when they lead to the moral and religious edification of their audience. Even many non-Jansenists, notably Bossuet, supported a total ban on Christian attendance at plays.

66. On the Christian critique of the dramatic profession, see Herbert Thurston, "Theatre," in *The Catholic Encyclopedia*, vol. 14 (New York: Appleton, 1912), 559–561.

67. See Blaise Pascal, "Divertissements," in *Oeuvres complètes*, ed. Louis Lafuma (Paris: Seuil, 1963), 516–518.

68. See Cousin, *Madame de Sablé*, 79–80.

69. La Rochefoucauld, *Oeuvres complètes*, 255.

Chapter III. Madame Deshoulières: A Naturalist Creed

1. See Madame and Mademoiselle Deshoulières, *Oeuvres*, 2 vols. (Paris: Stéréotype d'Hernan, 1803 [An XI]). This edition is cited internally in this chapter as *D*/volume/page. The translations from the French are my own.

2. See Pierre Leguay, "Des Houlières," in *Dictionnaire de Biographie française*, vol. 10 (Paris: Letouzey et Ané, 1965), 1387–1389. Earlier literary critics include Sauvigny, La Harpe, and Sainte-Beuve.

3. See Eustache Le Noble, *Le Triomphe de Madame des Houlières, reçue dixième muse au Parnasse* (Paris: Claude Mazuel, 1694).

4. Writing under the pseudonym "Amarylis," Deshoulières published in *Le mercure galant*, the leading literary periodical in Paris.

5. For a biographical sketch of Deshoulières, see Frédéric Lachèvre, *Les derniers libertins* (Paris: E. Champion, 1924), 25–63.

6. See Jean Hesnault (1611–1682), *Les oeuvres de Jean Dehénault . . . (le maître de madame des Houlières), précédées d'une notice par Frédéric Lachèvre* (Paris: Champion, 1922).

7. Pierre Gassendi (1592–1655), philosopher and Catholic priest. For a biographical sketch, see Lisa T. Sarasohn, *Gassendi's Ethics* (Ithaca: Cornell University Press, 1996), 1–29. Sarasohn argues that Gassendi attempted to reconcile Epicurean naturalism with Catholic orthodoxy. For example, Gassendi transforms the Epicurean account of moral behavior as the pursuit of pleasure and avoidance of pain by identifying the Beatific Vision as the highest pleasure open to humans. While following Gassendi in affirming God's existence, Deshoulières treats other Christian doctrines, such as those of human immortality and divine providence, with greater skepticism.

8. Esprit Fléchier (1632–1710), bishop of Nîmes; prolific author of works in history, oratory, poetry, and theology; renowned for funeral elegies. He was elected to the Acadèmie française in 1673. His major works include *Histoire de Théodose le Grand* (1679), *Panégyriques et autres sermons* (1710), and *Lettres choisies* (1715).

9. Jacques Vallée, sieur Des Barreaux (1602–1673), a poet celebrated for sonnets and a religious skeptic.

10. Jules Mascaron (1634–1703), bishop of Agen; renowned preacher. His major work is *Oraisons funèbres* (1704).

11. Isaac de Benserade (1613–1691), poet and dramatist; defender of the rationalist Bayle; elected to the Académie française in 1674.

12. Philippe Quinault (1635–1688), dramatic author and collaborator with Lulli on operas and ballets. His major works include *Proserpine* (1681), *Amadis* (1684), and *Roland* (1685).

13. Paul Pellisson (1624–1693), French civil servant allied with the party of Fouquet. He was the author of several historical works, including *Histoire de l'académie française jusqu'en 1652* (1653) and *Histoire de Louis XIV* (1749).

14. Gilles Ménage (1613–1692), lexicographer. His major work is *Dictionnaire étymologique* (1650).

15. Bernard de la Monnoye (1641–1728), jurist and prolific author. He was elected to the Académie française in 1713. Among his major works are *Les noëls bourgignons* (1700–1702) and *Poésies françaises* (1716).

16. See Eugène Asse, "Des Houlières," in *La Grande Encyclopédie*, vol. 14 (Paris: Grande Encyclopédie, 1960), 238–239.

17. See Nicolas Boileau-Despréaux, *Satires X*, in *Oeuvres complètes*, ed. Françoise Escal (Paris: Gallimard-Pléiade, 1966), 73–74.

18. See Mme Deshoulières, *Les poésies de Madame Deshoulières* (Paris: Veuve Mabre-Cramoisy, 1687). Subsequent editions of her poetry were published in 1688, 1694, 1695, 1702, 1703, 1707, 1709, 1724, 1732, 1745, 1747, 1753, 1754, 1759, 1762, 1764, 1777, 1780, 1799, and 1803.

19. See Madame and Mademoiselle Deshoulières, *Oeuvres*, 2 vols. (Paris: Stéréotype d'Hernan, 1803 [An XI].

20. Pierre Bayle, *Dictionnaire historique et critique*, 4th ed. (Amsterdam: Brunel, 1730), 2.721 b.

21. Ibid., 3.560 a.

22. See Voltaire, *Correspondance*, 13 vols., ed. Théodore Besterman (Paris: Gallimard-Pléiade, 1978–1993), 1.645; 4.794; 9.850; 10.875; 11.654, 11.762.

23. See Jean-Jacques Rousseau, *Correspondance complète de Rousseau*, 52 vols., ed. R. A. Leigh (Oxford: Voltaire Foundation, 1965–1998), 17.209, 222.

24. Antoine Adam, *Les Libertins au XVIIe siècle* (Paris: Buchet/Chastel, 1986), 252.

25. Ann-Marie-Louise d'Orléans, duchess of Montpensier, sympathizer with the Fronde, conducted her literary salon at the Palais du Luxembourg. Her chief literary works are *Mémoires* (1724), *Rélations de l'Île invisible* (1659), and *Divers Portraits* (1659).

26. Madeleine de Souvré, the marquise de Sablé (1599–1678), conducted salons at the Place Royal (1644–1655) and on the grounds of the Jansenist convent of Port-Royal (1655–1661, 1669–1678). See chapter 2.

27. Vincenza C. Zema Guidarelli, "The Salon of Madame de Sablé: Foyer of Literary Jansenism" (Ph.D. dissertation, Fordham University, 1979), 421.

28. See Lachèvre, *Derniers libertins*, 40.

29. See Henri Busson, *La religion des classiques (1660–1685)* (Paris: Presses Universitaries de France, 1948), 110–130.

Chapter IV. Madame de la Sablière: The Ethics of the Desert

1. The definitive biography is contained in Vicomte Menjot d'Elbenne, *Madame de la Sablière: Ses pensées Chrétiennes et ses lettres à l'Abbé de Rancé* (Paris: Plon, 1923), 1–246. This work is hereafter referred to as *MDS*. The subdivisions of the book's collection of Sablière's writings are cited internally as follows: *MC* (*Maximes Chrétiennes*); *PC* (*Pensées Chrétiennes*); *L* (*Lettres de Madame de Sablière*). The translations from the French are my own. For a contemporary English sketch of Sablière, see Glenda Wall, "Marguerite Hessein de la Sablière," in *An Encyclopedia of Continental Women Writers*, ed. K. Wilson (New York: Garland, 1991), 2.1086–1087.

2. Cited by Madame de Sévigné in "Lettre au Comte de Bussy-Rabutin et à Madame de

Coligny" (30 Juillet 1677), in Madame de Sévigné, *Lettres,* ed. Émile Gérard-Gailly (Paris: Gallimard-Pléiade, 1955), 2.315.

3. Antoine Rambouillet, sieur de La Sablière (1624–1679). His son Nicolas Rambouillet de la Sablière posthumously published his father's collected poems in *Madrigaux de M.D.L.S.* (Paris: Barbin, 1680). Popular with both the reading and the critical public, Monsieur Sablière's madrigals underwent numerous re-editions (1681, 1687, 1705, 1758) and were anthologized in numerous poetry collections (1692, 1720, 1752, 1784) in the *ancien régime.* Charles Nodier's scholarly edition, *Madrigaux de Monsieur de la Sablière,* ed. Charles Nodier (Paris: Delange, 1825), launched the contemporary interest in the work of Sablière.

4. The three children were Anne de Rambouillet, Mme de Muysson (1655–1714); Nicolas de Rambouillet, seigneur de la Sablière (1656–1718); and Marguerite de Rambouillet, Mme de Mésangère et de Nocé (1658–1714). In the wake of the Revocation of the Edict of Nantes (1685), both Nicolas and Anne suffered imprisonment, confiscation of goods, and exile because of their Protestant faith. Nicolas fled to Denmark and England, where he occupied a series of high civic posts. Anne fled to Holland, where she assisted refugees. Marguerite converted to Catholicism and participated in the salon life of Paris. Fontenelle dedicated *Entretiens sur la pluralité des mondes* to her.

5. Christina-Augusta, Queen of Sweden (1626–1689), conducted a prestigious philosophical salon in Stockholm during her reign (1632–1654). Participants included Descartes, Grotius, Vossius, and Saumaise. She renounced the throne and converted to Catholicism in 1654. Her maxims and historical works are collected in *Mémoires concernant Christine, reine de Suède,* ed. Johann Arckenholz, 4 vols. (Amsterdam: P. Mortier, 1754–1760).

6. Jean Sobiesky (1624–1696), distinguished military hero, ruled as Polish king under the title John III (1676–1696).

7. Charles Perrault (1628–1703) was an essayist and historian who established his reputation by his collection of tales. He was elected to the Académie française in 1671. His major work is *Les histoires et contes du temps passé avec des moralités* (Paris, 1697).

8. Paul Pellisson (1624–1693) was a historian who fulfilled numerous offices in the court of Louis XIV. Among his major works are *Histoire de l'académie française jusqu'en 1652* (1653) and *Histoire de Louis XIV* (1749).

9. Isaac de Benserade (1613–1691), a poet and dramatist, was elected to the Académie française in 1674.

10. Bernard Le Bovier de Fontenelle (1657–1757) was a dramatist, essayist, and philosopher, and a partisan of Descartes. He was elected to the Académie française in 1691. His major works include *Entretiens sur la pluralité des mondes* (1686); *Éléments de la géométrie de l'infini* (1727); and *Théorie des tourbillons cartésiens* (1752).

11. Marie de Rabutin-Chantal, marquise de Sévigné (1626–1696), was a woman of letters renowned posthumously for her letters to her daughter. Her major published work is *Lettres* (Paris: s.n., 1725).

12. Anne-Thérèse de Marguenal de Courcelles, marquise de Lambert (1647–1733), prolific essayist and the head of a powerful Parisian salon. Her major works were in education: *Avis d'une mère à son fils* (1734) and *Avis d'une mère à sa fille* (1734).

13. Jean Racine (1639–1699), dramatist, ally of Jansenists; he was elected to the Académie française in 1673. His major works include *Phèdre* (1677), *Esther* (1689), and *Athalie* (1691).

14. Jean-Baptiste Poquelin, alias Molière (1622–1673), comic dramatist. Among his major works are *Le malade imaginaire* (1673), *Le tartuffe* (1664), and *Le misanthrope* (1666).

15. Pierre-Daniel Huet (1630–1721) was an erudite prelate who published numerous works in Latin and in French concerning patristics, philosophy, and theology. He was elected to the Académie française in 1674, and consecrated bishop of Avranches in 1689. A passionate Cartesian in his youth, he later opposed the Cartesian school. His principal

philosophical works include *Censura philosophia Cartesianae* (Paris, 1689); *Nouveau mémoire pour servir à l'histoire du Cartésianisme* (Paris, 1692); and *Traité philosophique de la faiblesse de l'esprit humain* (Amsterdam, 1723).

16. Jacques Testu, abbé de Belval (1626–1706), a renowned court preacher and literary figure, was elected to the Académie française in 1665. His major work is *Les doctrines de la raison selon les maximes de Senèque* (1696).

17. Dominique Bouhors, S.J. (1628–1702) was a prolific author who specialized in works of linguistics, literary criticism, and hagiography. His major work is *Manière de bien penser dans les ouvrages d'esprit* (1687).

18. François Bernier (1620–1688) was a medical doctor, teacher, and philosopher. Renowned for his travels in Asia and for his comparative study of Asian religions, Bernier established an international scholarly reputation with the publication of *Histoire de la dernière révolution des États du Grand Mogul,* 4 vols. (Paris, 1670–1671). His major philosophical work is *Traité du libre et du volontaire* (Paris, 1688).

19. Joseph Sauveur (1653–1716) established himself as a specialist in applied mathematics, hydraulics, engineering, and acoustics. He held the chair of mathematics at the Collège Royal (1686); was elected to the Academy of Sciences (1696); and served as Inspector for the Royal Engineer Corps (1703). Among his major works are *Détermination d'un son fixe* (1702) and *Applications des sons harmoniques* (1707).

20. Gilles Personne de Roberval (1602–1675) pioneered research in integrated calculus, in cartography, and in weights and measures. He participated in the scientific-philosophical circle led by Père Mersenne. A professor of philosophy in the Collège Gervais, he was appointed to the chair of mathematics at Collège Royal (1634), and was elected to the Royal Academy of Sciences (1666).

21. Guichard-Joseph du Verney (1648–1730) was a popular professor of anatomy at Saint-Côme. His lectures and public experiments attracted large audiences. He was elected to the Académie royale des sciences (1674), and nominated to the chair of anatomy at the Jardin du Roi (1679). His principal work is *Traité de l'origine de l'ouïe* (Paris, 1683).

22. Giovanni Domenico Cassini (1625–1712) established himself as a distinguished astronomer and observatory director, first in Italy, then in France. His research advanced knowledge in planet rotation, in the moons of planets, and in comet structure. He served as professor of astronomy at the University of Bologna (1650–1669) and director of the Royal Observatory of Paris (1671–1712). His major work is *Opera astronomica* (1666).

23. See Marilyn Ogilvie-Bailey, "La Sablière, Marguerite Hessein de," in *Women in Science: Antiquity through the Nineteenth Century: A Biographical Dictionary* (Cambridge, Mass.: MIT Press, 1986), 118–119; "De la Sablière," *Sky & Telescope* 14, no. 1 (1954): 8.

24. See François Bernier, *Abrégé de la philosophie de M. Gassendi* (Lyon: Moulu, 1675).

25. See François Bernier, *Doutes sur quelques-uns des principaux chapitres de l'Abrégé de la philosophie de Gassendi* (Paris: 1682).

26. Originally published in the *Journal des Savants,* Bernier's essay was reprinted in *Mercure de France,* December 1722, 61–70.

27. Antoine Menjot, *Opuscules posthumes de M. Menjot* (Amsterdam: Desbordes, 1697), 134.

28. See Pierre Bayle, *Nouvelles de la république des lettres* (Amsterdam: Desbordes, 1685), 1008.

29. See Voltaire, "Lettre à M. R. à Cirey; June 20, 1738," in *Oeuvres de Voltaire,* ed. M. Beuchot (Paris: Didot, 1831), 53.164.

30. Jean de la Fontaine (1621–1695) was a prolific author who wrote in a wide variety of genres, including poetry, drama, opera libretto, and translations from the classics. He established his literary reputation as a master of the tale and of the fable. His major works include *Contes et nouvelles* (Paris: Barbin, 1665) and *Fables choisies en vers par M. de la Fontaine* (Paris: Barbin, 1668). He was elected to the Académie française in 1683.

31. La Fontaine, *Discours à Madame de la Sablière (sur L'Âme des Animaux),* critical edition by H. Busson (Paris: Droz, 1938), 50.

32. See La Fontaine, "Remerciement du Sieur de la Fontaine a l'Académie française," in *Oeuvres diverses,* ed. Pierre Clarac (Paris: Gallimard, 1958), 640–646.

33. Madame de Sévigné, "Lettre à Mme de Grignan (21 juin 1680)," in Madame de Sévigné, *Lettres,* 2.315.

34. For centuries Catholic devotional literature has represented Mme de la Sablière as a "Magdalen" of the *grand siècle,* a woman who publicly repented of her sexual sins after a dramatic conversion. For a modern example of this hagiographic approach to Sablière, see Hugh Francis Blunt, *The Great Magdalens* (New York: Macmillan, 1928).

35. Père René Rapin (1621–1687) was a Jesuit priest, poet, literary critic, and classicist. He published numerous books in both Latin and French. Among his major works are *Hortorum libri IV* (1665), *Observations sur Horace et Virgile* (1669), and *Réflexions sur la Poétique d'Aristote* (1674).

36. See Antoine Menjot, *Opuscules posthumes,* 200–201.

37. See Nicolas Boileau-Despréaux, "Satire X: Sur les Femmes," in *Oeuvres Complètes de Boileau,* ed. Françoise Escal (Paris: Plon, 1966), 1.160.

38. In her salon, Mme de la Sablière introduced a minor revolution in tea drinking. In order to preserve her eggshell teacups from overly hot tea, she began the custom of pouring milk into tea. See "1680—Madame de la Sablière" in "Tea History" (www.tealand.com/TeaHistory).

39. Jean-Armand le Bouthillier de Rancé (1626–1700), scion of a wealthy family, pursued a worldly ecclesiastical career. In 1637, he became a canon of the Cathedral of Notre Dame, the Abbot of the Cistercian Abbey of La Trappe, and the recipient of numerous other ecclesiastical benefices. After a period of conversion (1657–1662), he renounced his wealth and introduced a series of austere reforms at La Trappe. A prolific writer who had published an edition of Anacreon with Greek notes at the age of twelve, Abbot Rancé produced a series of influential books and pamphlets on ascetical practice. Although an explicit opponent of Jansenist theology, his rigorist penitential practices and his opposition to moral casuistry, which he condemned as laxist, indicated sympathy with Jansenist spirituality.

40. Rancé himself translated into French the works of St. Dorotheus, a Greek patristic and ascetical author. See Dorothée de Gaza, *Les instructions de saint Dorothée, père de l'Église grecque, et abbé d'un monastère de la Palestine,* trans. Armand le Bouthillier de Rancé (Paris: F. Muguet, 1686).

41. See *Réflexions ou sentences et maximes morales de Monsieur de la Rochefoucauld, Maximes de Madame la marquise de Sablé. Pensées diverses de M.L.D. et les Maximes Chrétiennes de M***** (Amsterdam: Pierre Mortier, 1705), 277–310.

42. See *Réflexions, sentences et maximes morales, mises en ordre, avec des notes politiques et historiques,* ed. Abraham Nicolas, Sieur Amelot de la Houssaye (Paris: Etienne Ganeau, 1725), 251–276.

43. See *Les pensées, maximes et réflexions morales de François VI, duc de la Rochefoucauld, avec des notes critiques, morales, politiques et historiques sur chacune de ses pensées, par Amelot de la Houssaye et l'abbé de la Roche, et des Maximes Chrétiennes par Madame de la Sablière* (Paris: Pissot, 1777).

44. See Wall, "Marguerite Hessein de la Sablière," 1086–1087; Vincenza C. Zema Guidarelli, "The Salon of Mme Sablé: Foyer of Literary Jansenism" (Ph.D. dissertation, Fordham University, 1979), 396–404; Joseph Bédier and Paul Hazard, *Littérature française* (Paris: Larousse, 1948), 1.435–437.

45. Rancé himself composed several works written in the form of maxims. See Armand Jean le Bouthillier de Rancé, *Maximes Chrétiennes et morales,* 2 vols. (Delft: H. van Rhyn, 1699).

46. For a summary of the major tenets of Catholic casuistry in the seventeenth century,

see Albert Jonsen and Stephen Toulmin, *The Abuse of Casuistry: A History of Moral Reasoning* (Berkeley: University of California Press, 1988) and Edmund Leites, ed., *Conscience and Casuistry in Early Modern Europe* (Cambridge: Cambridge University Press, 1988).

47. In the *Provinciales* (1656–1659), Blaise Pascal stated the tutiorist position in classic form. Starting with Provincial Letter no. 5, Pascal attacked the system of probabilism, especially as presented by the works of the Jesuit casuist Escobar. Like other Jansenists, Pascal feared that probabilism prevented the Christian from undertaking a rigorous search for the morally certain course of action and seduced the Christian into compromises that flattered the agent's vices. For the tutiorist, strict moral certitude concerning the proper course of conduct was allied to the struggle against self-illusion and moral decadence.

48. Devised to help Christians resolve a perplexed conscience, these systems of casuistry differed as to the degree of "probability" (technically, the level of "solid justifying reasons") a particular course of action should possess so that an upright moral agent might choose it. The probabilists argued that a proposed course of action needed only solid reasons to commend it as a reasonable choice. According to the probabilists, even if another course of action in a dilemma seemed *more* solid (*probable*), the agent could choose the *less* probable course, as long as there were still solid reasons justifying it. The equiprobabilists argued that in a dilemma one could choose a course of action only if the reasons justifying it were equal in gravity to those supporting the strongest of the other possible courses of actions. The probabiliorists argued that one was bound always to choose the most probable course of action, that is, that option with the most solid set of reasons justifying it. For a presentation of these various schools of moral philosophy, employed for the resolution of a doubtful conscience, see Austin Fagothey, *Right and Reason* (St. Louis, Mo.: C. V. Mosby Company, 1959), 218–221.

49. Centered around the person and teaching of Mme Guyon (1648–1717), French Quietism stressed radical simplicity and passivity in prayer: "the prayer of quiet." The movement minimized traditional devotions, systematic meditation, and ascetical efforts to cultivate virtue. Supporters claimed that the movement was only a prolongation of the "abandonment to divine providence" encouraged by St. François de Sales and other spiritual masters of the *école française*. Critics argued that the movement was antinomian, destructive of the moral life and of Church authority. The Archbishop of Paris condemned Mme Guyon's theories in 1696.

50. The concern about the moral consequences of Quietism is transparent in the major papal condemnations of the tendency in the seventeenth century. In 1687 Pope Innocent XI condemned a series of "quietist" theses allegedly defended by the Spanish priest Miguel de Molinos. In 1699 Pope Innocent XII condemned a series of "semi-quietist" positions allegedly supported by the French bishop Fénelon.

Chapter V. Mademoiselle de la Vallière: The Logic of Mercy

1. The most celebrated of the genre is Alexandre Dumas's novel *Louise de la Vallière*. In the Anglophone world, Sir Edward Bulwer Lytton's play *Duchess de la Vallière* (1837) helped to establish the sensationalized reputation of La Vallière.

2. This chapter uses the following edition of the works of and related to La Vallière: Louise de la Vallière, *Réflexions sur la miséricorde de Dieu par Mme de la Vallière; suivies de prières tirées de l'écriture sainte, et d'une prière de l'Abbé Gérard; précédées de lettres adressées au maréchal de Bellefonds, des sermons pour la vêture et la profession, et la vie pénitente, et d'une notice historique par M. Henriou* (Paris: Blaise, 1828). Hereafter this work is cited as *RMDMV*. Internal references to *Réflexions sur la miséricorde de Dieu* will be cited as *RMD*, and references to *Lettres adressées au maréchal de Bellefonds* will be cited as *L*. Translations from the French are my own.

3. The following sources have been consulted for this biographical sketch: Henri Carré, *Mademoiselle de La Vallière, de la cour de Louis XIV aux Grandes carmélites* (Paris: Hachette, 1938); Monique de Huertas, *Louise de la Vallière: De Versailles au Carmel* (Paris: Pygmalion/ Watelet, 1998); Jean Baptiste Eriau, *La Madeleine française: Louise de la Vallière dans sa famille, à la cour, au Carmel* (Paris: Nouvelles éditions latines, 1961); Stéphanie, comtesse de Genlis, *La Duchesse de la Vallière* (Paris: Maradan, 1818); Jules Auguste Lair, *Louise de la Vallière et la jeunesse de Louis XIV* (Paris: Plon-Nourrit, 1902); Joan Sanders, *La Petite: The Life of Louise de la Vallière* (Boston: Houghton Mifflin, 1959).

4. Jean-Armand le Bouthillier de Rancé (1636–1700), a religious reformer, began his ministry as an ecclesiastical careerist and continued so until his religious conversion (1657–1662). He later introduced an austere reform at the Cistercian Abbey of La Trappe and achieved fame as an author of ascetical books and pamphlets.

5. The writer Honoré, chevalier d'Urfé, marquis de Vallromey (1568–1625). His major work is the pastoral novel *Astrée,* published in successive volumes (1609, 1610, 1617).

6. Gaultier de Coste, seigneur de La Calprenède (1609–1663), poet, dramatist, and novelist. Among his major novels are *Cassandre* (1642–1650), *Cléopâtre* (1647–1658), and *Faramond* (1661–1670).

7. Marin Le Roy, sieur du Parc et de Gomberville (1600–1674), writer and historian. His major novels include *Polexandre* (1629), *La Cythérée* (1640).

8. Madeleine de Scudéry (1607–1701), novelist and essayist. Her major novels are *Artemène ou le Grand Cyrus* (1649–1653) and *Clélie* (1654–1661).

9. See Huertas, *Louise de la Vallière,* 128.

10. Antoine-Nompar de Caumont, comte de Lauzun (1633–1723), military officer, administrator, and courtier to both Louis XIV and England's James II.

11. Roger de Rabutin, comte de Bussy (1618–1693), soldier, Frondeur, and author; renowned for his impiety. His major work is *Histoire amoureuse des Gaules* (1659), a risqué satire of French aristocrats.

12. Isaac de Benserade (1613–1691), poet and dramatist, noted for skeptical satire.

13. Philippe de Voucillon, marquis de Dangeau (1638–1720), courtier, soldier, and poet. His major work is *Le journal de Dangeau,* 10 vols. (1684–1720).

14. The book was originally published anonymously ("By a penitent lady") in 1680; the author was quickly identified by seventeenth-century editors as Mlle de la Vallière, now Soeur Louise de la Miséricorde in Carmel. Internal evidence (stylistic and referential) confirmed the attribution, with which contemporary critics agree. See Huertas, *Louise de la Vallière,* 150 ff. Some earlier critics wrongly attributed the work to one or several of her spiritual directors: to Bossuet or to Bellefonds. The degree of the influence of Bossuet, Bellefonds, and Rancé on the theology of La Vallière remains in dispute. For the state of the question on this controversy, see Marcel Bernos and Sonia Branca-Rosoff, "Parole de femme, discours d'homme: À propos des Confessions de Louise de la Vallière," in *Correspondances: Mélanges offerts à Roger Duchêne,* ed. Wolfgang Leiner and Pierre Ronzeaud (Tübingen: Narr, 1992), 183–189.

15. See Jean-Christian Petitfils, *Louise de la Vallière* (Paris: Perrin, 1990), 304–318.

16. See ibid., 304.

17. See ibid., 305.

18. See ibid., 306.

19. See Romain Cornut, *Les réflexions de Madame de la Vallière répentante écrite par elle-même et corrigées par Bossuet,* 2d ed. (Paris: Didier, 1857).

20. See Marcel Langlois, *La conversion de Mlle de la Vallière et l'auteur véritable des Réflexions* (Paris: Plon, 1932).

21. See Eriau, *La Madeleine française,* 17–27.

22. See Petitfils, *Louise de la Vallière,* 307–309.

23. Langlois, *La conversion de Mlle de la Vallière*, 134–135.
24. See Cornut, *Les réflexions*, 3 ff.
25. See Matthew 15:21–28.
26. See John 8:8–42.
27. For a discussion of the historical evolution of the cult of St. Mary Magdalene, see J. E. Fallon, "St. Mary Magdalene," in *New Catholic Encyclopedia*, vol. 14 (New York: McGraw-Hill, 1967), 187–189.
28. See Luke 8:2–3.
29. See John 19:25; 20:1–2, 11–18.
30. See John 11.
31. See Luke 7:36–50.
32. Marie de Gournay, *Egalité entre les hommes et les femmes* (Paris: Milagros Palma, 1989), 85–86.
33. For a discussion of the Bossuet-Simon dispute, see E. E. Reynolds, *Bossuet* (Garden City, N.Y.: Doubleday, 1963), 90–91, 256–258.

Chapter VI. Madame de Maintenon: A Moral Pragmatism

1. The memoirs of the Saint-Cyr schoolmistress Mme du Pérou are typical of this hagiography. See Mme du Pérou, *Mémoires sur Mme de Maintenon* (Paris: Fulgence, 1846).
2. See Saint-Simon, *Mémoires et additions au Journal de Dagneau*, 8 vols., ed. Y. Coirault (Paris: Gallimard, 1983–1988).
3. See Émile Faguet, *Madame de Maintenon institutrice* (Paris: Lecène et Oudin, 1887).
4. See Octave Gréard, *Madame de Maintenon, extraits de ses lettres, avis* (Paris: Hachette, 1884).
5. See Jacques Prévot, *La première institutrice de France, Madame de Maintenon* (Paris: Belin, 1981).
6. This biographical sketch draws upon the following sources: Françoise Chandernagor, *L'allée du roi* (Paris: Juilliard, 1981); Madeleine Daniélou, *Madame de Maintenon, éducatrice* (Paris: Bloud et Gay, 1946); Marcel Langlois, *Madame de Maintenon* (Paris: Librairie Plon, 1932); Pierre-E. Leroy, "Introduction," in Madame de Maintenon, *Comment la sagesse vient aux filles*, ed. Pierre-E. Leroy and Marcel Loyau (Paris: Bartillat, 1998), 7–28.
7. Paul Scarron (1610–1660), comic poet, dramatist, and novelist. Among his major works are *Quelques vers burlesques* (1643), *Jodelet* (1645), and *Le Virgile travesti* (1648–1653).
8. Louis-Victor de Rochechouart, duc de Mortemart et de Vivonne (1636–1688), maréchal de France, decorated military officer, and essayist. He defended the ancients in the *querelle des anciens et des modernes*.
9. François Beauvillier, comte de Saint-Aignan (1610–1687), military officer and poet. He was elected to the Académie française in 1663.
10. Pierre Costar (1603–1660), literary pamphleteer. His principal work is *Défense des ouvrages de M. de Voiture* (1652).
11. Gilles Ménage (1613–1692), lexicographer. His major work is *Dictionnaire étymologique* (1650).
12. Isaac Benserade (1613–1691), poet renowned for sonnets and defender of the skeptical works of Pierre Bayle. He was elected to the Académie française in 1674. His major work is *Métamorphoses d'Ovide en rondeaux* (1676).
13. Jean Chapelain (1585–1674), literary critic and poet. He defended the moral and political value of the works of pagan antiquity. His principal work is *La pucelle* (1666).
14. Georges Brossin, chevalier de Méré (1610–1685), an essayist specializing in the rules

of politeness, celebrated the virtue of *honnêteté*. His major works (published posthumously) include *De la vraie honnêteté* and *De l'éloquence et de l'entretien*.

15. See Mlle de Scudéry, *Clélie,* 10 vols. (Paris: Augustin Courbé, 1654–1661), 5.1–3, where Scudéry treats Mme Scarron under the pseudonymn "Lyriane."

16. See Antoine Baudeau de Somaize, *Le dictionnaire des prétieuses* (Paris: Estienne Loyson, 1660), 205, where Somaize treats Mme Scarron under the pseudonymn "Stratonice."

17. See Maintenon, *Sur l'education des demoiselles,* in *Sagesse,* 254–258.

18. See Maintenon, *Sur l'education solide,* in *Sagesse,* 279–283.

19. Maintenon, "Lettre à Mme de Fontaines" (1691), cited in Daniélou, *Madame de Maintenon,* 94.

20. Mme de Pérou, *Mémoires,* cited in Daniélou, *Madame de Maintenon,* 102–103.

21. Many of Maintenon's manuscripts are conserved in the Bibliothèque municipale de Versailles under the numbers P.62–P.68 (7 vols.).

The most thorough published presentation of the works of Mme de Maintenon is the edition published in successive volumes by Théophile Lavallée. See Madame de Maintenon, *Conseils et instructions aux demoiselles pour leur conduite dans le monde,* ed. Théophile Lavallée, 2 vols. (Paris: Charpentier, 1857); *Entretiens sur l'éducation des filles* (Paris: Charpentier, 1854); *Lettres historiques et édifiantes,* 2 vols. (Paris: Charpentier, 1856); *Lettres sur l'éducation des filles* (Paris: Charpentier, 1854).

22. Maintenon, "Lettre à une maîtresse des novices" (1686), in *Sagesse,* 310.

23. Ibid., 311.

24. Ibid., 312.

25. Maintenon, "Conseils à Mme la Princesse de Savoie," in *Conseils,* 1.160.

26. See Daniélou, *Madame de Maintenon,* 154.

27. Maintenon, "Lettre aux Abbesses de Gomerfainte et de Bizy" (1713), cited in Daniélou, *Madame de Maintenon,* 154.

28. Maintenon, *Maximes,* in *Sagesse,* 125.

29. Maintenon, *Sur l'éducation des demoiselles* (1686), in Gréard, *Madame de Maintenon,* 5.

30. Ibid., 6.

31. By far the most influential work of the French Counter-Reformation, St. François de Sales's *Introduction à la vie dévote* (1608) argued that the laity needed to adapt its pious practices according to the specific duties of one's state of life. Opposed to moral rigorism, Sales argued that attendance at balls and cultivation of the fine arts, if done with moderation, were perfectly appropriate for the noblewoman. After the Bible, the *Introduction* is the work most cited by Maintenon in her writings. She insisted that every pupil at Saint-Cyr own her personal copy of the book. Numerous Maintenon conferences refer to the theories and examples proposed by De Sales.

32. See Maintenon, *Qu'il y a de la peine dans tous les états* (1708), in *Sagesse,* 152–155.

33. Maintenon, *Sur les vertus cardinales,* in *Conseils,* 1.259.

34. Ibid.

35. Ibid., 1.260.

36. Ibid., 1.261.

37. Ibid.

38. Ibid.

39. Maintenon, *Des vertus cardinales,* in Gréard, *Madame de Maintenon,* 114. Subsequent citations of Gréard are by page number in the text.

40. Maintenon, *Sur la politesse,* in Gréard, *Madame de Maintenon,* 181.

41. Maintenon, *Sur la civilité,* in *Sagesse,* 134.

42. Ibid.

43. Ibid., 135.

44. Ibid., 138.
45. Maintenon, *Sur la bonne gloire,* in *Conseils,* 1.71.
46. See ibid.
47. Ibid., 72.
48. Ibid.
49. Ibid., 73.
50. Ibid.
51. Ibid.
52. Maintenon, *Sur l'élévation,* in *Conseils,* 1.314.
53. Stoicism exercised a considerable influence in the philosophy of the French Renaissance. In the sixteenth century a series of translations made the works of Epictetus, Seneca, and Plutarch available to a wide audience. In the early seventeenth century the Stoic revival reached its zenith. Guillaume du Vair and Pierre Charron adapted the Stoic themes of moral duty, mastery of passions, and personal reasonableness to modern concerns. J. P. Camus, Bishop of Belley, was one of many authors to integrate Stoic moral theory into an explicitly Christian theology. By the middle of the seventeenth century the vogue for Stoicism had waned. Christian (Pascal) and skeptical (Deshoulières) authors dismissed the Stoic ethical system as rooted in pride. Mme de Maintenon made her first acquaintance with Stoic thought through her childhood study of Plutarch. The literary salons of Paris later initiated her into the contemporary debate between the partisans and the critics of Stoicism.
54. Maintenon, *Sur l'élévation,* in *Conseils,* 1.315.
55. Ibid., 1.316.
56. Ibid.
57. Maintenon, *Sur le bon esprit,* in *Conseils,* 1.187.
58. Ibid.
59. Ibid., 1.188.
60. Ibid.
61. Ibid., 1.189.
62. Ibid.
63. Ibid., 1.190.

Chapter VII. Conclusion: Unmasking Virtue

1. For a recent translation and commentary on the works of Anna Maria van Schurman, see Anna Maria van Schurman, *Whether a Christian Woman Should Be Educated and Other Writings from her Intellectual Circle,* ed. Joyce Irwin (Chicago: University of Chicago Press, 1998).
2. Marie de Gournay's most influential feminist essays are *L'Égalite des hommes et des femmes,* an argument for gender equality, and *Grief des dames,* an apology for the equal access of women to education and to culture. The Modern Language Association lists more than a hundred commentaries on Gournay's work in its bibliography. A recent philosophical commentary: Douglas Lewis, "Marie de Gournay and the Engendering of Equality," *Teaching Philosophy* 22, no. 1 (1999): 53–76.

Works Cited

Adam, Antoine. *Les Libertins au XVIIe siècle*. Paris: Buchet/Chastel, 1986.

Arnauld, Antoine. *De la fréquente communion*. 9th ed. Lyon: Plaignaud, 1683.

Arnauld, Antoine, and Pierre Nicole. *De la perpétuité de la foi de l'église catholique*. Paris: Chez l'Abbé M., 1841.

Asse, Eugène. "Des Houlières." In *La Grande Encyclopédie*, vol. 14, 238–239. Paris: Grande Encyclopédie, 1960.

Baker, Susan Read. *Collaboration et originalité chez La Rochefoucauld*. Gainesville: University of Florida Press, 1980.

Bayle, Pierre. *Dictionnaire historique et critique*. 4th ed., vols. 2–3. Amsterdam: Brunel, 1730.

———. *Nouvelles de la république des lettres*. Amsterdam: H. Desbordes, 1685.

Bédier, Joseph, and Paul Hazard. *Littérature française*, vol. 1. Paris: Larousse, 1948.

Bernier, François. *Abrégé de la philosophie de M. Gassendi*. Lyon: Moulu, 1675.

———. *Doutes sur quelques-uns des principaux chapitres de l'Abrégé de la philosophie de Gassendi*. Lyon: Chez Anisson, Posuel et Rigaud, 1682.

———. *Histoire de la dernière révolution des États du Grand Mogul*. 4 vols. Paris: Chez C. Barbin, 1670–1671.

———. *Traité du libre et du volontaire*. Amsterdam: H. Desbordes, 1685.

Bernos, Marcel, and Sonia Branca-Rosoff. "Parole de femme, discours d'homme: À Propos des Confessions de Louise de la Vallière." In *Correspondances: Mélanges offerts à Roger Duchêne*, ed. Wolfgang Leiner and Pierre Ronzeaud.Tübingen: Narr, 1992.

Bertière, Simone. *Les femmes du Roi-Soleil*. Paris: Éditions de Fallois, 1998.

Beugnot, Bernard. *Le discours de la retraite au XVIIe siècle*. Paris: Presses Universitaires de France, 1996.

Blunt, Hugh Francis. *The Great Magdalens*. New York: Macmillan, 1928.

Boileau-Despréaux, Nicolas. *Oeuvres complètes*. Edited by Françoise Escal. Paris: Gallimard, 1966.

Bouhours, Dominique. *Manière de bien penser dans les ouvrages d'esprit*. Paris: Mabre-Cramoisy, 1687.

Brégy, Charlotte Saumaize de Chazon, comtesse de. *Lettres et poésies*. Leyden: Antoine du Val, 1659.

Buffet, Marguerite. *Éloges des illustres scavantes tant anciennes que modernes*. Paris: Jean Cusson fils, 1668.

Busson, Henri. *La religion des classiques (1660–1685)*. Paris: Presses Universitaires de France, 1948.

Carré, Henri. *Mademoiselle de La Vallière, de la cour de Louis XIV aux Grandes carmelites*. Paris: Hachette, 1938.

Chandernagor, Françoise. *L'allée du roi*. Paris: Julliard, 1981.

Chapelain, Jean. *Lettres de Jean Chapelain*. Edited by Philippe Tamizey de Larroque. 2 vols. Paris: Imprimerie Nationale, 1880.

Chatounières, François de Grenaille, sieur de. *L'honneste fille*. 3 vols. Paris: Paslé, 1639 (vol. 1); Paris: Sommaville et Quinet, 1640 (vols. 2–3).

Christina of Sweden. *Mémoires concernant Christine, reine de Suède*. 4 vols. Edited by Johann Arckenholtz. 4 vols. Amsterdam: P. Mortier, 1754–1760.

Cognet, Louis. *Le Jansénisme*. Paris: Presses Universitaires de France, 1961.

Conrart, Valentin. *Mémoires sur l'histoire de son temps*.Paris: Monmergué, 1825.

Cornut, Romain. *Les réflexions de Madame de la Vallière répentante écrite par elle-même et corrigées par Bossuet*. 2d edition. Paris: Didier, 1857.

Cousin, Victor. *Madame de Sablé*. Paris: Didier, 1854.

D'Ailly, Nicolas, abbé. *Sentiments et maximes sur ce qui se passe dans la société civile*. Paris: s.n., 1697.

Daniélou, Madeleine. *Madame de Maintenon, éducatrice*. Paris: Bloud et Gay, 1946.

Descartes, René. *Oeuvres de Descartes*. Vol. 1. Edited by Charles Adam and Paul Tannery. Paris: Cerf, 1899.

Deshoulières, Antoinette du Ligier de la Garde, Mme. *Oeuvres*. 2 vols. Paris: Stéréotype d'Hernan, 1803 [An XI].

——. *Les poésies de Madame Deshoulières*. Paris: Veuve Mabre-Cramoisy, 1687.

Dorothée de Gaza. *Les instructions de saint Dorothée, père de l'Église grecque, et abbé d'un monastère de la Palestine*. Translated by J.-A. B. de Rancé. Paris: F. Muguet, 1686.

Eriau, Jean Baptiste. *La Madeleine française: Louise de la Vallière dans sa famille, à la cour, au Carmel*. Paris: Nouvelles éditions latines, 1961.

Fagothey, Austin. *Right and Reason*. St. Louis, Mo.: C. V. Mosby Company, 1959.

Faguet, Émile. *Madame de Maintenon institutrice*. Paris: Lecène et Oudin, 1887.

Fallon, J. E. "St. Mary Magdalene." In *New Catholic Encyclopedia*, vol. 14, 187–189. New York: McGraw-Hill, 1967.

Fontenelle, Bernard Le Bovier, M. de. *Éloge des savants*. Paris: Vrin, 1981.

Forge, Jean de la. *Cercle des femmes savantes*. Paris: Loyson, 1663.

Genlis, Stéphanie, comtesse de. *La Duchesse de la Vallière*. Paris: Maradan, 1818.

Gibson, Wendy. *Women in Seventeenth-Century France*. New York: St. Martin's Press, 1989.

Goldsmith, Elizabeth C. *"Exclusive Conversations": The Art of Interaction in Seventeenth-Century France*. Philadelphia: University of Pennsylvania Press, 1988.

Gournay, Marie de. *Égalité entre les hommes et les femmes*. Paris: Milagros Palma, 1989.

Gracián, Baltasar. *Oráculo manual y arte de prudencia: The Spanish Text and a New English Translation*. Edited by L. B. Walton. New York: Salloch, 1953.

Guidarelli, Vincenza C. Zema. "The Salon of Mme de Sablé: Foyer of Literary Jansenism." Ph.D. dissertation, Fordham University, 1979.

Harth, Erica. *Cartesian Women: Versions and Subversions of Rational Discourse in the Old Regime*. Ithaca, N.Y.: Cornell University Press, 1992.

Hesnault, Jean. *Les oeuvres de Jean Dehénault . . . (le maître de madame des Houlières), précédées d'une notice par Frédéric Lachèvre*. Paris: Champion, 1922.

Huertas, Monique de. *Louise de la Vallière: De Versailles au Carmel.* Paris: Pygmalion/Watelet, 1998.

Ivanoff, Nicolas. *La Marquise de Sablé et son salon.* Paris: Les Presses Modernes, 1927.

Jonsen, Albert, and Stephen Toulmin. *The Abuse of Casuistry: A History of Moral Reasoning.* Berkeley: University of California Press, 1988.

Krajewska, Barbara. *Mythes et découvertes: Le salon littéraire de Madame de Rambouillet dans les lettres des contemporains.* Paris and Seattle: Papers on French Seventeenth-Century Literature, 1990.

Lachèvre, Frédéric. *Les derniers Libertins.* Paris: E. Champion, 1924.

Lafond, Jean. *La Rochefoucauld: Maximes et réflexions.* Paris: Gallimard, 1978.

La Fontaine, Jean de. *Contes et nouvelles.* Paris: Barbin, 1665.

——. *Discours à Madame de la Sablière (Sur l'Âme des Animaux).* Critical edition by H. Busson. Paris: Droz, 1938.

——. *Fables choisies en vers par M. de la Fontaine.* Paris: Barbin, 1668.

——. *Oeuvres diverses.* Edited by Pierre Clarac. Paris: Gallimard, 1958.

Lair, Jules Auguste. *Louise de la Vallière et la jeunesse de Louis XIV.* Paris: Plon-Nourrit, 1902.

Langlois, Marcel. *La conversion de Mlle de la Vallière et l'auteur véritable des Réflexions.* Paris: Plon, 1932.

——. *Madame de Maintenon.* Paris: Plon, 1932.

La Rochefoucauld, François duc de. *Oeuvres complètes.* Edited by Louis Martin-Chauffier. Paris: Gallimard-Pléiade, 1950.

——. *Les pensées, maximes, et réflexions morales de François VI, duc de La Rochefoucauld, avec des notes critiques, morales, politiques et historiques sur chacune de ces pensées, par Amelot de La Houssaye et l'abbé de La Roche, et des Maximes chrétiennes par Madame de La Sablière.* Paris: Pissot, 1777.

La Vallière, Louise, Mlle de. *Réflexions sur la miséricorde de Dieu par Mme de la Vallière; suivies de prières tirées de l'écriture sainte, et d'une prière de l'Abbé Gérard; précédées de lettres adressées au maréchal de Bellefonds, des sermons pour la vêture et la profession, et la vie pénitente, et d'une notice historique par M. Henriou.* Paris: Blaise, 1828.

Leguay, Pierre. "Des Houlières." In *Dictionnaire de Biographie française,* vol. 10, 1387–1389. Paris: Letouzey et Ané, 1965.

Leites, Edmund, ed. *Conscience and Casuistry in Early Modern Europe.* Cambridge: Cambridge University Press, 1988.

Le Noble, Eustache. *Le Triomphe de Madame des Houlières, reçue dixième muse au Parnasse.* Paris: Claude Mazuel, 1694.

Leroy, Pierre-E. "Introduction." In Madame de Maintenon, *Comment la sagesse vient aux filles,* ed. Pierre-E. Leroy and Marcel Loyau, 7–28. Paris: Bartillat, 1998.

Lesclache, Louis de. *Abrégé de la philosophie en tables.* Paris: s.n., 1652.

Lewis, Douglas. "Marie de Gournay and the Engendering of Equality," *Teaching Philosophy* 22, no. 1 (1999): 53–76.

Lougée, Carolyn C. *Le Paradis des Femmes: Women, Salons, and Social Stratification in Seventeenth-Century France.* Princeton: Princeton University Press, 1976.

Maintenon, Françoise d'Aubigné, marquise de. *Comment la sagesse vient aux filles.* Edited by Pierre-E. Leroy and Marcel Loyau. Paris: Bartillat, 1998.

——. *Conseils aux demoiselles pour leur conduite dans le monde.* 2 vols. Edited by Théophile Lavallée. Paris: Charpentier, 1857.

——. *Entretiens sur l'éducation des filles*. Edited by Théophile Lavallée. Paris: Charpentier, 1854.

——. *Lettres historiques et édifiantes*. 2 vols. Edited by Théophile Lavallée. Paris: Charpentier, 1856.

——. *Lettres sur l'éducation des filles*. Edited by Théophile Lavallée. Paris: Charpentier, 1854.

——. *Madame de Maintenon, extraits de ses lettres, avis*. Edited by Octave Gréard. Paris: Hachette, 1884.

Malebranche, Nicolas. *Oeuvres complètes*, vol. 1. Edited by Geneviève Rodis-Lewis. Paris: Gallimard-Pléiade, 1979.

Ménage, Gilles. *Historia mulierum philosopharum*. Lugduni: Apud Anissonios, Joan, Poseul, et Claudium Rigaud, 1690.

Menjot, Antoine. *Opuscules posthumes de M. Menjot*. Amsterdam: Desbordes, 1685.

Menjot d'Elbenne. *Madame de la Sablière: Ses Pensées Chrétiennes et ses Lettres à l'Abbé de Rancé*. Paris: Plon, 1923.

Motteville, Mme de. *Mémoires*. 6 vols. Amsterdam: Chauguion, 1750.

Nicole, Pierre. *Traité de la Comédie*. Edited by Georges Couton. Paris: Les Belles Lettres, 1961.

Ogilvie-Bailey, Marilyn. "La Sablière, Marguerite Hessein de." In *Women in Science: Antiquity through the Nineteenth Century: A Biographical Dictionary*, 118–119. Cambridge, Mass.: MIT Press, 1986.

O'Neill, Eileen. "Disappearing Ink: Early Modern Women Philosophers and Their Fate in History." In *Philosophy in a Feminist Voice: Critiques and Reconstructions*, ed. Janet Kourany, 17–62. Princeton: Princeton University Press, 1998.

Pascal, Blaise. *Oeuvres complètes*. Edited by Jacques Chevalier. Paris: Gallimard-Pléaide, 1954.

Pascal, Jacqueline, Gilberte Pascal Périer, and Marguerite Périer. *Lettres, opuscules et mémoires de Madame Périer et de Jacqueline, soeurs de Pascal, et de Marguerite Périer, sa nièce, publiés sur les manuscrits originaux par M. P. Faugère*. Edited by M. P. Faugère. Paris: A. Vaton, 1845.

Pekacz, Jolanta K. *Conservative Tradition in Pre-Revolutionary France: Parisian Salon Women*. New York: Peter Lang, 1999.

Périer, Gilberte Pascal. *La vie de Monsieur Pascal suivi de La vie de Jacqueline Pascal*. Paris: La Table Ronde, 1994.

Pérou, Madame du. *Mémoires sur Mme de Maintenon*. Paris: Fulgence, 1846.

Petitfils, Jean-Christian. *Louise de la Vallière*. Paris: Perrin, 1990.

Picard, Roger. *Les salons littéraires et la société française 1610–1789*. New York: Brentano's, 1943.

Portefeuilles de Dr. Valant: Bibliothèque Nationale de France (Salle Richelieu), Fonds français, nos. 17044–17058.

Poullain de la Barre, François. *De l'égalité des deux sexes, discours psychique et moral, où l'on voit l'importance de se défaire des préjugés*. Paris: Jean du Puis, 1656.

Prévot, Jacques. *La première institutrice de France, Madame de Maintenon*. Paris: Belin, 1981.

Rancé, Armand Jean le Bouthillier de. *Maximes chrétiennes et morales*. 2 vols. Delft: H. van Rhyn, 1699.

Rapin, René. *Réflexions sur la Poétique d'Aristote*. Paris: Chez F. Muguet, 1674.

Rapley, Elizabeth. *The Dévotes: Women and Church in Seventeenth-Century France.* Kingston, Ontario: McGill-Queen's University Press, 1989.

Reynier, Gustave. *La femme au XVIIe siècle.* Paris: Plon, 1933.

Reynolds, E. E. *Bossuet.* Garden City, N.Y.: Doubleday & Co., 1963.

Rochechouart de Mortemart, Marie-Madeleine-Gabrielle de. *Recueil de divers écrits sur l'amour et l'amitié.* Paris: s.n., 1736.

Rohan, Marie-Éléonore de. *La morale du sage et paraphrase des psaumes de la pénitence.* Paris: Claude Barbin, 1667.

Rouhault, Jacques. *Oeuvres posthumes.* Paris: Deprez, 1682.

———. *Traité de physique.* Paris: Deprez, 1676.

Rousseau, Jean-Jacques. *Correspondance complète de Rousseau.* 52 vols. Edited by R. A. Leigh. Oxford: Voltaire Foundation, 1965–1998.

Sablé, Madeleine de Souvré, marquise de. *Maximes de Madame la Marquise de Sablé; suivies de Pensées de M.L.D.* Edited by Nicolas, Abbé d'Ailly. Paris: Mabre-Cramoisy, 1678.

———. *Maximes de Mme de Sablé.* Edited by Damase Jouaust. Paris: Librairie des Bibliophiles, 1870.

Sablière, Antoine Rambouillet, sieur de la. *Madrigaux de M.D.L.S.* Paris: Barbin, 1680.

———. *Madrigaux de Monsieur de la Sablière.* Edited by Charles Nodier. Paris: Delangle, 1825.

Sablière, Marguerite Hessein, Madame de la. *Maximes Chrétiennes, Pensées Chrétiennes,* and *Lettres.* In Menjot d'Elbenne, *Madame de la Sablière.* Paris: Plon, 1923.

———. *Maximes Chrétiennes.* In *Réflexions ou Sentences et maximes morales de Monsieur de la Rochefoucauld, Maximes de Madame la marquise de Sablé. Pensées diverses de M.L.D. et les Maximes chrétiennes de M****.* Amsterdam: Pierre Mortier, 1705.

———. *Maximes Chrétiennes.* In *Réflexions, sentences et maximes morales, mises en ordre, avec des notes politiques et historiques,* ed. Abraham-Nicolas, sieur Amelot de la Houssaye. Paris: Etienne Ganeau, 1725, 1743.

Saint-Simon. *Mémoires et additions au Journal de Dagneau.* 8 vols. Edited by Y. Coirault. Paris: Gallimard, 1983–1988.

Sainte-Beuve, Charles Augustin. *Port-Royal.* 3 vols. Edited by Maxime Le Roy. Paris: Gallimard, 1953–1955.

Sales, St. François de. *Introduction to the Devout Life.* Translated by John K. Ryan. Garden City, N.Y.: Doubleday, 1972.

Sanders, Joan. *La Petite: The Life of Louise de la Vallière.* Boston: Houghton Mifflin, 1959.

Sarasohn, Lisa T. *Gassendi's Ethics.* Ithaca, N.Y.: Cornell University Press, 1996.

Schurman, Anna Maria Van. *Whether a Christian Woman Should Be Educated and Other Writings from Her Intellectual Circle.* Translated and edited by Joyce Irwin. Chicago: University of Chicago Press, 1998.

Scudéry, Madeleine de. *Artamène ou le Grand Cyrus.* 10 vols. Paris: Courbé, 1650.

———. *Clélie.* 10 vols. Paris: Augustin Courbé, 1654–1661.

Segrais, Jean. *Oeuvres.* Geneva: Slatkine,1968.

Sévigné, Marie de Rabutin-Chantal, marquise de. *Lettres.* 3 vols. Edited by Émile Gérard-Gailly. Paris: Gallimard-Pléiade, 1953–1957.

Somaize, Antoine de Baudeau, sieur de. *Le grand dictionnaire des prétieuses, historique, poétique, géographique, cosmographique et armorique.* 2 vols. Paris: s.n., 1661.

Tallemant des Réaux. *Les historiettes.* 6 vols. Edited by Louis-Jean-Nicolas Monmerqué. Paris: Garnier frères, 1932.

Thurston, Herbert. "Theatre." In *The Catholic Encyclopedia,* vol. 14, 559–561. New York: Appleton, 1912.

Timmermans, Linda. *L'accès des femmes à la culture.* Paris: Champion, 1993.

Voltaire, François Marie Arouet de. *Correspondance.* 13 vols. Edited by Théodore Besterman. Paris: Gallimard-Pléiade, 1978–1993.

———. *Oeuvres de Voltaire.* Edited by M. Beuchot. Paris: Didot, 1831.

Wall, Glenda. "Marguerite Hessein de la Sablière." In *An Encyclopedia of Continental Women Writers,* ed. K. Wilson, 2.1086–1087. New York: Garland, 1991.

Index

Sablé, Madeleine de Souvré, Mme de
(*continued*)
  critique of, 42–44; and Deshoulières, 67,
  72; and Sablière, 81, 83, 96; salon of, 29–
  31; works of: *Maximes de Mme de Sablé,* 34–
  42
Sablé, Marie de, 22
Sablé, Philippe-Emmanuel de Laval, marquis de, 22
Sablière, Antoine de Rambouillet de la, 75–
  77
Sablière, Marguerite Hessein, Mme de la, 2,
  6, 9, 11–12, 15, 17–18, 158, 161, 163–165;
  biography of, 75–81; canon of, 81–83;
  critique of, 94–96; and Maintenon, 155;
  works of: *Maximes chrétiennes* 83–91; *Pensées chrétiennes,* 91–94
Sacraments, 3, 89–91, 96
Saint-Aignan, François Beauvillier, duc de,
  47, 126
Saint-Aignan, Madeleine Gaudon de la Rail-
  lière, marquise de, 76
Saint-Cyr, academy at, 3, 12, 160; and Maintenon, 124–125, 127–130, 142, 148. *See
  also* Royal Institute of Saint-Louis
Saint-Cyran, J. Duvergier de Hauranne, 4, 24
Saint-Pierre, Mme de
Saint Rémy, Jacques de Courtavel, marquis
  de, 98
Saint-Simon, Louis de Rouvroy, duc de, 124
Sainte-Beuve, Charles Augustin, 20, 103
Salamis, Princess of, 23
Salonnière, 11–13, 16, 126, 137, 153, 163–165
Salons: of Deshoulières, 47; and La Vallière,
  99, 100, 111, 113, 116–117, 119, 122–123;
  and Maintenon, 126, 141, 143, 151, 155;
  and philosophy, 2, 6, 10–13, 16, 158–159;
  and Sablé, 20, 22–24, 29–36, 43–44; of
  Sablière, 77
Salvation, 87, 96, 152
Samaritan woman, 105–109
Sauveur, Joseph, 77
Scarron, Paul, 125–126
Science, 3, 9, 42, 77
Scrupulosity, 28
Scudéry, Madeleine de, 11–13, 22–23, 46,
  99, 101, 123, 126, 129
Secularism, 15
Segrais, Jean, 23
Seminary, 3
Sentiment, 64–67
Septuagint, 113
Sermon on the Mount, 145

Sesmaisons, Père, 24
Sévigné, Marie de Rabutin-Chantal, mar-
  quise de, 11, 15, 23, 29, 77–79
Sibyls, 108
Simon, Richard, abbé, 113
Singlin, Antoine, abbé, 26
Skepticism, 6, 18, 161, 165; of Deshoulières,
  48–49; 68, 73; and La Vallière, 102, 111;
  and Sablé, 33, 42
Sloth, 84
Sobiesky, Jean; King of Poland, 77
Social criticism, 36–39, 43–44
Solitude, 90, 93, 95–96
Somaize, Antoine de Baudeau, sieur de, 126
Soteriology, 121–122
Sourdis, Marquis de, 29, 33
Souvré, Gilles de, 21
Spanish, 21–22, 46
States of life, 135, 156
Stoicism, 1, 7, 29, 150, 208 n.53
Stubbornness, 36, 84
Style, 35
Sur la civilité, 144–147
Sur l'élévation, 149–151
Sur le bon esprit, 151–154
Sur la bonne gloire, 147–149
Sur la politesse, 142–144
Sur les vertus cardinales, 138–142

Tallemant des Réaux, Gédéon, 22
Tasso, 50
Temperament, moral, 122
Temperance, 1, 16, 135–138, 140–141,
  155–156, 161
Teresa of Avila, Saint, 98, 100, 123
Tertullian, 81
Testu, Jacques, abbé
Theocentrism, 92, 115
Theology, 3–6, 82; 95; 160–161
Timmermans, Linda, 11
Transubstantiation, 3
Treatise, 3, 14
Trent, Council of, 3
Tutiorism, 89, 204 n.47

University, 3, 157–158
Ursulines, 3, 48, 125, 127

Valant, Docteur, 29
Vanity, 36, 69
Van Schurman, Anna Maria, 157–158
Vatier, Père, 7
Venus, 51